Fodor's Eleventh Edition

Sweden

W9-BEV-457

The complete guide, thoroughly up-to-date

Packed with details that will make your trip

The must-see sights, off and on the beaten path

What to see, what to skip

Mix-and-match vacation itineraries

City strolls, countryside adventures

Smart lodging and dining options

Essential local do's and taboos

Transportation tips, distances and directions

Key contacts, savvy travel tips

When to go, what to pack

Clear, accurate, easy-to-use maps

Books to read, videos to watch

Excerpted from *Fodor's Scandinavia*

Fodor's Travel Publicatio
www.fodors.com

Fodor's Sweden

EDITORS: Andrew Collins, Tania Inowlocki

Editorial Contributors: Lauren Myers, Devin Wilson
Editorial Production: Brian Vitunic
Maps: David Lindroth, *cartographer;* Rebecca Baer, Bob Blake, *map editors*
Design: Fabrizio La Rocca, *creative director;* Guido Caroti, *art director;* Jolie Novak, *photo editor*
Cover Design: Pentagram
Production/Manufacturing: Mike Costa
Cover Photograph: © Bildhuset AB/Photonica

Copyright

ISBN 0–679–00404–1

ISSN 1528–3070

11th Edition

Special Sales

Fodor's Travel Publications are available at special discounts for bulk purchases for sales promotions or premiums. Special editions, including personalized covers, excerpts of existing guides, and corporate imprints, can be created in large quantities for special needs. For more information, contact your local bookseller or write to Special Markets, Fodor's Travel Publications, 201 East 50th Street, New York, NY 10022. Inquiries from Canada should be directed to your local Canadian bookseller or sent to Random House of Canada, Ltd., Marketing Department, 2775 Matheson Boulevard East, Mississauga, Ontario L4W 4P7. Inquiries from the United Kingdom should be sent to Fodor's Travel Publications, 20 Vauxhall Bridge Road, London, England SW1V 2SA.

PRINTED IN THE UNITED STATES OF AMERICA

10 9 8 7 6 5 4 3 2 1

Important Tip

Although all prices, opening times, and other details in this book are based on information supplied to us at press time, changes occur all the time in the travel world, and Fodor's cannot accept responsibility for facts that become outdated or for inadvertent errors or omissions. So **always confirm information when it matters,** especially if you're making a detour to visit a specific place.

CONTENTS

Maps

ON THE ROAD WITH FODOR'S

THE TRIPS YOU TAKE this year and next are going to be significant trips, if only because they'll be your first in the new millennium. For that reason, if there was ever a time you needed excellent travel information, it's now. So we've pulled out all stops in preparing *Fodor's Sweden*, and we've scoured all corners of Sweden. Our goals: To discover the places that are truly worth your time and money and to unearth the fascinating facts that will help you view what you've traveled to see in a rich new light.

About Our Writer

Our success in helping to make your trip the best of all possible vacations is a credit to the hard work of our Sweden writer and our editors.

Devin Wilson is an American journalist and writer living in Stockholm. Having moved to Sweden three years ago, he has completed a circular journey begun by his grandparents who moved to the United States in the early 1900s. He works presently as a magazine editor for both Swedish and American publications.

Don't Forget to Write

We love feedback—positive and negative—and follow up on all suggestions. So contact the Sweden editor at editors@fodors.com or c/o Fodor's, 201 East 50th Street, New York, New York 10022. Have a wonderful trip!

Karen Cure

Karen Cure
Editorial Director

Stockholm

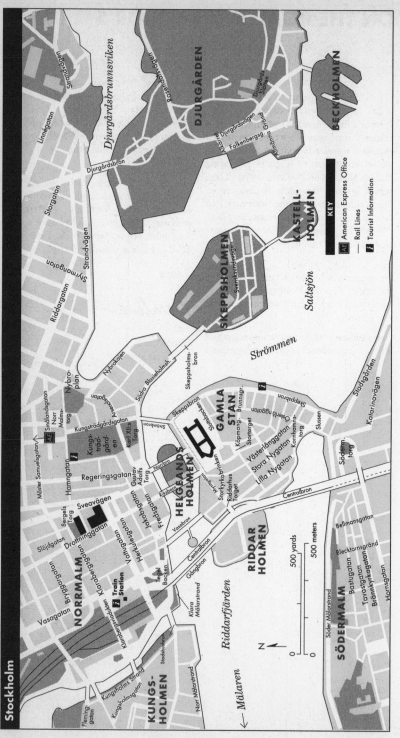

KEY

- **AE** American Express Office
- — Rail Lines
- ***i*** Tourist Information

Norwegian Sea

0 · 50 miles
0 · 75 km

Kiruna

E10

Gällivare

Jokkmokk

400

E10

Arjeplog

Haparanda

Töre

Arvidsjaur

Kalix

Tärnaby

45

E12

Sorsele

Luleå

Storuman

95

Piteå

Lycksele

Skellefteå

342

45

Åsela

92

Umeå

Strömsund

90

E4

Åre

Östersund

Tännäs

E14

Ljungan

Sundsvall

NORWAY

84

Idre

45

Hudiksvall

Gulf of Bothnia

70

Bollnäs

Mora

Söderhamn

62

Falun

80

Gävle

Borlänge

Fagersta

Avesta

E4

Uppsala

Karlstad

Västerås

E18

Stockholm

E18

Mellerud

Mälaren

Gulf of Finland

Strömstad

Vänern

E20

Örebro

E20

Uddevalla

Trollhättan

Norrköping

Gotska Sandön

ESTONIA

Göteborg

Vättern

Linköping

Baltic Sea

40

Jönköping

Visby

Gulf of Riga

Borås

Nässjö

E22

Oskarshamn

Gotland

Falkenberg

Värnamo

E6/E20

Halmstad

Växjö

Öland

23

Kalmar

LATVIA

Helsingborg

Karlskrona

Malmö

Kristianstad

DENMARK

LITHUANIA

Trelleborg

Ystad

FINLAND

Scandinavia

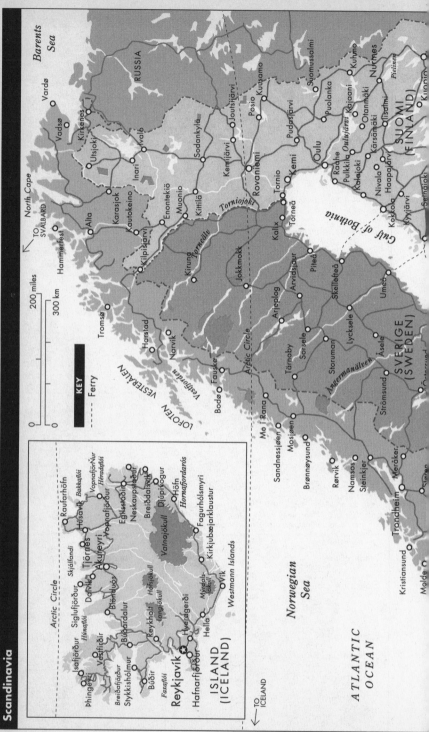

World Time Zones

Numbers below vertical bands relate each zone to Greenwich Mean Time (0 hrs.).
Local times frequently differ from these general indications,
as indicated by light-face numbers on map.

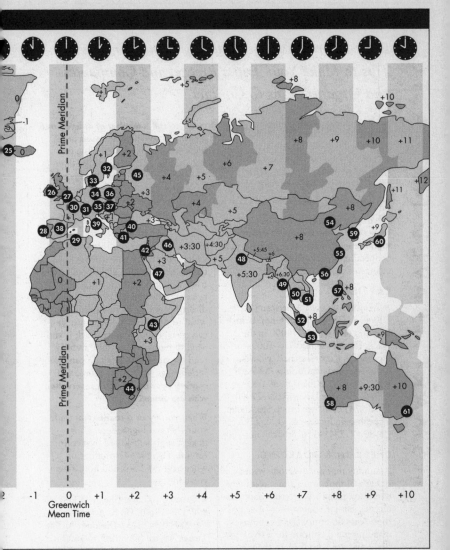

Greenwich
Mean Time

SMART TRAVEL TIPS A TO Z

Basic Information on Traveling in Sweden, Savvy Tips to Make Your Trip a Breeze, and Companies and Organizations to Contact

AIR TRAVEL

SAS, American, British Airways, TWA, and other major airlines serve Stockholm's Arlanda International Airport and Göteborg's Landvetter airport.

BOOKING YOUR FLIGHT

When you book look for nonstop flights and remember that "direct" flights stop at least once. Try to avoid connecting flights, which require a change of plane.

CARRIERS

➤ MAJOR AIRLINES: **American** (☎ 800/433–7300) to Stockholm. **British Airways** (☎ 020/88974000 in the U.K.). **Finnair** (☎ 800/950–5000) to Stockholm, Copenhagen, Reykjavík, Oslo. **Scandinavian Airlines (SAS)** (☎ 800/221–2350 in the U.S., ☎ 020/77344020 in the U.K., ☎ 08/727000 or 08/974175 in Sweden) to Stockholm, Copenhagen, Reykjavík, Oslo. **TWA** (☎ 800/892–4141) to Stockholm.

CHECK-IN & BOARDING

Assuming that not everyone with a ticket will show up, airlines routinely overbook planes. When that happens, airlines ask for volunteers to give up their seats. In return these volunteers usually get a certificate for a free flight and are rebooked on the next flight out. If there are not enough volunteers, the airline must choose who will be denied boarding. The first to get bumped are passengers who checked in late and those flying on discounted tickets, so get to the gate and check in as early as possible, especially during peak periods.

Always bring a government-issued photo I.D. to the airport. You may be asked to show it before you are allowed to check in.

CUTTING COSTS

The least-expensive airfares to Sweden must usually be purchased in advance and are nonrefundable. It's smart to call a number of airlines, and when you are quoted a good price, book it on the spot—the same fare may not be available the next day. Always check different routings and look into using different airports. Travel agents, especially low-fare specialists (☞ Discounts & Deals, *below*), are helpful.

Consolidators are another good source. They buy tickets for scheduled international flights at reduced rates from the airlines, then sell them at prices that beat the best fare available directly from the airlines, usually without restrictions. Sometimes you can even get your money back if you need to return the ticket. Carefully read the fine print detailing penalties for changes and cancellations, and confirm your consolidator reservation with the airline.

When you fly as a courier you trade your checked-luggage space for a ticket deeply subsidized by a courier service. There are restrictions on when you can book and how long you can stay.

➤ CONSOLIDATORS: **Cheap Tickets** (☎ 800/377–1000). **Up & Away Travel** (☎ 212/889–2345). **Discount Airline Ticket Service** (☎ 800/576–1600). **Unitravel** (☎ 800/325–2222). **World Travel Network** (☎ 800/409–6753).

ENJOYING THE FLIGHT

For more legroom request an emergency-aisle seat. Don't sit in the row in front of the emergency aisle or in front of a bulkhead, where seats may not recline. If you have dietary concerns, ask for special meals when booking. These can be vegetarian, low-cholesterol, or kosher, for example. On long flights, try to maintain a normal routine, to help fight jet lag. At night get some sleep. By day eat light meals, drink water (not alcohol), and move around the cabin to stretch your legs.

FLYING TIMES

Flying time from New York to Stockholm is 8 hours.

HOW TO COMPLAIN

If your baggage goes astray or your flight goes awry, complain right away. Most carriers require that you **file a claim immediately.**

➤ AIRLINE COMPLAINTS: U.S. Department of Transportation **Aviation Consumer Protection Division** (✉ C-75, Room 4107, Washington, DC 20590, ☎ 202/366–2220). **Federal Aviation Administration Consumer Hotline** (☎ 800/322–7873).

WITHIN SCANDINAVIA

Scandinavia is larger than it looks on a map, and many native travelers choose to fly between the capital cities, using trains and buses for domestic travel.

If you are traveling from south to north in Norway, Sweden, or Finland, flying is often a necessity: Stavanger in southern Norway is as close to Rome, Italy, as it is to the northern tip of Norway.

All major cities and towns in Sweden are linked with regular flights by Scandinavian Airlines System. Most Swedish airports are located a long way from city centers but are served by fast and efficient bus services. SAS also operates a limousine service at leading airports. For more information, contact SAS.

AIRPORTS

The major gateway to Sweden is **Arlanda International Airport** 41 km (26 mi) north of Stockholm.

➤ AIRPORT INFORMATION: Sweden **Arlanda International Airport** (☎ 011–46–8/797–6100).

BIKE TRAVEL

BIKES IN FLIGHT

Most airlines accommodate bikes as luggage, provided they are dismantled and boxed. For bike boxes, often free at bike shops, you'll pay about $5 (at least $100 for bike bags) from airlines. International travelers can sometimes substitute a bike for a piece of checked luggage at no charge; otherwise, the cost is about $100.

Domestic and Canadian airlines charge $25–$50.

BOAT & FERRY TRAVEL

Taking a ferry isn't only fun, it's often necessary in Scandinavia. Many companies arrange package trips, some offering a rental car and hotel accommodations as part of the deal.

Ferry crossings often last overnight. The trip between Copenhagen and Oslo, for example, takes approximately 16 hours, most lines leaving at about 5 PM and arriving about 9 the next morning. The direct cruise between Stockholm and Helsinki takes 12 hours, usually leaving at about 6 PM and arriving the next morning at 9. The shortest ferry route runs between Helsingør, Denmark, and Helsingborg, Sweden; it takes only 25 minutes.

An excellent way of seeing Sweden is from the many ferry boats that ply the archipelagoes and main lakes. In Stockholm, visitors should buy a special *Båtluffarkort* (Inter Skerries Card, SKr 250) from Waxholmsbolaget. This card allows you unlimited travel on the archipelago ferry boats for a 16-day period.

Highly popular four-day cruises are available on the Göta Canal, which makes use of rivers, lakes, and, on its last lap, the Baltic Sea. This lovely waterway, which links Göteborg on the west coast with Stockholm on the east, has a total of 65 locks, and you travel on fine old steamers, some of which date almost from the canal's opening in 1832. The oldest and most desirable is the *Juno*, built in 1874. Prices start at SKr 5,900 for a bed in a double cabin. For more information, contact the Göta Canal Steamship Company.

FARES & SCHEDULES

➤ BOAT & FERRY INFORMATION: **Color Line** (✉ Box 30, DK–9850 Hirsthals, Denmark, ☎ 45/99–56–20–00, FAX 45/99–56–20–20; Hjortneskaia, Box 1422 Vika, N–0115 Oslo, Norway, ☎ 47/22–94–44–00, FAX 47/22–83–04–30; c/o Bergen Line, Inc., 405 5th Ave., New York, NY 10022, ☎ 800/323–7436, FAX 212/983–1275; Tyne Commission Quay, North Shields NE29 6EA, Newcastle,

England, ☎ 091/296–1313, FAX 091/
296–1540). **Göta Canal Steamship
Company** (✉ Box 272, S401 24
Göteborg, ☎ 031/806315, FAX 031/
158311). **ScandLines** (✉ Box 1, DK–
300O Helsingør, Denmark, ☎ 45/33–
15–15–15, FAX 45/33–15–10–20;
Knutpunkten 44, S–252 78 Helsingborg, Sweden, ☎ 46/42–18–61–00,
FAX 46/42–18–74–10). **Waxholmsbolaget** (✉ Sodra Blasieholmsh wharf,
☎ 08/6795830).

FERRIES FROM ENGLAND

The chief operator between England
and many points within Scandinavia
is DFDS/Scandinavian Seaways, with
ships connecting Harwich and Newcastle to Göteborg and Amsterdam.

➤ MAJOR OPERATOR: **DFDS/Scandi-
navian Seaways** (✉ Sankt Annae
Plads 30, DK–1295 Copenhagen,
Denmark, ☎ 45/33–42–30–00, FAX
45/33–42–33–41; DFDS Travel Cen-
tre, 15 Hanover St., London W1R
9HG, ☎ 020/7409–6060, FAX 020/
7409–6035; Scandinavian Seaways,
DFDS Ltd., Scandinavia House,
Parkeston Quay, Harwich, Essex,
CO12 4QG, ☎ 191/293–6262;
DFDS Seaways USA Inc., 6555 NW
9th Ave., Suite 207, Fort Lauderdale,
FL 33309, ☎ 800/533–3755, FAX 305/
491–7958; Box 8895, Scandiahamnen, S–402 72 Göteborg, Sweden, ☎
46/31–650–610).

PLYING SCANDINAVIAN
WATERS

Connections from Denmark to Norway and Sweden are available
through DFDS and the Stena Line.
Fjord Line sails along the magnificent
west coast of Norway. Connections to
the Faroe Islands from Norway and
Denmark are available through the
Smyril Line. Silja Line and Viking
Line offer a variety of cruises to
Finland, with departures from Stockholm to Mariehamn in the Åland
archipelago, lTurku (Åbo) and
Helsinki (Helsingfors), and a crossing
from Umeå to Vaasa.

➤ MAJOR OPERATORS: **DFDS Seaways**
(☞ *above*). **Stena Line** (✉ Trafikham-
nen, DK–9900 Frederikshavn, Denmark, ☎ 45/96–20–02–00, FAX 45/96–
20–02–80; Jernbanetorget 2, N–0154
Oslo 1, Norway, ☎ 47/23–17–90–00,
FAX 47/23–17–90–60; Scandinavia AB,

S–405 19 Göteborg, Sweden, ☎ 46/
31–704–0000, FAX 46/31–241–038).
Fjord Line (✉ Skoltegrunnskaien,
Box 7250, N–5020 Bergen, Norway,
☎ 47/55–54–88–00, FAX 47/55–54–
86–01). **Smyril Line** (☞ DFDS Seaways, *above*; or J. Brocksgøta 37,
Box 370, FO-110 Tórshavn, Faroe
Islands, ☎ 298/31–59–00, FAX 298/
31–57–07; Slottsgate 1, Box 4135
Dreggen, N–5023 Bergen, Norway,
☎ 47 /55–32–09–70, FAX 47/55–96–
02–72). **Silja Line** (✉ Kungsgatan 2,
S–111 43 Stockholm, Sweden, ☎ 46/
8–666–3512, FAX 46/8–611–9162; c/o
Scandinavian Seaways, Parkeston
Quay Scand. House, Harwich, Essex,
England CO12 4QG, ☎ 44/255–
240–240, FAX 44/255–244–382).

CAR FERRIES

Travel by car in Scandinavia often
necessitates travel by ferry. Some
well-known vehicle and passenger
ferries run between Dragør, Denmark
(just south of Copenhagen), and
Limhamn, Sweden (just south of
Malmö); between Helsingør, Denmark, and Helsingborg, Sweden; and
between Copenhagen and Göteborg,
Sweden. On the Dragør/Limhamn
ferry (ScandLines), taking a car one-
way costs SKr 395 (about $60 or
£39). The Helsingør/Helsingborg
ferry (ScandLines also) takes only 25
minutes; taking a car along one-way
costs SKr 330 (about $50 or £33).
Fares for round-trip are cheaper, and
on weekends the Öresund Runt pass
(for crossing between Dragoør and
Limhamn one way and Helsingborg
and Helsingoør the other way) costs
only SKr 495 (about $75 or £49).

➤ MAJOR OPERATORS: **Stena Line**
(Sweden, ☎ 46–31/775–00–00).
ScandLines (☞ *above*).

BUS TRAVEL

Bus tours can be effective for smaller
regions within Sweden, Finland, and
Denmark, but all have excellent train
systems, which offer much greater
coverage in less time than buses.
Detailed information on bus routes is
available through local tourist of-
fices.There is, however, excellent bus
service between all major towns and
cities. Consult the Yellow Pages under
Bussresearrangörer for the telephone
numbers of the companies concerned.

Recommended are the services offered to different parts of Sweden from Stockholm by **Swebus** (✉ Cityterminalen, Klarabergsviadukten 72).

BUSINESS HOURS

BANKS

Banks are officially open weekdays 9:30 AM to 3 PM, but many stay open until 5 on most days and until 6 on Thursdays. The bank at Arlanda International Airport is open every day with extended hours, and the Forex and Valuta Specialisten currency-exchange offices also have extended hours.

MUSEUMS

The opening times for museums vary widely, but most are open from 10 AM to 4 PM weekdays and over the weekend but are closed on Monday. Consult the guide in *På Stan*, the entertainment supplement published in *Dagens Nyheter*'s Friday edition, or *Stockholm This Week*.

SHOPS

Shops are generally open weekdays from 9 AM, 9:30 AM, or 10 AM until 6 PM and Saturday from 9 AM to 1 or 4 PM. Most of the large department stores stay open later in the evenings, and some open on Sunday. Several supermarkets open on Sunday, and there are a number of late-night food shops such as the 7-Eleven chain. **Systembolaget,** Sweden's liquor monopoly and only place to buy alcohol and wine, is open weekdays *only* from 10–6, with extended hours until 7 on Thursdays.

CAMERAS & PHOTOGRAPHY

➤ PHOTO HELP: **Kodak Information Center** (☎ 800/242–2424). *Kodak Guide to Shooting Great Travel Pictures,* available in bookstores or from Fodor's Travel Publications (☎ 800/533–6478; $16.50 plus $4 shipping).

EQUIPMENT PRECAUTIONS

Always **keep your film and tape out of the sun.** Carry an extra supply of batteries, and **be prepared to turn on your camera or camcorder** to prove to security personnel that the device is real. Always **ask for hand inspection of film,** which becomes clouded after successive exposures to airport X-ray machines, and **keep videotapes away from metal detectors.**

CAR RENTAL

Major car-rental companies such as Avis, Bonus, Budget, Europcar/Inter-Rent, Hertz, and OK have facilities in all major towns and cities as well as at airports. It is worth shopping around for special rates. Various service stations also offer car rentals, including Q8, Shell, Statoil, and Texaco. See the Yellow Pages under *Biluthyrning* for telephone numbers and addresses.

Rates in Stockholm begin at $110 a day and $210 a week for an economy car without air-conditioning, and with a manual transmission and unlimited mileage.

➤ MAJOR AGENCIES: **Alamo** (☎ 800/522–9696; 020/8759–6200 in the U.K.). **Avis** (☎ 800/331–1084; 800/879–2847 in Canada; 02/9353–9000 in Australia; 09/525–1982 in New Zealand). **Budget** (☎ 800/527–0700; 0144/227–6266 in the U.K.). **Dollar** (☎ 800/800–6000; 020/8897–0811 in the U.K., where it is known as Eurodollar; 02/9223–1444 in Australia). **Hertz** (☎ 800/654–3001; 800/263–0600 in Canada; 0990/90–60–90 in the U.K.; 02/9669–2444 in Australia; 03/358–6777 in New Zealand). **National InterRent** (☎ 800/227–3876; 0345/222525 in the U.K., where it is known as Europcar InterRent).

CUTTING COSTS

To get the best deal **book through a travel agent who will shop around.** Do **look into wholesalers,** companies that do not own fleets but rent in bulk from those that do and often offer better rates than traditional car-rental operations. Payment must be made before you leave home.

➤ WHOLESALERS: **Auto Europe** (☎ 207/842–2000 or 800/223–5555, FAX 800–235–6321). **Europe by Car** (☎ 212/581–3040 or 800/223–1516, FAX 212/246–1458). **DER Travel Services** (✉ 9501 W. Devon Ave., Rosemont, IL 60018, ☎ 800/782–2424, FAX 800/282–7474 for information; 800/860–9944 for brochures). **Kemwel Holiday Autos** (☎ 914/825–3000 or 800/678–0678, FAX 914/381–8847).

INSURANCE

When driving a rented car you are generally responsible for any damage to or loss of the vehicle. Before you rent see what coverage your personal auto-insurance policy and credit cards already provide.

Collision policies that car-rental companies sell for European rentals usually do not include stolen-vehicle coverage. Before you buy it, check your existing policies—you may already be covered.

REQUIREMENTS & RESTRICTIONS

Ask about age requirements: Several countries require drivers to be over 20 years old, but some car-rental companies require that drivers be at least 25. In Scandinavia your own driver's license is acceptable for a limited time; check with the country's tourist board before you go. An International Driver's Permit is a good idea; it's available from the American or Canadian automobile association, or, in the United Kingdom, from the Automobile Association or Royal Automobile Club.

SURCHARGES

Before you pick up a car in one city and leave it in another **ask about drop-off charges or one-way service fees,** which can be substantial. Note, too, that some rental agencies charge extra if you return the car before the time specified in your contract. To avoid a hefty refueling fee **fill the tank just before you turn in the car,** but be aware that gas stations near the rental outlet may overcharge.

CAR TRAVEL

If you are planning on traveling from Denmark to Sweden after June 2000, you're in luck: The new Malmö–Copenhagen bridge will simplify car travel and make train connections possible between the two countries. Ferry service to Malmö and Helsingborg will remain an option after the bridge is complete.

Excellent, well-marked roads make driving a great way to explore Sweden—but beware that gasoline costs more than $1 per liter of lead-free gas, roughly four times the typical U.S. price. Ferry costs can be steep, and reservations are vital. Tolls on some major roads add to the expense, as do the high fees for city parking; tickets for illegal parking are painfully costly.

Also be aware that there are relatively low legal blood-alcohol limits and tough penalties for driving while intoxicated in Scandinavia. Penalties include suspension of the driver's license and fines or imprisonment and are enforced by random police road-blocks in urban areas on weekends. In addition, an accident involving a driver with an illegal blood-alcohol level usually voids all insurance agreements, so the driver becomes responsible for his own medical bills and damage to the cars.

In a few remote areas, especially in Sweden, road conditions can be unpredictable, and careful planning is required for safety's sake. It is wise to **use a four-wheel-drive vehicle** and to **travel with at least one other car** in these areas.

Keep your headlights on at all times; this is required by law in most of Scandinavia. Also by Scandinavian law, everyone, including infants, must **wear seat belts.**

Sweden has an excellent highway network of more than 80,000 km (50,000 mi). The fastest routes are those with numbers prefixed with an *E* (for "European"), some of which are the equivalent of American highways or British motorways.

AUTO CLUBS

➤ IN AUSTRALIA: **Australian Automobile Association** (☎ 02/6247–7311).

➤ IN CANADA: **Canadian Automobile Association** (CAA, ☎ 613/247–0117).

➤ IN NEW ZEALAND: **New Zealand Automobile Association** (☎ 09/377–4660).

➤ IN THE U.K.: **Automobile Association** (AA, ☎ 0990/500–600). **Royal Automobile Club** (RAC, ☎ 0990/722–722 for membership; 0345/121–345 for insurance).

➤ IN THE U.S.: **American Automobile Association** (☎ 800/564–6222).

EMERGENCY ASSISTANCE

The **Larmtjänst** organization, run by a confederation of Swedish insurance companies, provides a 24-hour breakdown service. Its phone numbers are listed in the Yellow Pages.

GASOLINE

Sweden has some of the highest gasoline rates in Europe, about SKr 8 per liter at press time. Lead-free gasoline is readily available. Gas stations are self-service: Pumps marked SEDEL are automatic and accept SKr 20 and SKr 100 bills; pumps marked KASSA are paid for at the cashier; the KONTO pumps are for customers with Swedish gas credit cards.

MAP

If you plan on extensive road touring, consider buying the *Vägatlas över Sverige,* a detailed road atlas published by the Mötormännens Riksförbund, available at bookstores for around SKr 270.

PARKING

Parking meters and, increasingly, timed ticket machines, operate in larger towns, usually between 8 AM and 6 PM. The fee varies from about SKr 6 to SKr 35 per hour. Parking garages in urban areas are mostly automated, often with machines that accept credit cards; LEDIGT on a garage sign means space is available. Try to avoid getting a parking ticket, which can slap you with a fine of SKr 300 to SKr 700.

ROAD CONDITIONS

All main and secondary roads are well surfaced, but some minor roads, particularly in the north, are gravel.

RULES OF THE ROAD

Drive on the right, and, no matter where you sit in a car, seat belts are mandatory. You must also have at least low-beam headlights on at all times. Signs indicate five basic speed limits, ranging from 30 kph (19 mph) in school or playground areas to 110 kph (68 mph) on long stretches of *E* roads.

CHILDREN IN SWEDEN

In Sweden children are to be seen *and* heard and are genuinely welcome in most public places. If you are renting a car don't forget to **arrange for a car seat** when you reserve.

DISCOUNTS

Children are entitled to discount tickets (often as much as 50% off) on buses, trains, and ferries throughout Sweden, as well as reductions on special City Cards. Children under 12 pay half-price and children under 2 pay 10% on SAS and Linjeflyg round-trips. The only restriction on this discount is that the family travel together and return to the originating city in Scandinavia at least two days later. With the Scanrail Pass (☞ Cutting Costs *in* Train Travel, *below*)—good for rail journeys throughout Scandinavia—children under 4 (on lap) travel free; those 4–11 pay half-fare and those 12–25 can get a Scanrail Youth Pass, providing a 25% discount off of the adult fare.

FLYING

If your children are two or older **ask about children's airfares.** As a general rule, infants under two not occupying a seat fly at greatly reduced fares or even for free. When booking **confirm carry-on allowances** if you're traveling with infants. In general, for babies charged 10% of the adult fare, you are allowed one carry-on bag and a collapsible stroller; if the flight is full the stroller may have to be checked or you may be limited to less.

Experts agree that it's a good idea to use safety seats aloft for children weighing less than 40 pounds. Airlines set their own policies: U.S. carriers usually require that the child be ticketed, even if he or she is young enough to ride free, since the seats must be strapped into regular seats. Do **check your airline's policy about using safety seats during takeoff and landing.** And since safety seats are not allowed just everywhere in the plane, get your seat assignments early.

When reserving, **request children's meals or a freestanding bassinet** if you need them. But note that bulkhead seats, where you must sit to use the bassinet, may lack an overhead bin or storage space on the floor.

LODGING

Most hotels in Sweden allow children under a certain age to stay in their

SMART TRAVEL TIPS A TO Z

parents' room at no extra charge, but others charge for them as extra adults; be sure to **find out the cutoff age for children's discounts.**

SIGHTS & ATTRACTIONS

Places that are especially good for children are indicated by a rubber duckie icon in the margin.

CONSUMER PROTECTION

Whenever shopping or buying travel services in Sweden, **pay with a major credit card** so you can cancel payment or get reimbursed if there's a problem. If you're doing business with a particular company for the first time, **contact your local Better Business Bureau and the attorney general's offices** in your state and the company's home state, as well. Have any complaints been filed? Finally, if you're buying a package or tour, always **consider travel insurance** that includes default coverage (☞ Insurance, *below*).

➤ LOCAL BBBs: **Council of Better Business Bureaus** (✉ 4200 Wilson Blvd., Suite 800, Arlington, VA 22203, ☎ 703/276–0100, ℻ 703/525–8277).

CUSTOMS & DUTIES

When shopping, **keep receipts** for all purchases. Upon reentering the country, **be ready to show customs officials what you've bought.** If you feel a duty is incorrect or object to the way your clearance was handled, note the inspector's badge number and ask to see a supervisor. If the problem isn't resolved, write to the appropriate authorities, beginning with the port director at your point of entry.

Travelers 21 or older entering Sweden from no-EU countries may import duty-free: 1 liter of liquor and 2 liters of fortified wine; 2 liters of wine or 15 liters of beer; 200 cigarettes or 100 grams of cigarillos or 50 cigars or 250 grams of tobacco; 50 grams of perfume; ¼ liter of aftershave; and other goods up to the value of SKr 1,700. Travelers from the United Kingdom or other EU countries may import duty-free: 1 liter of liquor or 3 liters of fortified wine; 5 liters of wine; 15 liters of beer; 300 cigarettes or 150 cigarillos or 75 cigars or 400 grams of tobacco; and other goods, including perfume and aftershave, of any value.

IN SWEDEN

Limits on what you can bring in duty-free vary from country to country. **Check with individual country tourist boards for limits on alcohol, cigarettes, and other items.** Also be careful to check before bringing food of any kind into Iceland.

IN AUSTRALIA

Australia residents who are 18 or older may bring home $A400 worth of souvenirs and gifts (including jewelry), 250 cigarettes or 250 grams of tobacco, and 1,125 ml of alcohol (including wine, beer, and spirits). Residents under 18 may bring back $A200 worth of goods. Prohibited items include meat products. Seeds, plants, and fruits need to be declared upon arrival.

➤ INFORMATION: **Australian Customs Service** (Regional Director, ✉ Box 8, Sydney, NSW 2001, ☎ 02/9213–2000, ℻ 02/9213–4000).

IN CANADA

Canadian residents who have been out of Canada for at least 7 days may bring home C$500 worth of goods duty-free. If you've been away less than 7 days but more than 48 hours, the duty-free allowance drops to C$200; if your trip lasts 24–48 hours, the allowance is C$50. You may not pool allowances with family members. Goods claimed under the C$500 exemption may follow you by mail; those claimed under the lesser exemptions must accompany you. Alcohol and tobacco products may be included in the 7-day and 48-hour exemptions but not in the 24-hour exemption. If you meet the age requirements of the province or territory through which you reenter Canada, you may bring in, duty-free, 1.14 liters (40 imperial ounces) of wine or liquor *or* 24 12-ounce cans or bottles of beer or ale. If you are 16 or older you may bring in, duty-free, 200 cigarettes and 50 cigars. Check ahead of time with Revenue Canada or the Department of Agriculture for policies regarding meat products, seeds, plants, and fruits.

You may send an unlimited number of gifts worth up to C$60 each duty-free to Canada. Label the package UNSOLICITED GIFT—VALUE UNDER $60. Alcohol and tobacco are excluded.

➤ INFORMATION: **Revenue Canada** (✉ 2265 St. Laurent Blvd. S, Ottawa, Ontario K1G 4K3, ☎ 613/993–0534; 800/461–9999 in Canada).

IN NEW ZEALAND

Homeward-bound residents 17 or older may bring back $700 worth of souvenirs and gifts. Your duty-free allowance also includes 4.5 liters of wine or beer; one 1,125-ml bottle of spirits; and either 200 cigarettes, 250 grams of tobacco, 50 cigars, or a combination of the three up to 250 grams. Prohibited items include meat products, seeds, plants, and fruits.

➤ INFORMATION: **New Zealand Customs** (Custom House, ✉ 50 Anzac Ave., Box 29, Auckland, New Zealand, ☎ 09/359–6655, FAX 09/359–6732).

IN THE U.K.

If you are a U.K. resident and your journey was wholly within the European Union (EU), you won't have to pass through customs when you return to the United Kingdom. If you plan to bring back large quantities of alcohol or tobacco, check EU limits beforehand. From countries outside the EU, including, Sweden, you may import, duty-free, 200 cigarettes or 50 cigars; 1 liter of spirits or 2 liters of fortified or sparkling wine or liqueurs; 2 liters of still table wine; 60 milliliters of perfume; 250 milliliters of toilet water; plus £136 worth of other goods, including gifts and souvenirs.

➤ INFORMATION: **HM Customs and Excise** (✉ Dorset House, Stamford St., Bromley Kent BR1 1XX, ☎ 020/7202–4227).

IN THE U.S.

U.S. residents who have been out of the country for at least 48 hours (and who have not used the $400 allowance or any part of it in the past 30 days) may bring home $400 worth of foreign goods duty-free. U.S. residents 21 and older may bring back 1 liter of alcohol duty-free. In addition, regardless of your age, you are allowed 200 cigarettes and 100 non-Cuban cigars. Antiques, which the U.S. Customs Service defines as objects more than 100 years old, enter duty-free, as do original works of art done entirely by hand, including paintings, drawings, and sculptures.

You may also send packages home duty-free: up to $200 worth of goods for personal use, with a limit of one parcel per addressee per day (and no alcohol or tobacco products or perfume worth more than $5); label the package PERSONAL USE and attach a list of its contents and their retail value. Do not label the package UNSOLICITED GIFT or your duty-free exemption will drop to $100. Mailed items do not affect your duty-free allowance on your return.

➤ INFORMATION: **U.S. Customs Service** (inquiries, ✉ 1300 Pennsylvania Ave. NW, Washington, DC 20229, ☎ 202/927–6724; complaints, ✉ Office of Regulations and Rulings, 1300 Pennsylvania Ave. NW, Washington, DC 20229; registration of equipment, ✉ Registration Information, 1300 Pennsylvania Ave. NW, Washington, DC 20229, ☎ 202/927–0540).

DINING

Sweden's major cities offer a full range of dining choices, from traditional to international restaurants. Restaurants in smaller towns stick to traditional local fare. Local dishes can be very good, especially in the seafood and game categories, but bear in mind that northern climes beget exceptionally hearty, and heavy, meals. Sausage appears in a thousand forms, likewise potatoes. Some particular northern tastes can seem very different, such as the fondness for pickled and fermented fish—to be sampled carefully at first—and a universal obsession with sweet pastries, ice cream, and chocolate. Other novelties for the visitor might be the use of fruit in main dishes and soups, or sour milk on breakfast cereal, or preserved fish paste as a spread for crackers, or the prevalence of tasty, whole-grain crisp breads and hearty rye breads. The Swedish *smörgåsbord* is often the traveling diner's best bet, providing you find an authentic sampling. They include fresh fish and vegetables alongside meat and starches, and are also among the lower-priced menu choices.

Restaurant meals are a big-ticket item throughout Sweden, but there are ways to keep the cost of eating down. Take full advantage of the large, buffet breakfast usually included in the cost of a hotel room. At lunch, look for the "menu" that offers a set two- or three-course meal for a set price, or limit yourself to a hearty appetizer. Some restaurants now include a trip to the salad bar in the dinner price. At dinner, pay careful attention to the price of wine and drinks, since the high tax on alcohol raises these costs considerably. For more information on affordable eating, *see* Money Matters, *below*.

Properties indicated by an ✕🏠 are lodging establishments whose restaurant warrants a special trip.

RESERVATIONS & DRESS

Reservations are always a good idea: we mention them only when they're essential or are not accepted. Book as far ahead as you can, and reconfirm as soon as you arrive. We mention dress only when men are required to wear a jacket or a jacket and tie.

DISABILITIES & ACCESSIBILITY

Facilities for travelers with disabilities in Sweden are generally good, and most of the major tourist offices offer special booklets and brochures on travel and accommodations.

LODGING

Best Western offers properties with wheelchair-accessible rooms in Stockholm. If wheelchair-accessible rooms are not available, ground-floor rooms are provided.

When discussing accessibility with an operator or reservations agent **ask hard questions.** Are there any stairs, inside *or* out? Are there grab bars next to the toilet *and* in the shower/tub? How wide is the doorway to the room? To the bathroom? For the most extensive facilities meeting the latest legal specifications **opt for newer accommodations.**

➤ Wheelchair-Friendly Chain: **Best Western** (☎ 800/528–1234).

TRANSPORTATION

➤ Complaints: **Disability Rights Section** (✉ U.S. Department of Justice, Civil Rights Division, Box 66738, Washington, DC 20035-6738, ☎ 202/514–0301; 800/514–0301; 202/514–0301 TTY; 800/514–0301 TTY, ℻ 202 /307–1198) for general complaints. **Aviation Consumer Protection Division** (☞ Air Travel, *above*) for airline-related problems. **Civil Rights Office** (✉ U.S. Department of Transportation, Departmental Office of Civil Rights, S-30, 400 7th St. SW, Room 10215, Washington, DC 20590, ☎ 202/366–4648, ℻ 202/366–9371) for problems with surface transportation.

TRAVEL AGENCIES

In the United States, although the Americans with Disabilities Act requires that travel firms serve the needs of all travelers, some agencies specialize in working with people with disabilities.

➤ Travelers with Mobility Problems: **Access Adventures** (✉ 206 Chestnut Ridge Rd., Rochester, NY 14624, ☎ 716/889–9096), run by a former physical-rehabilitation counselor. **Accessible Journeys** (✉ 35 W. Sellers Ave., Ridley Park, PA 19078, ☎ 610/521–0339 or 800/846–4537, ℻ 610/521–6959). **CareVacations** (✉ 5-5110 50th Ave., Leduc, Alberta T9E 6V4, ☎ 780/986–6404 or 877/ 478–7827, ℻ 780/986–8332) has group tours and is especially helpful with cruise vacations. **Flying Wheels Travel** (✉ 143 W. Bridge St., Box 382, Owatonna, MN 55060, ☎ 507/ 451–5005 or 800/535–6790, ℻ 507/ 451–1685). **Hinsdale Travel Service** (✉ 201 E. Ogden Ave., Suite 100, Hinsdale, IL 60521, ☎ 630/325– 1335, ℻ 630/325–1342).

DISCOUNTS & DEALS

Be a smart shopper and **compare all your options** before making decisions. A plane ticket bought with a promotional coupon from travel clubs, coupon books, and direct-mail offers may not be cheaper than the least expensive fare from a discount ticket agency. And always keep in mind that what you get is just as important as what you save.

DISCOUNT RESERVATIONS

To save money **look into discount-reservations services** with toll-free numbers, which use their buying power to get a better price on hotels, airline tickets, even car rentals. When booking a room, always **call the hotel's local toll-free number** (if one is available) rather than the central reservations number—you'll often get a better price. Always ask about special packages or corporate rates.

When shopping for the best deal on hotels and car rentals **look for guaranteed exchange rates,** which protect you against a falling dollar. With your rate locked in, you won't pay more, even if the price goes up in the local currency.

➤ AIRLINE TICKETS: ☎ **800/FLY–4–LESS.**

➤ HOTEL ROOMS: **Steigenberger Reservation Service** (☎ 800/223–5652). **Travel Interlink** (☎ 800/888–5898).

PACKAGE DEALS

Don't confuse packages and guided tours. When you buy a package, you travel on your own, just as though you had planned the trip yourself. Fly/drive packages, which combine airfare and car rental, are often a good deal. If you **buy a rail/drive pass** you may save on train tickets and car rentals. All Eurail- and Europass holders get a discount on Eurostar fares through the Channel Tunnel. Also check rates for Scanrail Passes (☞ Cutting Costs *in* Train Travel, *below*).

ELECTRICITY

To use your U.S.-purchased electric-powered equipment **bring a converter and adapter.** The electrical current in Scandinavia is 220 volts, 50 cycles alternating current (AC); wall outlets take Continental-type plugs, with two round prongs.

If your appliances are dual-voltage you'll need only an adapter. Don't use 110-volt outlets, marked FOR SHAVERS ONLY, for high-wattage appliances such as blow-dryers. Most laptops operate equally well on 110 and 220 volts and so require only an adapter.

EMERGENCIES

Ambulance, fire, and police assistance is available 24 hours in Sweden; dial 112.

EMBASSIES

➤ EMBASSIES IN STOCKHOLM: **Australia** (✉ Sergels Torg 12, ☎ 08/6132900). **Canada** (✉ Tegelbacken 4, Box 16129, 10323 Stockholm, ☎ 08/4533000). **U.K.** (✉ Skarpög. 68, 11593 Stockholm, ☎ 08/6719000). **U.S.** (✉ Strandv. 101, 11589 Stockholm, ☎ 08/7835300).

GAY & LESBIAN TRAVEL

➤ GAY- AND LESBIAN-FRIENDLY TRAVEL AGENCIES: **Different Roads Travel** (✉ 8383 Wilshire Blvd., Suite 902, Beverly Hills, CA 90211, ☎ 323/651–5557 or 800/429–8747, FAX 323/651–3678). **Kennedy Travel** (✉ 314 Jericho Turnpike, Floral Park, NY 11001, ☎ 516/352–4888 or 800/237–7433, FAX 516/354–8849). **Now Voyager** (✉ 4406 18th St., San Francisco, CA 94114, ☎ 415/626–1169 or 800/255–6951, FAX 415/626–8626). **Skylink Travel and Tour** (✉ 1006 Mendocino Ave., Santa Rosa, CA 95401, ☎ 707/546–9888 or 800/225–5759, FAX 707/546–9891), serving lesbian travelers.

INSURANCE

The most useful travel insurance plan is a comprehensive policy that includes coverage for trip cancellation and interruption, default, trip delay, and medical expenses (with a waiver for preexisting conditions).

Without insurance you will lose all or most of your money if you cancel your trip, regardless of the reason. Default insurance covers you if your tour operator, airline, or cruise line goes out of business. Trip-delay covers expenses that arise because of bad weather or mechanical delays. Study the fine print when comparing policies.

If you're traveling internationally, a key component of travel insurance is coverage for medical bills incurred if you get sick on the road. Such expenses are not generally covered by Medicare or private policies. U.K. residents can buy a travel-insurance policy valid for most vacations taken during the year in which it's purchased (but check pre-existing-condi-

SMART TRAVEL TIPS A TO Z

tion coverage). Always **buy travel policies directly from the insurance company**; if you buy it from a cruise line, airline, or tour operator that goes out of business you probably will not be covered for the agency or operator's default, a major risk. Before you make any purchase **review your existing health and homeowner's policies** to find what they cover away from home.

➤ TRAVEL INSURERS: In the U.S. Access America (✉ 6600 W. Broad St., Richmond, VA 23230, ☎ 804/285–3300 or 800/284–8300), **Travel Guard International** (✉ 1145 Clark St., Stevens Point, WI 54481, ☎ 715/345–0505 or 800/826–1300). In Canada **Voyager Insurance** (✉ 44 Peel Center Dr., Brampton, Ontario L6T 4M8, ☎ 905/791–8700; 800/668–4342 in Canada).

➤ INSURANCE INFORMATION: In the U.K. the **Association of British Insurers** (✉ 51–55 Gresham St., London EC2V 7HQ, ☎ 020/7600–3333, ℻ 020/7696–8999). In Australia the **Insurance Council of Australia** (☎ 03/9614–1077, ℻ 03/9614–7924).

LANGUAGE

Despite the fact that four of the five Scandinavian tongues are in the Germanic family of languages, it is a myth that someone who speaks German can understand Danish, Icelandic, Swedish, and Norwegian. Fortunately, English is widely spoken in Scandinavia. German is the most common third language. English becomes rarer outside major cities, and it's a good idea to **take along a dictionary or phrase book.** Even here, however, anyone under the age of 50 is likely to have studied English in school.

Danish, Norwegian, and Swedish are similar, and fluent Norwegian and Swedish speakers can generally understand each other. While Finns must study Swedish (the second national language) in school, they much prefer to speak English with their Scandinavian counterparts.

Characters special to these three languages are the Danish "ø" and the Swedish "ö," pronounced a bit like a very short "er," similar to the French "eu"; "æ" or "ä," which sounds like

the "a" in "ape" but with a glottal stop, or the "a" in "cat," depending on the region, and the "å" (also written "aa"), which sounds like the "o" in "ghost." The important thing about these characters isn't that you pronounce them correctly—foreigners usually can't—but that you know to look for them in the phone book at the very end. Mr. Søren Åstrup, for example, will be found after "Z." Æ or Ä and ø or Ö follow. The Swedish letter "K" softens to a "sh" sound next to certain vowels such as the Ö—beware when pronouncing place names such as Enköping (sounds like "Enshöping").

After "z" in the Swedish alphabet come "å," "ä," and "ö," something to bear in mind when using the phone book. Another oddity in the phone book is that v and w are interchangeable; Wittström, for example, comes before Vittviks, not after.

LODGING

The lodgings we list are the cream of the crop in each price category. We always list the facilities that are available—but we don't specify whether they cost extra. When pricing accommodations, always ask what's included and what costs extra.

In the larger cities, lodging ranges from first-class business hotels run by SAS, Sheraton, and Scandic to good-quality tourist-class hotels, such as RESO, Best Western, Scandic Budget, and Sweden Hotels, to a wide variety of single-entrepreneur hotels. In the countryside, look for independently run inns and motels. Before you leave home, **ask your travel agent about discounts** (☞ Hotels, *below*), including summer hotel checks for Best Western, Scandic, and Inter Nor hotels, a summer Fjord pass in Norway, and enormous year-round rebates at SAS hotels for travelers over 65. All EuroClass (business class) passengers can get discounts of at least 10% at SAS hotels when they book through SAS.

Two things about hotels usually surprise North Americans: the relatively limited dimensions of Scandinavian beds and the generous size of Scandinavian breakfasts. Scandinavian double beds are often about 60 inches wide or slightly less, close in size to the U.S. queen size. King-size beds (72 inches wide) are difficult to find and, if available, require special reservations.

Older hotels may have some rooms described as "double," which in fact have one double bed plus one foldout sofa big enough for two people. This arrangement is occasionally called a combi-room but is being phased out.

Many older hotels, particularly the country inns and independently run smaller hotels in the cities, do not have private bathrooms. Ask ahead if this is important to you.

Scandinavian breakfasts resemble what many people would call lunch, usually including breads, cheeses, marmalade, hams, lunch meats, eggs, juice, cereal, milk, and coffee. Generally, the farther north you go, the larger the breakfasts become. Breakfast is usually included in hotel rates.

Make reservations whenever possible. Even countryside inns, which usually have space, are sometimes packed with vacationing Europeans.

Ask about high and low seasons when making reservations, since different countries define their tourist seasons differently. Some hotels lower prices during tourist season, whereas others raise them during the same period. Sweden virtually shuts down during the entire month of July, so make your hotel reservations in advance, especially if staying outside the city areas during July and early August. Some hotels close during the winter holidays as well; call ahead for information.

Assume that hotels operate on the European Plan (EP, with no meals) unless we specify that they use the Continental Plan (CP, with a Continental breakfast daily), Modified American Plan (MAP, with breakfast and dinner daily), or the Full American Plan (FAP, with all meals).

Sweden offers a variety of accommodations from simple bed-and-breakfasts, camp sites, and hostels to hotels of the highest international standard. Prices are normally on a per-room basis and include all taxes and service charges and usually breakfast. What-

ever their size, almost all Swedish hotels provide scrupulously clean accommodation and courteous service.

HOME EXCHANGES

If you would like to exchange your home for someone else's **join a home-exchange organization,** which will send you its updated listings of available exchanges for a year and will include your own listing in at least one of them. It's up to you to make specific arrangements.

➤ EXCHANGE CLUBS: **HomeLink International** (✉ Box 650, Key West, FL 33041, ☎ 305/294–7766 or 800/638–3841, FAX 305/294–1448; $93 per year). **Intervac U.S.** (✉ Box 590504, San Francisco, CA 94159, ☎ 800/756–4663, FAX 415/435–7440; $83 for catalogues).

CAMPING

There are 760 registered campsites nationwide, many close to uncrowded bathing places and with fishing, boating, or canoeing; they may also offer bicycle rentals. Prices range from SKr 70 to SKr 130 per 24-hour period. Many campsites also offer accommodations in log cabins at various prices, depending on the facilities offered. Most are open between June and September, but about 200 remain open in winter for skiing and skating enthusiasts. The Sveriges Campingvärdarnas Riksförbund publishes, in English, an abbreviated list of sites; contact the office for a free copy.

➤ CONTACT: **Sveriges Campingvärdarnas Riksförbund** (Swedish Campsite Owners' Association or SCR, ✉ Box 255, S451 17 Uddevalla, ☎ 0522/642440, FAX 0522/642430).

CHALET RENTAL

With 250 chalet villages with high standards, Sweden enjoys popularity with its chalet accommodations, often arranged on the spot at tourist offices. Many are organized under the auspices of the Swedish Touring Association. Scandinavian Seaways in Göteborg arranges package deals that combine a ferry trip from Britain across the North Sea and a stay in a chalet village.

➤ CONTACTS: **Swedish Touring Association** (STF; ☎ 08/4632200, FAX 08/

6781938). **Scandinavian Seaways** (☎ 031/650600; within the U.K., 191/2936262) in Göteborg arranges package deals that combine a ferry trip from Britain across the North Sea and a stay in a chalet village.

HOSTELS

No matter what your age you can **save on lodging costs by staying at hostels.** In some 5,000 locations in more than 70 countries around the world, Hostelling International (HI), the umbrella group for a number of national youth-hostel associations, offers single-sex, dorm-style beds and, at many hostels, couples rooms and family accommodations. Membership in any HI national hostel association, open to travelers of all ages, allows you to stay in HI-affiliated hostels at member rates (one-year membership is about $25 for adults; hostels run about $10–$25 per night). Members also have priority if the hostel is full; they're eligible for discounts around the world, even on rail and bus travel in some countries.

➤ ORGANIZATIONS: **Australian Youth Hostel Association** (✉ 10 Mallett St., Camperdown, NSW 2050, ☎ 02/9565–1699, ℻ 02/9565–1325). **Hostelling International—American Youth Hostels** (✉ 733 15th St. NW, Suite 840, Washington, DC 20005, ☎ 202/783–6161, ℻ 202/783–6171). **Hostelling International—Canada** (✉ 400–205 Catherine St., Ottawa, Ontario K2P 1C3, ☎ 613/237–7884, ℻ 613/237–7868). **Youth Hostel Association of England and Wales** (✉ Trevelyan House, 8 St. Stephen's Hill, St. Albans, Hertfordshire AL1 2DY, ☎ 01727/855215 or 01727/845047, ℻ 01727/844126). **Youth Hostels Association of New Zealand** (✉ Box 436, Christchurch, New Zealand, ☎ 03/379–9970, ℻ 03/365–4476). Membership in the U.S. $25, in Canada C$26.75, in the U.K. £9.30, in Australia $44, in New Zealand $24.

HOTELS

Sweden offers Inn Checks, or prepaid hotel vouchers, for accommodations ranging from first-class hotels to country cottages. These vouchers, which must be purchased from travel agents or from the Scandinavian Tourist Board (☞ Visitor Informa-

tion, *below*) before departure, are sold individually and in packets for as many nights as needed and offer savings of up to 50%. Most countries also offer summer bargains for foreign tourists. For further information about Scandinavian hotel vouchers, contact the Scandinavian Tourist Board.

ProSkandinavia checks can be used in 430 hotels across Scandinavia (excluding Iceland) for savings up to 50%, for reservations made usually no earlier than 24 hours before arrival, although some hotels allow earlier bookings. One check costs about $40 U.S. Two checks will pay for a double room at a hotel, one check for a room in a cottage. The checks can be bought at many travel agencies in Scandinavia or ordered from ProSkandinavia. All hotels listed have private bath unless otherwise noted.

The official annual guide, *Hotels in Sweden,* published by and available free from the Swedish Travel and Tourism Council (☞ Visitor Information, *below*), gives comprehensive information about hotel facilities and prices. Countryside Hotels is comprised of 35 select resort hotels, some of them restored manor houses or centuries-old inns. Hotellcentralen is an independent agency that makes advance telephone reservations for any Swedish hotel at no cost. The Sweden Hotels group has about 100 independently owned hotels and its own classification scheme—*A, B,* or *C*—based on facilities.

➤ CONTACTS: **ProSkandinavia** (✉ Nedre Slottsgate 13, N-0157 Oslo, Norway, ☎ 47–22/42–50–06, ℻ 47–22/42–06–57, www.proskandinavia. com). **Countryside Hotels** (✉ Box 69, 830 13 Åre, ☎ 0647/51860, ℻ 0647/51920). **Hotellcentralen** (✉ Central Station, 111 20, ☎ 08/7892425, ℻ 08/7918666).

➤ HOTEL NUMBERS: **Adams Mark** (☎ 800/444/2326). **Baymont Inns** (☎ 800/428–3438). **Best Western** (☎ 800/528–1234 in the U.S., 08/330600 or 020/792752 in Sweden). **Choice** (☎ 800/221–2222). **Clarion** (☎ 800/252–7466). **Colony** (☎ 800/777–1700). **Comfort** (☎ 800/228–5150). **Days Inn** (☎ 800/325–2525). **Dou-**

bletree and Red Lion Hotels (☎ 800/
222–8733). Embassy Suites (☎ 800/
362–2779). Fairfield Inn (☎ 800/
228–2800). Forte (☎ 800/225–5843).
Four Seasons (☎ 800/332–3442).
Hilton (☎ 800/445–8667). Holiday
Inn (☎ 800/465–4329). Howard
Johnson (☎ 800/654–4656). Hyatt
Hotels & Resorts (☎ 800/233–1234).
Inter-Continental (☎ 800/327–0200).
La Quinta (☎ 800/531–5900). Mar-
riott (☎ 800/228–9290). Le Meridien
(☎ 800/543–4300). Nikko Hotels
International (☎ 800/645–5687).
Omni (☎ 800/843–6664). Quality
Inn (☎ 800/228–5151). Radisson (☎
800/333–3333). Radisson SAS (☎
020/797592 in Sweden). Ramada (☎
800/228–2828). Renaissance Hotels
& Resorts (☎ 800/468–3571). RESO
(☎ 08/4114040 in Sweden). Ritz-
Carlton (☎ 800/241–3333). Scandic
(☎ 08/6105050 in Sweden). Sheraton
(☎ 800/325–3535). Sleep Inn (☎
800/753–3746). Sweden Hotels (☎
08/7898900 in Sweden). Westin
Hotels & Resorts (☎ 800/228–3000).
Wyndham Hotels & Resorts (☎ 800/
822-4200).

MAIL

Postcards and letters up to 20 grams
can be mailed for SKr 7 to destinations
within Europe, SKr 8 to the United
States and the rest of the world.

MONEY MATTERS

Costs are high in Sweden where so
many things must be imported. Be
aware that sales taxes can be very
high, but foreigners can get some
refunds by shopping at tax-free stores
(☞ Taxes, *below*). City cards can
save you transportation and entrance
fees in many of the larger cities.

You can **reduce the cost of food by
planning.** Breakfast is often included
in your hotel bill; if not, you may
wish to buy fruit, sweet rolls, and a
beverage for a picnic breakfast. Electrical devices for hot coffee or tea
should be bought abroad, though, to
conform to the local current. **Opt for
a restaurant lunch instead of dinner,**
since the latter tends to be significantly more expensive. Instead of beer
or wine, **drink tap water**—liquor can
cost four times the price of the same
brand in a store—but do specify tap
water, as the term "water" can refer

to soft drinks and bottled water,
which are also expensive. Throughout
Scandinavia, the tip is included in the
cost of your meal.

In most of Scandinavia, liquor and
strong beer (over 3% alcohol) can be
purchased only in state-owned shops,
at very high prices, during weekday
business hours, usually 9:30 to 6 and in
some areas on Saturdays until mid-
afternoon. A midsize bottle of whiskey
in Sweden, for example, can easily cost
SKr 250 (about $35). Weaker beers
and ciders are usually available in
grocery stores in Scandinavia.

Prices throughout this guide are given
for adults. Substantially reduced fees
are almost always available for children, students, and senior citizens. For
information on taxes, *see* Taxes, *below.*

ATMS

The 1,200 or so blue Bankomat cash
dispensers nationwide have been
adapted to take some foreign cards,
including MasterCard, Visa, and
bank cards linked to the Cirrus network. For more information, contact
Bankomat Centralen (☎ 08/
7257240) in Stockholm or your local
bank. **American Express** (✉ Birger
Jarlsg. 1, ☎ 020/793211 toll-free),
has cash and traveler's check dispensers; there's also an office at
Stockholm's Arlanda airport.

➤ ATM LOCATIONS: **Cirrus** (☎ 800/
424–7787).

CREDIT CARDS

Throughout this guide, the following
abbreviations are used: **AE,** American
Express; **DC,** Diner's Club; **MC,**
MasterCard; and **V,** Visa.

CURRENCY

The unit of currency is the krona
(plural kronor), which is divided into
100 öre and is written as SKr or SEK.
The 10-öre coin was phased out in
1991, leaving only the 50-öre, SKr 1,
and SKr 5 coins. These have been
joined by an SKr 10 coin. Bank notes
are at present SKr 20, 50, 100, 500,
and 1,000. At press time (winter
2000), the exchange rate was SKr
8.44 to the dollar, SKr 13.73 to the
pound, and SKr 5.81 to the Canadian
dollar. **Since rates fluctuate daily, you**

SMART TRAVEL TIPS A TO Z

should check them at the time of your departure.

CURRENCY EXCHANGE

For the most favorable rates, **change money through banks.** Although ATM transaction fees may be higher abroad than at home, ATM rates are excellent because they are based on wholesale rates offered only by major banks. You won't do as well at exchange booths in airports or rail and bus stations, in hotels, in restaurants, or in stores. To avoid lines at airport exchange booths **get a bit of local currency before you leave home.**

Traveler's checks and foreign currency can be exchanged at banks all over Sweden and at post offices displaying the NB EXCHANGE sign.

➤ EXCHANGE SERVICES: **International Currency Express** (☎ 888/842–0880 on East Coast; 888/278–6628 on West Coast). **Thomas Cook Currency Services** (☎ 800/287–7362 for telephone orders and retail locations).

SAMPLE PRICES

Cup of coffee, SKr 15–SKr 20; a beer, SKr 30–SKr 45; mineral water, SKr 10–SKr 20; cheese roll, SKr 20–SKr 40; pepper steak à la carte, SKr 120–SKr 160; cheeseburger, SKr 40; pizza, starting at SKr 30.

TRAVELER'S CHECKS

Do you need traveler's checks? It depends on where you're headed. If you're going to rural areas and small towns, go with cash; traveler's checks are best used in cities. Lost or stolen checks can usually be replaced within 24 hours. To ensure a speedy refund, buy your own traveler's checks—don't let someone else pay for them: irregularities like this can cause delays. The person who bought the checks should make the call to request a refund.

OUTDOOR ACTIVITIES AND SPORTS

BIKING

Rental costs average around SKr 90 per day. Tourist offices and **Svenska Turistförening** (Swedish Touring Association or STF, ⊠ Box 25, 101 20 Stockholm, ☎ 08/4632200, FAX 08/6781938) have information about cycling package holidays that include bike rentals, overnight accommodations, and meals. The bicycling organization, **Cykelfrämjandet** (National Cycle Association, ⊠ Torsg. 31, Box 6027, 102 31 Stockholm, ☎ 08/321680 Mon.–Thurs. 9–noon, FAX 08/310503), publishes a free English-language guide to cycling trips.

BOATING AND SAILING

STF, in cooperation with Telia (Sweden's PTT, or Postal, Telephone, and Telegraph authority), publishes an annual guide in Swedish to all the country's marinas. It is available from **Telia Infomedia** (☎ 08/6341700) or in your nearest Telebutik. **Svenska Kanotförbundet** (Swedish Canoeing Association, ⊠ Idrotts Hus, 123 87 Farsta, ☎ 08/6056565) publishes a similar booklet.

GOLFING

Sweden has 365 golf clubs; you can even play by the light of the midnight sun at Boden in the far north. **Svenska Golfförbundet** (Swedish Golfing Association, ⊠ Box 84, 182 11 Danderyd, ☎ 08/6221500, FAX 08/7558439) publishes an annual guide in Swedish; it costs around SKr 100, including postage.

SKIING

There are plenty of downhill and cross-country facilities in Sweden. The best-known resorts are in the country's western mountains: Åre in the north, with 29 lifts; Idre Fjäll, to the south of Åre, offering accommodations for 10,000; and Sälen in the folklore region of Dalarna. You can ski through May at Riksgränsen in the far north.

TENNIS

Contact **Svenska Tennisförbundet** (Swedish Tennis Association, ⊠ Lidingöv. 75, Box 27915, 115 94 Stockholm, ☎ 08/6679770, FAX 08/6646606).

PACKING

Bring a folding umbrella and a lightweight raincoat, as it is common for the sky to be clear at 9 AM, rainy at 11 AM, and clear again in time for lunch. **Pack casual clothes,** as Swedes tend to dress more casually than their Continental brethren. If you have trouble sleeping when it is light or are sensitive to strong sun, **bring an eye mask and dark sunglasses;** the sun rises as early as 4 AM in some areas, and the far-northern latitude causes it to slant at angles unseen elsewhere on the globe. Bring bug repellent if you plan to venture away from the capital cities; large mosquitoes can be a real nuisance on summer evenings throughout Sweden.

In your carry-on luggage **bring an extra pair of eyeglasses or contact lenses** and **enough of any medication you take** to last the entire trip. You may also want your doctor to write a spare prescription using the drug's generic name, since brand names may vary from country to country. In luggage to be checked, **never pack prescription drugs or valuables.** To avoid customs delays, carry medications in their original packaging. And don't forget to copy down and carry addresses of offices that handle refunds of lost traveler's checks.

CHECKING LUGGAGE

How many carry-on bags you can bring with you is up to the airline. Most allow two, but not always, so make sure that everything you carry aboard will fit under your seat, and get to the gate early. Note that if you have a seat at the back of the plane, you'll probably board first, while the overhead bins are still empty.

If you are flying internationally, note that baggage allowances may be determined not by piece but by weight— generally 88 pounds (40 kilograms) in first class, 66 pounds (30 kilograms) in business class, and 44 pounds (20 kilograms) in economy.

Airline liability for baggage is limited to $1,250 per person on flights within the United States. On international flights it amounts to $9.07 per pound or $20 per kilogram for checked baggage (roughly $640 per 70-pound bag) and $400 per passenger for unchecked baggage. You can buy additional coverage at check-in for about $10 per $1,000 of coverage, but it excludes a rather extensive list of items, shown on your airline ticket.

Before departure **itemize your bags' contents** and their worth, and label the bags with your name, address, and phone number. (If you use your home address, cover it so that potential thieves can't see it readily.) Inside each bag **pack a copy of your itinerary.** At check-in **make sure that each bag is correctly tagged** with the destination airport's three-letter code. If your bags arrive damaged or fail to arrive at all, file a written report with the airline before leaving the airport.

PASSPORTS & VISAS

When traveling internationally **carry a passport even if you don't need one** (it's always the best form of ID), and **make two photocopies of the data page** (one for someone at home and another for you, carried separately from your passport). If you lose your passport promptly call the nearest embassy or consulate and the local police.

ENTERING SWEDEN

All U.S. citizens, even infants, need only a valid passport to enter any Scandinavian country for stays of up to three months.

PASSPORT OFFICES

The best time to apply for a passport or to renew is during the fall and winter. Before any trip, check your passport's expiration date, and, if necessary, renew it as soon as possible.

➤ AUSTRALIAN CITIZENS: **Australian Passport Office** (☎ 131–232).

➤ CANADIAN CITIZENS: **Passport Office** (☎ 819/994–3500 or 800/567–6868).

➤ NEW ZEALAND CITIZENS: **New Zealand Passport Office** (☎ 04/494–0700 for information on how to apply; 04/474–8000 or 0800/225–050 in New Zealand for information on applications already submitted).

➤ U.K. CITIZENS: **London Passport Office** (☎ 0990/210–410) for fees and documentation requirements and to request an emergency passport.

➤ U.S. CITIZENS: **National Passport Information Center** (☎ 900/225–5674; calls are 35¢ per minute for automated service, $1.05 per minute for operator service).

SMART TRAVEL TIPS A TO Z

SENIOR-CITIZEN TRAVEL

To qualify for age-related discounts **mention your senior-citizen status up front** when booking hotel reservations (not when checking out) and before you're seated in restaurants (not when paying the bill). When renting a car ask about promotional car-rental discounts, which can be cheaper than senior-citizen rates.

TRAIN TRAVEL

Travelers over 60 can buy a **SeniorRail Card** for about $27 in Sweden. It gives 30% discounts on train travel in 21 European countries for a whole year from purchase. Certain countries may offer even greater discounts.

➤ EDUCATIONAL PROGRAMS: **Elderhostel** (✉ 75 Federal St., 3rd fl., Boston, MA 02110, ☎ 877/426–8056, FAX 877/426–2166). **Interhostel** (✉ University of New Hampshire, 6 Garrison Ave., Durham, NH 03824, ☎ 603/862–1147 or 800/733–9753, FAX 603/862–1113).

SHOPPING

Prices in Sweden are never low, but quality is high, and specialties are sometimes less expensive here than elsewhere. Swedish crystal is one of the items to look for. Keep an eye out for sales, called *rea* in Swedish.

STUDENTS IN SWEDEN

➤ STUDENT IDs & SERVICES: **Council on International Educational Exchange** (CIEE, ✉ 205 E. 42nd St., 14th fl., New York, NY 10017, ☎ 212/822–2600 or 888/268–6245, FAX 212/822–2699) for mail orders only, in the U.S. **Travel Cuts** (✉ 187 College St., Toronto, Ontario M5T 1P7, ☎ 416/979–2406 or 800/667–2887) in Canada.

TAXES

VALUE-ADDED TAX (V.A.T.)

One way to beat high prices is to **take advantage of tax-free shopping.** Throughout Scandinavia, you can make major purchases free of tax if you have a foreign passport. Ask about tax-free shopping when you make a purchase for $50 (about £32) or more. When your purchases exceed a specified limit (which varies from country to country), you receive a special export receipt. Keep the parcels intact and take them out of the country within 30 days of purchase. When you leave the last EU country visited, you can obtain a refund of the V.A.T. (called *moms* all over Scandinavia) in cash from a special office at the airport, or, upon arriving home, you can send your receipts to an office in the country of purchase to receive your refund by mail. Citizens of EU countries are not eligible for the refund.

All hotel, restaurant, and departure taxes and V.A.T. are automatically included in prices. V.A.T. is 25%; non-EU residents can obtain a 15% refund on goods of SKr 200 or more. To receive your refund at any of the 15,000 stores that participate in the tax-free program, you'll be asked to fill out a form and show your passport. The form can then be turned in at any airport or ferry customs desk. Keep all your receipts and tags; occasionally, customs authorities ask to see your purchases, so pack them where they will be accessible.

Note: Tax-free sales of alcohol, cigarettes, and other luxury goods has been abolished among EU countries, with the Scandinavian countries among the last to adopt these regulations. The Aland islands, however, are not part of the EU customs union and allows tax-free sales for ferries in transit through its ports. All Sweden–Finland ferry routes now pass through the islands, de facto continuing the extremely popular tax-free sales for tourists. Air travel to the Scandinavia EU member states (Sweden, Finland, Denmark), as well as Norway, no longer allows tax-free sales.

Europe Tax-Free Shopping is a V.A.T. refund service that makes getting your money back hassle-free. E.T.S. is Europe-wide and has 90,000 affiliated stores. In participating stores, **ask for the E.T.S. refund form** (called a Shopping Cheque). As is true for all customs forms, when leaving the European Union you get them stamped by the customs official. Then you take them to the E.T.S. counter and they will refund your money right there in cash, by check, or a refund to your credit card. All that convenience will cost you 20%—but then it's done.

➤ VAT REFUNDS: **Global Refund** (⊠ 707 Summer St., Stamford, CT 06901, ☎ 800/566–9828).

TELEPHONES

Post offices do not have telephone facilities, but there are plenty of pay phones, and long-distance calls can be made from special telegraph offices called *Telebutik,* marked TELE.

COUNTRY & AREA CODES

The country code for Sweden is 46. When dialing a Swedish number from abroad, drop the initial 0 from the local area code. The country code is 1 for the U.S. and Canada, 61 for Australia, 64 for New Zealand, and 44 for the U.K.

DIRECTORY ASSISTANCE AND OPERATOR INFORMATION

For international calls, the operator assistance number is ☎ 0018; directory assistance is ☎ 07977. Within Sweden, dial ☎ 90130 for operator assistance and ☎ 118118 for directory assistance.

INTERNATIONAL CALLS

To make an international call, dial 00 followed by the country code, and then your number. AT&T, MCI, and Sprint access codes make calling long distance relatively convenient, but you may find the local access number blocked in many hotel rooms. First ask the hotel operator to connect you. If the hotel operator balks ask for an international operator, or dial the international operator yourself. One way to improve your odds of getting connected to your long-distance carrier is to travel with more than one company's calling card (a hotel may block Sprint, for example, but not MCI). If all else fails call from a pay phone.

➤ ACCESS CODES: **AT&T USADirect** (☎ 020/795611 Sweden). **MCI Call USA** (☎ 020/795922 Sweden). **Sprint Express** (☎ 020/799011 Sweden).

LOCAL CALLS

A local call costs a minimum of SKr 2. For calls outside the locality, dial the area code (see telephone directory). Public phones are of three types: one takes SKr 1 and SKr 5 coins (newer public phones also accept SKr 10 coins); another takes only credit cards; and the last takes only the prepaid *Telefonkort*.

A *Telefonkort* (telephone card), available at Telebutik, Pressbyrån (large blue-and-yellow newsstands), or hospitals, costs SKr 35, SKr 60, or SKr 100. If you're making numerous domestic calls, the card saves money. Many of the pay phones in downtown Stockholm and Göteborg take only these cards, so it's a good idea to carry one.

TIPPING

In addition to the 12% value-added tax, most hotels usually include a service charge of 15%; it is not necessary to tip unless you have received extra services. Similarly, a service charge of 13% is usually included in restaurant bills. It is a custom, however, to leave small change when buying drinks. Taxi drivers and hairdressers expect a tip of about 10%.

TOURS & PACKAGES

On a prepackaged tour or independent vacation everything is prearranged so you'll spend less time planning—and often get it all at a good price.

BOOKING WITH AN AGENT

Travel agents are excellent resources. But it's a good idea to collect brochures from several agencies because some agents' suggestions may be influenced by relationships with tour and package firms that reward them for volume sales. If you have a special interest **find an agent with expertise in that area**; ASTA (☞ Travel Agencies, *below*) has a database of specialists worldwide.

Make sure your travel agent knows the accommodations and other services of the place they're recommending. Ask about the hotel's location, room size, beds, and whether it has a pool, room service, or programs for children, if you care about these. Has your agent been there in person or sent others whom you can contact?

Do some homework on your own, too: Local tourism boards can provide information about lesser-known and small-niche operators, some of which may sell only direct.

BUYER BEWARE

Each year consumers are stranded or lose their money when tour operators—even large ones with excellent reputations—go out of business. So **check out the operator.** Ask several travel agents about its reputation, and try to **book with a company that has a consumer-protection program.** (Look for information in the company's brochure.) In the United States, members of the National Tour Association and United States Tour Operators Association are required to set aside funds to cover your payments and travel arrangements in case the company defaults. It's also a good idea to choose a company that participates in the American Society of Travel Agents' Tour Operator Program (TOP); ASTA will act as mediator in any disputes between you and your tour operator.

Remember that the more your package or tour includes the better you can predict the ultimate cost of your vacation. Make sure you know exactly what is covered, and **beware of hidden costs.** Are taxes, tips, and transfers included? Entertainment and excursions? These can add up.

➤ TOUR-OPERATOR RECOMMENDATIONS: **American Society of Travel Agents** (☞ Travel Agencies, *below*). **National Tour Association** (NTA, ✉ 546 E. Main St., Lexington, KY 40508, ☎ 606/226–4444 or 800/682–8886). **Stockholm Sightseeing** (✉ Skeppsbron 22, ☎ 08/58714000). **United States Tour Operators Association** (USTOA, ✉ 342 Madison Ave., Suite 1522, New York, NY 10173, ☎ 212/599–6599 or 800/468–7862, FAX 212/599–6744).

TRAIN TRAVEL

Statens Järnvägar, or SJ, the state railway company, has a highly efficient network of comfortable, electric trains. On nearly all long-distance routes there are buffet cars and, on overnight trips, sleeping cars and couchettes in both first and second class. Seat reservations are advisable, and on some trains—indicated with *R, IN,* or *IC* on the timetable—they are compulsory. An extra fee of SKr 15 is charged to reserve a seat on a

trip of less than 150 km (93 mi); on longer trips there is no extra charge. Reservations can be made right up to departure time. The **high-speed X2000 train** has been introduced on several routes; the Stockholm–Göteborg run takes just under three hours. Travelers younger than 19 years travel at half-fare. Up to two children younger than 12 years may travel free if accompanied by an adult.

From London, the British Rail European Travel Center can be helpful in arranging connections to Sweden's SJ (Statens Järnvägar).

➤ INFORMATION: **British Rail European Travel Center** (✉ Victoria Station, London, ☎ 020/78342345). **Statens Järnvägar (SJ)** (✉ Central Station, Vasag. 1, ☎ 08/7622000 or 020/757575; 020/757575 for reservations).

CUTTING COSTS

For SKr 150 you can buy a *Reslustkort,* which gets you 50% reductions on *röda avgångar* ("red," or off-peak, departures).

Consider a Scanrail Pass, available for travel in Sweden, Norway, and Finland for both first- and second-class train travel: you may have five days of unlimited travel in a 15-day period ($222 first-class/$176 second-class); 10 days of unlimited travel in a month ($354/$248); or one month of consecutive day unlimited train travel ($516/$414). With the Scanrail Pass, you also enjoy travel bonuses, including free or discounted ferry, boat, and bus travel and a Hotel Discount Card that allows 10–30% off rates for select hotels June–August. Passengers 12–25 can **buy Scanrail Youth Passes** ($167 first-class/$132 second-class, five travel days in 15 days; $266/$213 for 10 travel days in a month; $387/$311 for one month of unlimited travel). Those over 55 can **take advantage of the Scanrail 55+** Pass, which offers the travel bonuses of the Scanrail Pass and discounted travel ($198 first-class/$157 second-class, five days; $315/$253 10 days; $459/$368 one month). Buy Scanrail passes through Rail Europe and travel agents.

For car and train travel, price the Scanrail'n Drive Pass: in 15 days you can get five days of unlimited train travel and three days of car rental (choice of three car categories) with unlimited mileage in Denmark, Finland, Norway, and Sweden. You can purchase extra car rental days and choose from first- or second-class train travel. Rates for two adults (compact car $315 first-class/$275 second-class), are considerably lower (about 25%) than for single adults.

In Scandinavia, you can **use Eurail-Passes,** which provide unlimited first-class rail travel, in all of the participating countries, for the duration of the pass. If you plan to rack up the miles, get a standard pass. These are available for 15 days ($522), 21 days ($678), one month ($838), two months ($1,188), and three months ($1,468). Eurail- and EuroPasses are available through travel agents and Rail Europe. The Eurail and InterRail passes are both valid in Sweden. SJ also organizes reduced-cost package trips in conjunction with local tourist offices. Details are available at any railway station or from SJ.

In addition to standard EurailPasses, **ask about special rail-pass plans.** Among these are the Eurail YouthPass (for those under age 26), the Eurail SaverPass (which gives a discount for two or more people traveling together), a Eurail FlexiPass (which allows a certain number of travel days within a set period), the Euraildrive Pass, and the EuroPass Drive (which combines travel by train and rental car).

Whichever pass you choose, remember that you must **purchase your pass before you leave** for Europe.

Many travelers assume that rail passes guarantee them seats on the trains they wish to ride. Not so. You need to **book seats ahead even if you are using a rail pass;** seat reservations are required on some European trains, particularly high-speed trains, and are a good idea on trains that may be crowded—particularly in summer on popular routes. You will also need a reservation if you purchase sleeping accommodations.

※ ➤ WHERE TO BUY RAIL PASSES: **Rail Europe** (✉ 226–230 Westchester Ave., White Plains, NY 10604, ☎ 914/682–5172, 800/848–7245, or 800/438–7245; 2087 Dundas East, Suite 105, Mississauga, Ontario L4X 1M2, ☎ 416/602–4195). **DER Tours** (✉ Box 1606, Des Plaines, IL 60017, ☎ 800/782–2424, FAX 800/282–7474). **CIT Tours Corp.** (✉ 342 Madison Ave., Suite 207, New York, NY 10173, ☎ 212/697–2100 or 800/248–8687, or 800/248–7245 in western U.S.).

TRANSPORTATION AROUND SCANDINAVIA

Vast distances between cities and towns make air transportation a cost-efficient mode of travel in Scandinavia. SAS is Scandinavia's major air carrier; it also operates domestic lines in Norway, Sweden, and Denmark. SAS offers discount packages for travel among the Scandinavian capitals, as well as reduced domestic fares in the summer. Finnair is also expanding its routes in Scandinavia.

Trains—comfortable, clean, and fast—are good for covering large distances in Scandinavia. Remember to ask for a smoking or nonsmoking seat or compartment. You should inquire with your travel agent about Scanrail Passes for travel within the region.

Another means of getting around Scandinavia's countries is to go by ferry. These huge vessels offer a combination of efficient travel (you sleep aboard and wake up in your destination the next morning) and amenities approaching what you might expect on a cruise ship: luxury dining, gambling, a sauna and pool, and entertainment. Travelers should beware, however, that the noise level may be high and the crowd is usually very lively.

If you prefer the freedom of planning an itinerary and traveling at your own pace, a rental car is a good, albeit expensive, alternative. Most major car rental companies operate in Scandinavia. Roads are generally good, but allow plenty of time for navigating the region's winding highway network. Scandinavia enforces some of the most strict drinking-and-driving laws in the world—a drunk driver could end up in jail after one offense.

SMART TRAVEL TIPS A TO Z

Public transportation in Scandinavia's cities is safe, fast, and inexpensive. Some cities, including the capitals, offer day passes reducing the cost of buses and train travel.

Taxis in Scandinavia are safe, clean, *and* expensive. All taxis should be clearly marked and have a meter inside; unmarked taxis—usually operated illegally by unlicensed drivers—are not recommended. A 10% tip is a friendly gesture, but by no means necessary. Most taxis accept major credit cards and cash.

TRAVEL AGENCIES

A good travel agent puts your needs first. Look for an agency that has been in business at least five years, emphasizes customer service, and has someone on staff who specializes in your destination. In addition **make sure the agency belongs to a professional trade organization.** The American Society of Travel Agents (ASTA), with 27,000 agents in some 170 countries, is the largest and most influential in the field. Operating under the motto "Integrity in Travel," it maintains and enforces a strict code of ethics and will step in to help mediate any agent-client disputes if necessary. ASTA also maintains a Web site that includes a directory of agents. Note that if a travel agency is also acting as your tour operator, *see* Buyer Beware *in* Tours & Packages, *above.*

➤ Local Agent Referrals: American Society of Travel Agents (ASTA, ☎ 800/965–2782 24-hr hot line, FAX 703/684–8319, www.astanet.com). Association of British Travel Agents (✉ 68–271 Newman St., London W1P 4AH, ☎ 020/7637–2444, FAX 020/7637–0713). Association of Canadian Travel Agents (✉ 1729 Bank St., Suite 201, Ottawa, Ontario K1V 7Z5, ☎ 613/521–0474, FAX 613/521–0805). Australian Federation of Travel Agents (✉ Level 3, 309 Pitt St., Sydney 2000, ☎ 02/9264–3299, FAX 02/9264–1085). Travel Agents' Association of New Zealand (✉ Box 1888, Wellington 10033, ☎ 04/499–0104, FAX 04/499–0786).

VISITOR INFORMATION

➤ Scandinavian Tourist Boards: U.S.: Scandinavian Tourist Board (✉ 655 3rd Ave., New York, New York 10017-5617, ☎ 212/949–2333 or 212/8859700, FAX 212/983–5260 or 212/6970835).

U.K.: Swedish Travel and Tourism Council (✉ 73 Welbeck St., London W1M 8AN, ☎ 020/7935–9784, FAX 020/7935–5853).

Sweden: Swedish Travel and Tourism Council (✉ Box 3030, Kungsg. 36, 103 61 Stockholm, ☎ 08/7255500, FAX 08/7255531). Stockholm Information Service at Sweden House (Sverigehuset, ✉ Hamng. 27, Box 7542, 103 93 Stockholm, ☎ 08/7892490).

➤ U.S. Government Advisories: U.S. Department of State (✉ Overseas Citizens Services Office, Room 4811 N.S., 2201 C St. NW, Washington, DC 20520; ☎ 202/647–5225 for interactive hot line; 301/946–4400 for computer bulletin board; FAX 202/647–3000 for interactive hot line); enclose a self-addressed, stamped, business-size envelope.

WEB SITES

Do **check out the World Wide Web** when you're planning. You'll find everything from up-to-date weather forecasts to virtual tours of famous cities. Fodor's Web site www.fodors.com, is a great place to start your online travels.

FERRY OPERATORS

Color Line (www.colorline.com), Fjord Line (www.fjordline.com), ScandLines (www.scandlines.com), Scandinavian Seaways (www.scansea.com), Silja Line (www.silja.com), Smyril Line (www.smyril-line.fo), Stena Line (www.stenaline.dk), Viking Line (www.vikingline.fi)

DANISH RESOURCES

Tourism information (general, www.dt.dk; oriented toward North American visitors, www.visitdenmark.dt.dk; oriented toward British and Irish visitors, www.dtb.dt.dk).

SWEDISH RESOURCES

Tourism information (general English-speaking information, www.gosweden.org; general information,

www.visit-sweden.com or
www.sverigeturism.se/smorgasbord).

WHEN TO GO

The Swedish tourist season runs from
mid-May through mid-September and
peaks in June, July, and August, when
daytime temperatures are often in the
70s (21°C to 26°C) and sometimes
rise into the 80s (27°C to 32°C).
Many attractions close in late August,
when the schools reopen at the end of
the Swedish vacation season. The
weather can be glorious in the spring
and fall, and many visitors prefer
sightseeing when there are fewer
people around. In general, the
weather is not overly warm, and a
brisk breeze and brief rainstorms are
possible anytime. Nights can be chilly,
even in summer.

Visit in summer if you want to experience the delightfully long summer
days. In Stockholm, the weeks just
before and after Midsummer offer
almost 24-hour light, whereas in the
far north, above the Arctic Circle, the
sun doesn't set between the end of
May and the middle of July. Many
attractions extend their hours during
the summer, and many shut down
altogether when summer ends. Fall,
spring, and even winter are pleasant,
despite the area's reputation for
gloom. The days become shorter
quickly, but the sun casts a golden
light not seen farther south. On dark
days, fires and candlelight will warm
you indoors.

Away from the protection of the Gulf
Stream, Sweden experiences very
cold, clear weather that attracts
skiers; even Stockholm's harbor, well
south in Sweden but facing the Baltic
Sea, freezes over completely.

CLIMATE

The following are average daily
maximum and minimum temperatures for Stockholm.

➤ FORECASTS: **Weather Channel Connection** (☎ 900/932–8437), 95¢ per
minute from a Touch-Tone phone.

STOCKHOLM

Jan.	30F	−1C	May	57F	14C	Sept.	59F	15C
	23	−54		3	6		48	9
Feb.	30F	−1C	June	66F	19C	Oct.	48F	9C
	23	−5		52	11		41	5
Mar.	37F	3C	July	72F	22C	Nov.	41F	5C
	25	−4		57	14		34	1
Apr.	46F	8C	Aug.	68F	20C	Dec.	36F	2C
	34	1		55	13		28	−2

FESTIVALS AND SEASONAL EVENTS

➤ JAN. 13: **Knut** signals the end of
Christmas festivities and "plunder-
ing" of the Christmas tree: Trinkets
are removed from the tree, edible
ornaments gobbled up, and the tree
itself thrown out.

➤ FEB. (FIRST THURS., FRI., AND SAT.):
A **market** held in Jokkmokk features
both traditional Sami-Lapp artifacts
and plenty of reindeer. On **Shrove
Tuesday** special buns called *semlor*—
lightly flavored with cardamom, filled
with almond paste and whipped
cream—are traditionally placed in a
dish of warm milk, topped with
cinnamon, and eaten.

➤ MAR. (FIRST SUN.): The **Vasaloppet
Ski Race** treks 88 km (55 mi) from
Sälen to Mora in Dalarna, and attracts entrants from all over the
world.

➤ APR.: On **Maundy Thursday,** which
marks the beginning of Easter celebrations, small girls dress up as
witches and hand out "Easter letters"
for small change or candy. *Påskris,*
twigs tipped with brightly dyed
feathers, decorate homes. On April
30, for the **Feast of Valborg,** bonfires
are lit to celebrate the end of winter.
The liveliest celebrations involve the
students of the university cities of
Uppsala, 60 km (37 mi) north of

Stockholm, and Lund, 16 km (10 mi) north of Malmö.

➤ MAY 1: **Labor Day** marches and rallies are held nationwide, and politicians give speeches at the town square. *Tjejtrampet,* one of the world's largest bicycle races for women, takes place in May as well, along with the start of the season at the Drottningholm Court Theater.

➤ JUNE 6: **National Day** is celebrated, with parades, speeches, and band concerts nationwide.

➤ JUNE: In early June, the **Restaurant Festival** fills Kungsträgården with booths offering inexpensive international cuisine, and the **Orient Festival** brings Arabic dance, music, food, and culture to Djurgården. Also in June is the **Stockholm Marathon. Midsummer's Eve and Day** celebrations are held on the Friday evening and Saturday that fall between June 20 and 26. Swedes raise maypoles decorated with floral garlands and sing, play games, and dance all night long.

➤ AUG.: **Stockholm Water Festival** celebrates the city's clean water environment with water-sports performances, a fireworks competition, and many other events all over town. Crayfish are considered a delicacy in Sweden, and the second Wednesday of August marks the **Crayfish premiere,** when friends gather to eat them at outdoor parties.

➤ NOV.: The **Stockholm Film Festival** brings world-class films, directors, and actors to the city. The **Stockholm**

Open tennis tournament and the **Stockholm International Horse Show** are other big draws.

➤ NOV. 11: **St. Martin's Day** is celebrated primarily in the southern province of Skåne. Roast goose is served, accompanied by *svartsoppa,* a bisque made of goose blood and spices.

➤ DEC.: For each of the four weeks of **Advent,** leading up to Christmas, a candle is lit in a four-pronged candelabra. The **Stockholm International Poetry Festival** features poets from around the globe.

➤ DEC. 10: **Nobel Day** sees the presentation of the Nobel prizes by King Carl XVI Gustaf at a glittering banquet held in the Stockholm City Hall.

➤ DEC. 13: On **Santa Lucia Day** young girls are selected to be "Lucias"; they wear candles—today usually electric substitutes—in their hair and sing hymns with their handmaidens and "star boys" at ceremonies around the country.

➤ DEC. 24: **Christmas Eve** is the principal day of Christmas celebration. Traditional Christmas dishes include ham, rice porridge, and *lutfisk* (dried ling that is soaked in lye and then boiled).

➤ DEC. 31: **New Year's Eve** is the Swedes' occasion to set off an astounding array of fireworks. Every household has its own supply, and otherwise quiet neighborhood streets are full of midnight merrymakers.

1 DESTINATION: SWEDEN

SWEDISH SPECTACULAR

SWEDEN REQUIRES THE VISI-
TOR to travel far, in terms of
both distance and attitude.
Approximately the size of California, Sweden reaches as far north as the Arctic
fringes of Europe, where glacier-topped
mountains and thousands of acres of pine,
spruce, and birch forests are broken here
and there by wild rivers, countless pristine lakes, and desolate moorland. In the
more populated south, roads meander
through mile after mile of softly undulating
countryside, skirting lakes and passing
small villages with their ubiquitous sharp-
pointed church spires. Here, the lush
forests that dominate Sweden's northern
landscape have largely fallen to the plow.

Once the dominant power of the region, Sweden has traditionally looked mostly inward,
seeking to find its own, Nordic solutions.
During the cold war, it tried with considerable success to steer its famous "Middle
Way" between the two superpowers, both
economically and politically. Its citizens
were in effect subjected to a giant social ex-
periment aimed at creating a perfectly just
society, one that adopted the best aspects
of both socialism and capitalism.

In the late 1980s, as it slipped into the worst
economic recession since the 1930s, Sweden made adjustments that lessened the
role of its all-embracing welfare state in
the lives of its citizens. Although fragile,
the conservative coalition, which defeated
the long-incumbent Social Democrats in
the fall of 1991, attempted to make further cutbacks in welfare spending as the
country faced one of the largest budget
deficits in Europe. In a kind of nostalgic
backlash, the populace voted the Social
Democrats back into power in 1994, hop-
ing to recapture the party's policy of cra-
dle-to-grave protection. The world economy
hasn't exactly cooperated, and the country's budget deficit is only now crawling
back to parity. An influx of immigrants
is reshaping what was once a homogeneous
society. As a result, the mostly blond,
blue-eyed Swedes may now be more open
to the outside world than at any other time
in their history. Indeed, another major

change was Sweden's decision to join the
European Union (EU) as of January 1995,
a move that represents a radical break
with its traditional independent stance
on international issues. So far, the domestic benefits of membership are not
tangible, but the country's exporting industries have made considerable gains.

The country possesses stunning natural assets. In the forests, moose, deer, bears,
and lynx roam, coexisting with the whine
of power saws and the rumble of automatic
logging machines as mankind exploits a
natural resource that remains the country's economic backbone. Environmental
awareness, however, is high. Fish abound
in sparkling lakes and tumbling rivers,
sea eagles and ospreys soar over myriad
pine-clad islands in the archipelagoes off
the east and west coasts.

The country is Europe's fourth largest,
482,586 square km (173,731 square mi)
in area, and its population of 8.7 million
is thinly spread. If, like Greta Garbo—one
of its most famous exports—you enjoy
being alone, you've come to the right
place. A law called Allemansrätt guaran-
tees public access to the countryside; NO
TRESPASSING signs are seldom seen.

Sweden stretches 1,563 km (977 mi) from
the barren Arctic north to the fertile plains
of the south. Contrasts abound, but they are
neatly tied together by a superbly efficient
infrastructure, embracing air, road, and rail.
You can catch salmon in the far north and,
thanks to the excellent domestic air network, have it cooked by the chef of your luxury hotel in Stockholm later the same day.

The seasons contrast savagely: Sweden is
usually warm and exceedingly light in the
summer, then cold and dark in the winter. The sea may freeze, and in the north,
iron railway lines may snap.

Sweden is also an arresting mixture of
ancient and modern. The countryside is
dotted with runic stones recalling its Viking
past: trade beginning in the 8th century
eastward to Kiev and as far south as Constantinople and the Mediterranean, expanding to the British Isles in the 9th
through 11th centuries, and settling in

Normandy in the 10th century. Small timbered farmhouses and maypoles around which villagers still dance at Midsummer in their traditional costumes evoke both the pagan early history and the more recent agrarian culture.

Many of the country's cities are sci-fi modern, their shop windows filled with the latest in consumer goods and fashions, but Swedes are reluctant urbanites: their hearts and souls are in the forests and the archipelagoes, and to there they faithfully retreat in the summer and on weekends to take their holidays, pick berries, or just listen to the silence. The skills of the woodcarver, the weaver, the leather worker, and the glassblower are all highly prized. Similarly, Swedish humor is earthy and slapstick. Despite the praise lavished abroad on introspective dramatic artists such as August Strindberg and Ingmar Bergman, it is the simple trouser-dropping farce that will fill Stockholm's theaters, the scatological joke that will get the most laughs.

Again, despite the international musical success of the Swedish rock groups Ace of Base, Roxette, and Abba, the domestic penchant is more often for the good, old-fashioned dance band. Gray-haired men in pastel sweaters playing saxophones are more common on TV than heavy-metal rockers. Strangely, in ultramodern concert halls and discos, it is possible to step back in time to the 1950s, if not the 1940s.

Despite the much-publicized sexual liberation of Swedes, the joys of hearth and home are most prized in what remains in many ways an extremely conservative society. Conformity, not liberty, is the real key to the Swedish character. However, the good of the collective is slowly being replaced by that of the individual as socialism begins to lose its past appeal.

At the same time, Swedes remain devoted royalists and patriots, avidly following the fortunes of King Carl XVI Gustaf, Queen Silvia, and their children in the media, and raising the blue-and-yellow national flag each morning on the flagpoles of their country cottages. Few nations, in fact, make as much of an effort to preserve and defend their natural heritage. It is sometimes difficult in cities such as Stockholm, Göteborg, or Malmö to realize that you are in an urban area. Right in the center of Stockholm, thanks to a cleanup program in the 1970s, you can fish for salmon or go for a swim. In Göteborg's busy harbor, you can sit aboard a ship bound for the archipelago and watch fish jump out of the water; in Malmö hares hop around in the downtown parks. It is this pristine quality of life that can make a visit to Sweden a step out of time, a relaxing break from the modern world.

–Updated by Devin Wilson

NEW AND NOTEWORTHY

Scandinavia's largest country, Sweden has always been politically independent and commercially prolific, but despite strong exports, domestically Swedes are still fighting the effects of the worst economic recession to hit the country since the 1930s. The downturn began in the late '80s and shook the very foundations of Sweden's social structure.

Although the economy bounced back a bit in the mid-'90s, perhaps due in part to Sweden's entry into the EU in January 1995, the end of the decade has presented another downturn, and this has caused some of Sweden's large companies to struggle. Smaller businesses, on the other hand, particularly those focused on the Internet and related technologies, are flourishing.

But this is good news for you, as the weak krona means that Sweden has become a relatively inexpensive place to vacation, although hotel and restaurant prices are still relatively higher than those in the United States.

Travel between Arland airport and Stockholm has been greatly improved with the completion of the Arlanda Express, a high-speed train service that started running in August 1999. The train, which leaves every 15 minutes, travels at speeds of up to 200 kph (135 mph) and completes the trip in just 20 minutes. Tickets cost SKr 120. The southern tip of Sweden, particularly the city of Malmö, is currently preparing for a major change as the bridge across Øresund from Sweden to Denmark nears its scheduled completion date in June 2000. The economic and environmental impact of the bridge is yet to be seen, but it's certain that tourist travel will be enhanced as both car and train traffic begin to replace the ferry services.

WHAT'S WHERE

In Sweden, streamlined, ultramodern cities give way to lush forests and timbered farmhouses, and modern western European democracy coexists with strong affection for a monarchy. With 449,964 square km (171,263 square mi) for only 8.8 million residents, almost all have room to live as they choose.

Stockholm, one of Europe's most beautiful capitals, is built on 14 small islands. Bustling, skyscraper-lined boulevards are a short walk from twisting medieval streets in this modern yet pastoral city. South of the city, in the densely forested Småland province, are isolated villages whose names are bywords when it comes to fine crystal glassware: Kosta, Orrefors, Boda, and Strömbergshyttan. Skåne, the country's southernmost province, is an area of fertile plains, sand beaches, scores of castles and manor houses, thriving farms, medieval churches, and summer resorts.

Sweden's second-largest city, Göteborg, is on the west coast. A Viking port in the 11th century, today the city is home to the Scandinavium indoor arena; Nordstan, one of Europe's largest indoor shopping malls; and Liseberg, Scandinavia's largest amusement park. A cruise on the Göta Canal provides a picturesque coast-to-coast journey through the Swedish countryside.

Dalarna, the central region of Sweden, is considered the most typically Swedish of all the country's 24 provinces, a place of forests, mountains, and red-painted wooden farmhouses and cottages by the shores of pristine, sun-dappled lakes. The north of Sweden, Norrland, is a place of wide-open spaces. Golden eagles soar above snowcapped crags; huge salmon fight their way up wild, tumbling rivers; rare orchids bloom in Arctic heathland; wild rhododendrons splash the land with color.

PLEASURES AND PASTIMES

Beaches

Beaches in Sweden range from wide, sandy strands to steep, rocky shores, from ocean-front to lakefront, from resorts to remote nature preserves. Beaches are wide and sandy on the western side of the country, steep and rocky on the eastern side. The area most favored for the standard sunbathing and wave-frolicking vacation is known as the Swedish Riviera, on the coast south of Göteborg.

Camping

As soon as the winter frost abates, the Swedes migrate en masse to the country, with camping and sports gear in tow. Of the 760 registered campsites nationwide, many offer fishing, boating, or canoeing, and about 200 remain open in winter for skiing and skating. Many campsites also offer accommodations in log cabins at various prices.

Dining

The nation's standard home-cooked meal is basically peasant fare—sausages, potatoes, and other hearty foods to ward off the winter cold. Yet Sweden has also produced the *smörgåsbord,* a generous and artfully arranged buffet featuring both hot and cold dishes. Fish—fresh, smoked, or pickled—is a Swedish specialty; herring and salmon both come in myriad traditional and new preparations.

Recently, restaurants in the larger cities have begun offering innovative dishes that combine the ingredients and simplicity of traditional Swedish cuisine with Mediterranean, Asian, and Caribbean influences, a fusion trend that dovetails an increase in the number of foreign restaurants popping up throughout Sweden. Despite the popularity of such culinary endeavors, you'll have no problem finding *Husmanskost* (home-cooking) recipes, which are often served in restaurants as a *dagens rätt* (daily special) at lunch. Examples are *pyttipanna* (literally, "bits in the pan"—beef and potato hash topped with a fried egg), *Janssons frestelse* ("Jansson's Temptation"—gratin of potatoes with anchovy), or pea soup with pancakes, a traditional meal on Thursday.

Look for *kräftor* (crayfish), boiled with dill, salt, and sugar, then cooled overnight; they are most popular in August. Swedes eat kräftor with hot buttered toast, caraway seeds, and schnapps or beer. Autumn heralds an exotic assortment of mushrooms and wild berries. Trout and salmon are common, as are various cuts of elk and reindeer. To the foreign palate, the best of Norrland's culinary specialties is undoubtedly *löjrom*, pinkish caviar from a species of Baltic herring, eaten with chopped onions and sour cream, and the various desserts made from the cloudberries that thrive here.

CATEGORY	COST*
$$$$	over SKr 500
$$$	SKr 250–SKr 500
$$	SKr 120–SKr 250
$	under SKr 120

Prices are per person for a two-course meal, including service charge and tax but not wine.

Fishing

It is not unusual to see a fisherman landing a thrashing salmon from the quayside in central Stockholm. Outside the city limits, the country is laced with streams and lakes full of fish, and there's excellent deep-sea fishing off the Baltic coast.

Lodging

Service in a Swedish hotel, no matter the price category, is always unfailingly courteous and efficient. You'll find that accommodations on the expensive side offer great charm and beauty, but the advantages of location held by less luxurious establishments shouldn't be overlooked. The woodland setting of a camper's *stuga* (small wooden cottage) may be just as desirable and memorable as the gilded antiques of a downtown hotel.

In summer many discounts, special passes, and summer packages are available. Your travel agent or the Swedish Travel and Tourism Council (in New York) will have full details. The Scandic Hotel Summer Check plan enables you to pay for accommodations in advance with checks costing SKr 530 each for one night in a double room. Depending on the hotel you choose, you may also have to purchase a PlussCheck for SKr 125. Sweden Hotel's Nordic Hotel Pass costs SKr 90 and gives discounts of 15% to 50% from June 20 to August 17 and on weekends year-round.

Vandrarhem (hostels), also scrupulously clean and well run, are more expensive than elsewhere in Europe. The Swedish Touring Association (STF) has 394 hostels and cabins nationwide, most with four- to six-bed family rooms, around 100 with running hot and cold water. They are open to anyone regardless of age. Prices are about SKr 100 per night for members of STF or organizations affiliated with Hostelling International. Nonmembers are charged an additional SKr 35 per night. STF publishes an annual hostel handbook. The Swedish Hostel Association also has a Web site with information in English (www.svif.se).

CATEGORY	COST*
$$$$	over SKr 1,400
$$$	SKr 1,100–SKr 1,400
$$	SKr 850–SKr 1,100
$	under SKr 850

All prices are for a standard double room, including breakfast and tax.

Sailing

Deep at heart, modern Swedes are still seafaring Vikings. Sweden's cultural dependence on boats runs so deep that a popular gift at Christmas is candles containing creosote, providing the comforting scent of dock and hull for when sailors can't be on their boats—which is most of the year. In summer, thousands of craft jostle among the islands of the archipelago and clog the lakes and rivers. Statistics claim there are more than 250,000 boats in the Stockholm archipelago alone. Boating opportunities for visitors are plentiful, from hourly rentals to chartered cruises in anything from kayaks to motor launches to huge luxury ferry liners.

Tennis

When Björn Borg began to win Wimbledon with almost monotonous regularity, Sweden became a force in world tennis. As such, the country is filled with indoor and outdoor courts, and major competitions, notably the Stockholm Open, take place regularly. One of the most unusual is the annual Donald Duck Cup, in Båstad, for children ages 11 to 15; ever since the young Björn won a Donald Duck trophy, the tournament has attracted thousands of youngsters who hope to imitate his success.

GREAT ITINERARIES

Sweden consists of 24 counties. In the southeast is Stockholm, the capital. The industrial seaport city of Göteborg and the neighboring west coastal counties of Bohuslän and Halland (the so-called Swedish Riviera) form another region, along with Värmland and Dalsland on the Norwegian border. The southernmost part of Sweden, a lovely mix of farmland, forests, and châteaus, includes Skåne, Småland, Blekinge, Västergötland, Östergötland, and the island of Öland. Dalarna, the country's heartland, is centered on Lake Siljan and the town of Mora; this is where Swedish folklore and traditions are most visible. The northern half of Sweden, called Norrland and including the counties of Lappland and Norrbotten, is a great expanse consisting mostly of mountains and wilderness; here the hardy Sami herd reindeer and hardy tourists come to see the midnight sun.

Sampling all of Sweden's far-flung variety is best suited to a traveler with either no time constraints or an exceedingly generous purse. The few representative stops below, however, can make even a short visit worthwhile.

If You Have 3 Days

Spend two days in the capital city, **Stockholm**; one of these days may be spent on a boat trip in the archipelago or on Lake Mälaren. On the third day either visit **Göteborg**—a port town since the Viking era, marked with attractive boulevards, canals, and important museums—by a high-speed train, or fly to **Mora**, in the heart of Sweden's folklore country, Dalarna.

If You Have 5 Days

Start with two days in **Stockholm**; add a third day for a side trip to **Uppsala**, Sweden's principal university town, along the banks of the Fyris River. On day four, fly to **Mora** and rent a car for a drive around Lake Siljan. On day five, fly to **Göteborg**.

If You Have 10 Days

You can tackle this itinerary using public transportation. Start with three days in **Stockholm**; on day four, take the high-speed train to **Göteborg** and stay two nights; on day six, take the train to **Kalmar** with Sweden's best preserved Renaissance castle, via **Växjö**. From Kalmar, catch the ferry to **Gotland**. On day eight, return to Stockholm. Spend day nine either flying to **Mora** or **Kiruna**, the northernmost city in Sweden. Return to Stockholm on day ten.

When to Tour Sweden

The official tourist season—when hotel rates generally go down and museum and castle doors open up—runs from mid-May through mid-September. This is Sweden's balmiest time of year; summer days are sunny and warm, nights refreshingly cool. (Summer is also mosquito season, especially in the north, but also as far south as Mora.) The colors of autumn fade out as early as September, when the rainy season begins. Winter comes in November and stays through March, and sometimes longer, but winter days can be magnificent when the snow is fresh and the sky is a brilliant Nordic blue. April brings spring, and by the middle of June the whole country goes mad for Midsummer Day.

FODOR'S CHOICE

Flavors

★ **Ulriksdals Wärsdhus, Stockholm.** The lunchtime smörgåsbord is renowned at this restaurant in an 1868 country inn. $$$$

★ **The Place, Göteborg.** Sample delicious and exotic dishes, from smoked breast of pigeon to beef tartar with caviar. $$$

★ **Örtagården, Stockholm.** This delightful vegetarian, no-smoking restaurant is above the Östermalmstorg food market. $

★ **Wedholms Fisk, Stockholm.** Traditional Swedish fare here, especially the fresh fish, is simple but outstanding. $$$

Comforts

★ **Berns, Stockholm.** This 132-year-old hotel employs discreet lighting, modern Italian furniture, and swank marble, granite, and wood inlays to create a wonderful art deco atmosphere. $$$$

★ **Marina Plaza, Helsingborg.** The use of space, style, and elegance—especially in the lofty lobby atrium—lends a decidedly modern appeal to this lodging. $$$

Castles and Churches

★ **Drottningholms Slott, Stockholm.** One of the most delightful European palaces embraces all that was best in the art of living practiced by mid-18th-century royalty.

★ **Kalmar Slott, Småland.** The "Key to the Realm" during the Vasa era, this Renaissance palace commands the site of an 800-year-old fortress on the Baltic shore.

★ **Kungliga Slottet, Stockholm.** In this magnificent granite edifice, you can tour the State Apartments, the Royal Armory, and the Treasury, where the crown jewels are kept.

Museums

★ **Skansen, Stockholm.** Farmhouses, windmills, barns, and churches are just some of the buildings brought from around the country for preservation at this museum.

★ **Vasa Museet, Stockholm.** Visit the Vasa, a warship that sank on its maiden voyage in 1628, was raised nearly intact in 1961, and now resides in its own museum.

★ **Zorn Museet, Mora.** Many fine paintings by Anders Zorn (1860–1920), Sweden's leading Impressionist painter, are displayed in this museum next to the beautiful house he built in his hometown.

Special Moments

★ Dogsledding in Norrland

★ Watching a Lucia procession at Christmastime

★ A summer sailing trip in the Stockholm archipelago

2   STOCKHOLM

OSITIONED WHERE the waters of Lake Mälaren rush into the Baltic, Stockholm is one of Europe's most beautiful capitals. Nearly 1.6 million people now live in the greater Stockholm area, yet it remains a quiet, almost pastoral city.

Built on 14 small islands joined by bridges crossing open bays and narrow channels, Stockholm is a handsome, civilized city filled with parks, squares, and airy boulevards, yet it is also a bustling, modern metropolis. Glass-and-steel skyscrapers abound, but you are never more than a five-minute stroll from twisting medieval streets and waterside walkways.

The first written mention of Stockholm dates from 1252, when a powerful regent named Birger Jarl (d. 1266) built a fortified castle and township here. King Gustav Vasa (1496–1560) took it over in 1523, and King Gustavus Adolphus (1594–1632) made it the heart of an empire a century later.

During the Thirty Years' War (1618–48), Sweden gained importance as a Baltic trading state, and Stockholm grew commensurately. But by the beginning of the 18th century, Swedish influence had begun to wane and Stockholm's development had slowed. It did not revive until the Industrial Revolution, when the hub of the city moved north from Gamla Stan.

Nowadays most Stockholmers live in high-rise suburbs that branch out to the pine forests and lakesides around the capital. They are linked by a highly efficient infrastructure of roads, railways, and one of the safest subway systems in the world. Air pollution is minimal, and the city streets are relatively clean and safe.

EXPLORING STOCKHOLM

Although Stockholm is built on a group of islands adjoining the mainland, the waterways between them are so narrow, and the bridges so smoothly integrated, that the city really does feel more or less continuous. The island of Gamla Stan and its smaller neighbors, Riddarholmen and Helgeandsholmen, form what can be called the town center. South of Gamla Stan, Södermalm spreads over a wide area, where the many art galleries and bars attract a slightly bohemian crowd. North of Gamla Stan is Norrmalm, the financial and business heart of the city. West of Norrmalm is the island of Kungsholmen, site of Stadshuset, the City Hall, and most of the city government offices. East of Norrmalm is Östermalm, an old residential neighborhood where many of the embassies and consulates are found. Finally, between Östermalm and Södermalm lies the island of Djurgården, once a royal game preserve, now the site of lovely parks and museums such as Skansen, the open-air cultural heritage park.

Numbers in the text correspond to numbers in the margin and on the Stockholm map.

Modern Stockholm

The area bounded by Stadshuset, Hötorget, Stureplan, and the Kungliga Dramatiska Teatern (nicknamed Dramaten) is essentially Stockholm's downtown, where the city comes closest to feeling like a bustling metropolis. Shopping, nightlife, business, traffic, dining, festivals—all are at their most intense in this part of town.

A Good Walk

Start at the redbrick **Stadshuset** ①, a powerful symbol of Stockholm. Cross the bridge to Klara Mälarstrand and follow the waterfront to

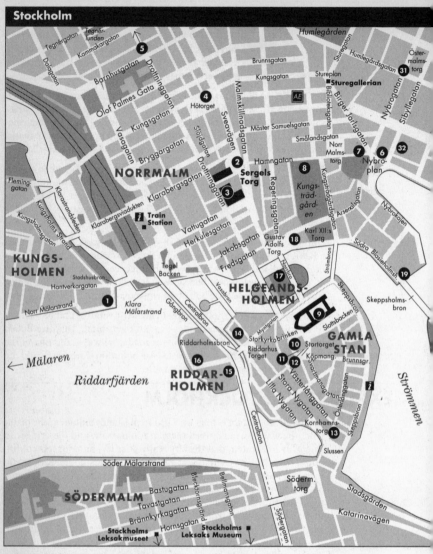

ÖSTERMALM

Kommendörsgatan
Karlaplan
Millesgården
N. DJURGÅRDEN

Karlavägen

Linnégatan

Narvavägen

Banérgatan

Oxenstiernsgatan

Gärdevägen

Storgatan

Linnégatan

30

Riddargatan
Skeppargatan
Grevgatan
Styrmangatan
Storgatan

Oscars
Kyrka

Strandvägen

33

Strandvägen

Djurgårdsbron

Djurgårdsbrunnsviken

23

24

Rosendalsvägen

29

22

28

Hazeliusbacken

DJURGÅRDEN

20 21

Alkärret

Djurgårdsvägen

Sirishovsvägen

KEPPSHOLMEN

Svensksundsvägen

26

Falkenb. G.

25

Djurgårds Slätten

Sottidsbacken
Singelbacken

27

Allmänna Gränd

KASTELL-
HOLMEN

Baltic→

Saltsjön

BECKHOLMEN

N

KEY		0		500 yards

AE American Express
Office

0   500 meters

i Tourist Information

Drottninggatan, onto which you'll make a left and continue along this popular shop-lined pedestrian street north to the hub of the city, **Sergels Torg** ②. The **Kulturhuset** ③ is in the imposing glass building on the southern side of Sergels Torg. Continuing north on Drottninggatan, you'll come to the market-filled **Hötorget** ④. The intersection of Kungsgatan and Sveavägen, at the corner of Konserthuset, is one of the busiest pedestrian crossroads in town.

Head north up Sveavägen for a brief detour to see the spot where Prime Minister Olof Palme was assassinated in 1986. A plaque has been laid on the right-hand side of the street, just before the intersection with Olof Palmes Gata; his grave is in Adolf Fredrik's Kyrkogård, a few blocks farther on. Continue north along Sveavägen, and turn left up Tegnérgatan to find **Strindbergsmuseet Blå Tornet** ⑤, where playwright August Strindberg lived from 1908 to 1912. Return to Hötorget by way of Drottninggatan.

Next, walk east along Kungsgatan, one of Stockholm's main shopping streets, to Stureplan, where you'll find Sturegallerian, an elegant mall (☞ Shopping, *below*). Head southeast along Birger Jarlsgatan—named for the nobleman generally credited with founding Stockholm around 1252— where there are still more interesting shops and restaurants. When you reach Nybroplan, take a look at the grand **Kungliga Dramatiska Teatern** ⑥.

Heading west up Hamngatan, stop in at **Hallwylska Museet** ⑦ for a tour of the private collection of Countess von Hallwyl's treasures. Continue along Hamngatan to **Kungsträdgården** ⑧, a park since 1562. Outdoor cafés and restaurants are clustered by this leafy spot, a summer venue for public concerts and events. At the northwest corner of the park you will find Sverigehuset, or Sweden House, the tourist center (☞ Visitor Information *in* Stockholm A to Z, *below*); on the opposite side of Hamngatan is the NK department store (☞ Shopping, *below*).

TIMING

Allow about 4½ hours for the walk, plus an hour each for guided tours of Stadshuset and Hallwylska Museet (Sept.–June, Sun. only). Note the Strindbergsmuseet Blå Tornet is closed Monday.

Sights to See

⑦ **Hallwylska Museet** (Hallwyl Museum). This private late-19th-century palace with imposing wood-panel rooms houses a collection of furniture, paintings, and musical instruments in a bewildering mélange of styles assembled by Countess von Hallwyl, who left it to the state on her death. ✉ *Hamng. 4,* ☎ *08/6664499.* ☞ *SKr 60.* ☉ *Guided tours only. Tours in English July and Aug., daily at 1; Sept.–June, Sun. at 1.*

④ **Hötorget** (Hay Market). Once the city's hay market, this is now a popular gathering place with an excellent outdoor fruit and vegetable market. Also lining the square are the Konserthuset (Concert Hall), the PUB department store, and a multiscreen cinema Filmstaden Sergel (☞ Nightlife and the Arts, *below*). ✉ *Just west of Sveaväg.*

NEED A
BREAK?

Stop at **Kungshallen** (✉ Hötorget opposite Filmstaden Sergel, ☎ 08/ 218005) and choose from an array of international goodies. Or, get a window table at the café inside Filmstaden Sergel.

③ **Kulturhuset** (Culture House). Since it opened in 1974, architect Peter Celsing's cultural center, which sits like a glass and stone barn on the south side of Sergels Torg, has become a symbol of Stockholm and of the growth of modernism in Sweden. Stockholmers are divided on the aesthetics of this building—most either love it or hate it. You'll find an array of exhibitions for children and adults, a library, a theater, a cyber-café, a youth center, an exhibition center, and a restaurant. Head to Café Panorama, on the top floor, to savor a jumbo salad and a great view of Sergels Torg down below. ⊠ *Sergels Torg 3,* ☏ *08/50831400. Call for details.*

⑥ Kungliga Dramatiska Teatern (Royal Dramatic Theater). Locally known as Dramaten, the national theater stages plays by the likes of Strindberg and Bergman in a grand, appealing building whose facade and gilded statuary look out over the city harbor. The theater gave its first performance in 1788 when it was located at Bollhuset on Slottsbacken, next to the Royal Palace. It later moved to Kungsträdgården, spent some time in the Opera House, and ended up at its present location in 1908. Performances are in Swedish. ⊠ *Nybroplan,* ☏ *08/6670680.*

⊘ ⑧ Kungsträdgården (King's Garden). This is one of Stockholm's smallest yet most central parks. Once the royal kitchen garden, it now hosts a large number of festivals and events each season. The park comes replete with numerous cafés and restaurants, a playground, and an ice-skating rink in winter. ⊠ *Between Hamng. and the Operan.*

❷ Sergels Torg. Named after Johan Tobias Sergel (1740–1814), one of Sweden's greatest sculptors, this busy junction in Stockholm's center is dominated by modern, functional buildings and a sunken pedestrian square with subterranean connections to the rest of the neighborhood.

★ ❶ Stadshuset (City Hall). The architect Ragnar Östberg, one of the founders of the National Romantic movement, completed Stockholm's City Hall in 1923. Headquarters of the city council, the building is functional but ornate: its immense **Blå Hallen** (Blue Hall) is the venue for the Nobel Prize dinner, Stockholm's principal social event. A trip to the top of the 348-ft tower, most of which can be achieved by elevator, is rewarded by a breathtaking panorama of the city and Riddarfjärden. ⊠ *Hantverkarg. 1,* ☏ *08/50829059.* ☙ *SKr 40, tower SKr 15.* ☉ *Guided tours only, daily 10–4:30. Tours in English, June–Aug., daily 10, 11, noon, 2; Sept., daily 10, noon, 2; Oct.–May, daily 10 and noon.*

NEED A BREAK? After climbing the Stadshuset tower, relax on the fine grass terraces that lead down to the bay and overlook Lake Mälaren. Or, have lunch in **Stadshuskällaren** (City Hall Cellar, ☏ 08/6505454), where the annual Nobel Prize banquet is held. You can also head a few blocks down Hantverkargatan to find several good small restaurants.

❺ Strindbergsmuseet Blå Tornet (Strindberg Museum, Blue Tower). Hidden away over a grocery store, this museum is dedicated to Sweden's most important author and dramatist, August Strindberg (1849–1912), who resided here from 1908 until his death. The interior has been expertly reconstructed with authentic furnishings and other objects, including one of his pens. The museum also houses a library, printing press, and picture archives, and it is the site of literary, musical, and theatrical events. ⊠ *Drottningg. 85,* ☏ *08/4115354.* ☙ *SKr 35.* ☉ *Sept.–May, Tues. 11–7, Wed.–Fri. 11–4, weekends noon–4. June–Aug., Tues.–Fri. 11–4, weekends noon–4.*

Gamla Stan and Skeppsholmen

Gamla Stan (Old Town) sits on a cluster of small islands between two of Stockholm's main islands and is the site of the medieval city. Just east of Gamla Stan is the island of Skeppsholmen, whose narrow, twisting cobbled streets are lined with superbly preserved old buildings.

A Good Walk

Start at the waterfront edge of Kungsträdgården and cross Strömsbron to the **Kungliga Slottet** ⑨, where you can see the changing of the guard

STOCKHOLM'S ARCHITECTURAL PROCESSION

AS IN MANY OTHER SWEDISH CITIES, a single afternoon walk in Stockholm offers a journey through centuries of architectural change and innovation. There are, of course, the classics. Take Kungliga Slottet (Royal Palace) on Gamla Stan. Designed by Nicodemus Tessin and built between 1690 and 1704, it's a rather austere palace— no domes, no great towers—and yet it commands a certain respect sitting so regally over the water. Nearby, on Riddarholmen, observe the gorgeous, medieval Riddarholmskyrkan (Riddarholm Church), with its latticed spire pointed toward the heavens. And let's not forget Drottningholm, a 17th-century chateau-esque structure— also designed by Tessin—that has been the home of the royal family since 1981. Also at Drottningholm is the Court Theater (1766), which, remarkably, still contains its original decor and fully functional stage machinery.

Stadshuset (City Hall) is also a must-see on any architectural walking tour. Completed in 1923, the building contains more than 8 million bricks and 19 million gilded mosaic tiles. Each year the Nobel Prize ceremony is held in the building's Blå Hallen (Blue Hall). Built a few years later is Stadsbiblioteket (City Library), designed by Eric Gunnar Asplund— one of Sweden's most renowned architects. The library's eye-pleasing yet simple design foreshadows the *Funkis* (Functionalist) movement that Gunnar helped spearhead in the 1920s and '30s.

Skattehuset (Tax House), also known as SkatteScrapan (a play on "skyscraper") is hard to miss, looming mercilessly as it does over Södermalm. Completed in the early 1950s as part of an attempt to consolidate the nation's tax offices, the singularly dull gray 25-story building is often criticized for having ruined the southern skyline of Stockholm. But for the annual siege of thousands of Stockholmers flooding it with last-minute tax declarations every May, the building sees few visitors.

Farther south of the city, another architectural oddity plagues or enhances, depending on whom you ask, the skyline. Globen, the world's largest spherical building, looks something like a colossal golf ball, or a futuristic space-station still awaiting its launch into orbit. Unveiled in 1988, it's the main arena in Stockholm for indoor sporting events (especially hockey) and rock concerts. Despite debates concerning its aesthetic (or lack there of), a look at the cables and beams inside reveals Globen's architecture marvel.

Another much debated architectural undertaking is Hötorgscity, across from the highly influential Kulturhuset at Sergels Torg. This post-war compound of five 18-story buildings was constructed in the mid-'50s (see the aforementioned description of SkatteScrapan to get a sense of its appearance) and was intended to house retail stores and offices, thus fulfilling downtown Stockholm's focus of the era on commerce. The project failed. A significant chunk of historic Stockholm was lost. Vandalized by ne'er-do-wells and ignored by prospective tenants, the buildings were shut down in the ë70s, although today there is a renewed interest in the top floors of the buildings, especially among young business owners.

What is most striking about the buildings that comprise Stockholm's architectural portfolio is their collective diversity. You'll glean a particularly remarkable sense of them if you visit them all in one day. Centuries of history involving both failures and successes are reflected in the styles these structures represent. Every building in Stockholm, new or old, tells a story.

at noon every day. Walk up the sloping cobblestone drive called Slotts-backen and bear right past the Obelisk to find the main entrance to the palace. Stockholm's 15th-century Gothic cathedral, **Storkyrkan** ⑩, stands at the top of Slottsbacken, but its entrance is at the other end, on Trångsund.

Following Källargränd from the Obelisk or Trångsund from Storkyrkan, you will reach the small square, **Stortorget** ⑪, marvelously atmospheric amid magnificent old merchants' houses. The **Stockholms Fondbörs** ⑫ fronts the square.

Walk past Svartmangatan's many ancient buildings, including the Tyska Kyrkan, or German Church, with its resplendent oxidized cop-per spire and airy interior. Continue along Svartmangatan, take a right on Tyska Stallplan to Prästgatan, and just to your left you'll find Mårten Trotzigs Gränd; this picturesque, lamplit alley stairway leads downhill to **Järntorget** ⑬. From here you can take Västerlånggatan back north across Gamla Stan, checking out the pricey fashion boutiques, galleries, and souvenir shops along the way.

Cut down Storkyrkobrinken to the 17th-century Dutch Baroque **Rid-darhuset** ⑭. A short walk takes you over Riddarholmsbron to Rid-darholmen—Island of Knights—on which stands **Riddarholmskyrkan** ⑮. Also on Riddarholmen is the white 17th-century palace that houses the **Svea Hovrätt** ⑯. Returning across Riddarholmsbron, take Mynt-gatan back toward Kungliga Slottet and turn left at Mynttorget to cross the bridge and pass through the refurbished stone **Riksdagshuset** ⑰ on Helgeandsholmen, Holy Ghost Island. Another short bridge puts you on Drottninggatan; take a right onto Fredsgatan and walk to Gustav Adolfs Torg.

The **Operan** ⑱ occupies the waterfront between Gustav Adolfs Torg and Kungsträdgården. A little farther along on Strömgatan, a host of tour boats dock in front of the stately Grand Hotel. Pass the Grand and visit the **Nationalmuseum** ⑲. Cross the footbridge to the idyllic island of Skeppsholmen, where you'll find the **Östasiatiska Museet** ⑳, with a fine collection of Buddhist art. On Skeppsholmen you will also find the **Moderna Museet** ㉑. The adjoining island, Kastellholmen, is a pleasant place for a stroll, especially on a summer evening, with views of the Baltic harbor and Djurgården's lighted parks.

TIMING

Allow three hours for the walk, and double that if you want to tour the various parts of the palace. The Nationalmuseum and Östasiatiska Museet will take up to an hour each to view. Note that Kungliga Slot-tet is closed Monday off-season, and Stockholms Leksakmuseum, Moderna Museet, Nationalmuseum, and Östasiatiska Museet are al-ways closed Monday. The Riddarhuset is open weekdays only; off-sea-son, hit the Riddarholmskyrkan on a Wednesday or weekend.

Sights to See

⑬ **Järntorget** (Iron Square). Named after its original use as an iron and copper marketplace, this square was also the venue for public execu-tions. ⊠ *Intersection of Västerlångg. and Österlångg.*

OFF THE
BEATEN PATH

STOCKHOLMS LEKSAKMUSEUM – In Södermalm, Stockholm's Toy Museum has a collection of toys and dolls from all over the world, as well as a children's theater with clowns, magicians, storytellers, and puppet shows. The museum is near the Mariatorget subway station, two stops south of Gamla Stan. ⊠ *Mariatorget 1, Södermalm,* ☎ *08/6416100.* ⊡ *SKr 40.* ☉ *Tues.–Fri. 10–4, weekends noon–4.*

★ ❾ **Kungliga Slottet** (Royal Palace). Designed by Nicodemus Tessin, the Royal Palace was completed in 1760 and replaced the previous palace that had burned here in 1697. Just three weeks later, Tessin—who had also designed the previous incarnation, submitted his drawings for the new palace to the Swedish government. The rebuilding was finally completed, exactly according to Tessin's designs, 60 years later. The four facades of the palace each have a distinct style: the west is the King's, the east the Queen's, the south belongs to the nation, and the north represents royalty in general. Watch the changing of the guard in the curved terrace entrance. And view the palace's fine furnishings and Gobelin tapestries on a tour of the **Representationsvän** (State Apartments); to survey the crown jewels, which are no longer used in this self-consciously egalitarian country, head to the **Skattkammaren** (Treasury). The **Livrustkammaren** (Royal Armory) has an outstanding collection of weaponry, coaches, and royal regalia. Entrances to the Treasury and Armory are on the Slottsbacken side of the palace. ⊠ *Gamla Stan,* ☎ *08/4026130 State Apartments, 08/4026130 Treasury, 08/6664475 Royal Armory.* ▣ *State Apartments SKr 50, Treasury SKr 50, Royal Armory SKr 50.* ☉ *State Apartments and Treasury, May–Aug., daily 10–4; Sept.–Apr., Tues.–Sun. noon–3. Armory, May–Aug., daily 11–4; Sept.–May, Tues.–Sun. 11–4.*

㉑ **Moderna Museet** (Museum of Modern Art). Reopened in its original venue on Skeppsholmen, the museum's excellent collection includes works by Picasso, Kandinsky, Dalí, Brancusi, and other international artists. You can also view examples of significant Swedish painters and sculptors and an extensive section on photography. The building itself is something to be seen, designed by award-winning Spanish architect Rafael Moneo, with seemingly endless hallways of blond wood and walls of glass. ⊠ *Skeppsholmen,* ☎ *08/51955200,* ▣ *SKr 60.* ☉ *Tues.–Thurs. 11–10, Fri.–Sun. 11–6.*

⑲ **Nationalmuseum** (National Museum). The musueum's collection of paintings and sculptures comprises about 12,500 works, including works by Rembrandt and other important masters. The print and drawing department is also impressive, with a nearly complete collection of Edouard Manet prints. Art from Sweden and other Nordic countries are given priority, but other parts of the world are also well represented. ⊠ *Södra Blasieholmshamnen,* ☎ *08/6664250.* ▣ *SKr 60.* ☉ *Tues. 11–8, Wed.–Sun. 11–5; Jan.–Feb., Tues. and Thurs. 11–8, Wed.–Sun. 11–5.*

⑱ **Operan** (Opera House). Stockholm's Baroque Opera House is almost more famous for its restaurants and bars than for its opera and ballet productions. It has been one of Stockholm's artistic and literary watering holes since the first Operakällaren restaurant (☞ Dining, *below*) opened on the site in 1787. ⊠ *Gustav Adolfs Torg,* ☎ *08/248240.*

⑳ **Östasiatiska Museet** (Museum of Far Eastern Antiquities). If you have an affinity for Asian disciplines, don't miss this fascinating collection of Chinese and Japanese Buddhist sculptures and artifacts. ⊠ *Skeppsholmen,* ☎ *08/6664250.* ▣ *SKr 40.* ☉ *Tues. noon–8, Wed.–Sun. noon–5.*

⑮ **Riddarholmskyrkan** (Riddarholm Church). Dating from 1270, the Grey Friars monastery is the second-oldest structure in Stockholm and the burial place for Swedish kings for more than four centuries. The most famous figures interred within are King Gustavus Adolphus, hero of the Thirty Years' War, and the warrior King Karl XII, renowned for his daring invasion of Russia, who died in Norway in 1718. The latest of the 17 Swedish kings to be put to rest here was Gustav V, in 1950. The various rulers' sarcophagi, usually embellished with their monograms, are visible in the small chapels given over to the various dynasties. The redbrick structure, distinguished by its delicate iron fretwork spire, is rarely used for services. ⊠ *Riddarholmen,* ☎ *08/4026130.* ⬚ *SKr 20.* ⊙ *May–Aug., daily 10–4; Sept., weekends noon–3.*

⑭ **Riddarhuset** (House of Nobles). Completed in 1674, the House of Nobles was used for parliamentary assemblies and administration during the four-estate parliamentary period that lasted until 1866. Since then, Swedish nobility have continued to meet here every three years for administrative meetings. Hanging from its walls are 2,325 escutcheons, representing all the former noble families of Sweden. Thanks to the building's excellent acoustic properties, Riddarhuset is often used for concerts. ⊠ *Riddarhustorget,* ☎ *08/7233990.* ⬚ *SKr 40.* ⊙ *Weekdays 11:30–12:30.*

⑰ **Riksdagshuset** (Parliament Building). When in session, the Swedish Parliament meets in this 1904 building. Above the entrance, the architect placed scultptures of a peasant, a burgher, a clergyman, and a nobleman. Take a tour of the building and you will not only learn about Swedish government, but also see various works of art. In the former First Chamber are murals by Otte Sköld illustrating different periods in the history of Stockholm, and in the current First Chamber a massive tapestry by Elisabet Hasselberg Olsson, *Memory of a Landscape,* hangs above the podium. ⊠ *Riksg. 3A,* ☎ *08/7864000.* ⬚ *Free.* ⊙ *Tours in English late June–late Aug., weekdays 12:30 and 2:30; late Aug.–late June, weekends 1:30. Call ahead for bookings.*

⑫ **Stockholms Fondbörs** (Stockholm Stock Exchange). The Swedish Academy meets at the Stock Exchange every year to decide the winner of the Nobel Prize for Literature. The Stock Exchange itself is computerized and rather quiet. There are no tours in English, but there is a film about the Stock Exchange in Swedish. ⊠ *Källargränd 2,* ☎ *08/ 6138892.* ⊙ *Group tours by appointment only.*

⑩ **Storkyrkan** (Great Church). Swedish kings were crowned in the 15th-century Great Church as late as 1907. Today, its main attractions are a dramatic wooden statue of Saint George slaying the dragon, carved by Bernt Notke of Lübeck in 1489, and the *Parhelion,* a painting of Stockholm dating from 1520, the oldest in existence. ⊠ *Trångsund 1,* ☎ *08/7233016.* ⊙ *Sept.–Apr., daily 9–4; May–Aug. daily 9–6.*

⑪ **Stortorget** (Great Square). Here in 1520, the Danish king Christian II ordered a massacre of Swedish noblemen, paving the way for a national revolt against foreign rule and the founding of Sweden as a sovereign state under King Gustav Vasa, who ruled from 1523 to 1560. One legend holds that if it rains heavily enough on the anniversary of the massacre, the old stones still run red.

NEED A BREAK?
Of the cafés, pubs, and restaurants just south along Västerlånggatan, **Grå Munken** (Gray Monk, ⊠ Västerlång. 18, at Stora Gråmunkegränd) truly merits a leisurely coffee and pastry stop.

⑯ **Svea Hovrätt** (Swedish High Court). The Swedish High Court commands a prime site on the island of Riddarholmen, on a quiet and restful quayside. Sit on the water's edge and watch the boats on Riddarfjärden (Bay of Knights) and, beyond it, Lake Mälaren. From here you can see the lake, the stately arches of Västerbron (West Bridge) in the distance, the southern heights, and above all the imposing profile of the City Hall, which appears almost to be floating on the water. At the quay you may see one of the Göta Canal ships. ⊠ *Riddarholmen.* ⊙ *Not open to the public.*

Djurgården and Skansen

Djurgården is Stockholm's pleasure island: on it you will find the outdoor museum Skansen, the Gröna Lund amusement park, and the *Vasa*, a 17th-century warship raised from the harbor bed in 1961, as well as other delights.

A Good Walk

You can approach Djurgården from the water aboard the small ferries that leave from Slussen at the southern end of Gamla Stan or from Nybrokajen, or New Bridge Quay, in front of the Kungliga Dramatiska Teatern. Alternatively, starting at the theater, stroll down the Strandvägen quayside—taking in the magnificent old sailing ships and the fine views over the harbor—and cross Djurgårdsbron, or Djurgården Bridge, to the island. As you turn immediately to the right, your first port of call should be the **Vasa Museet** ㉒, with a dramatic display of the splendid 17th-century warship. Especially if you have kids in tow, visit the fairy tale house, **Junibacken** ㉓, just off Djurgårdsbron. Return to the main street, Djurgårdsvägen, to find the entrance to the **Nordiska Museet** ㉔, worth a visit for an insight into Swedish folklore.

Continue on Djurgårdsvägen to the amusement park **Gröna Lund Tivoli** ㉕, where Stockholmers of all ages come to play. Beyond the park, cross Djurgårdsvägen to **Skansen** ㉖.

From Skansen, continue following Djurgårdsvägen to Prins Eugens Väg, and follow the signs to the beautiful late-nineteenth-century **Waldemarsudde** ㉗. On the way back to Djurgårdsbron, follow the small street called Hazeliusbacken to the charmingly archaic **Biologiska Museet** ㉘. From the museum walk toward Djurgårdsbron and then take a right on Rosendalsvägen. Follow the signs to **Rosendals Trädgårder** ㉙, which comprise beautiful gardens and a delightful café. From here you can stroll back along the water toward the city.

TIMING

Allow half a day for this tour, unless you're planning to turn it into a full-day event with lengthy visits to Skansen, Junibacken, and Gröna Land Tivoli. The Vasa Museet warrants two hours, and the Nordiska and Biologiska museums need an hour each. Waldemarsudde requires another half hour. Gröna Lund Tivoli is closed from mid-September to late April. Note the Nordiska Museet closes Monday, and the Biologiska Museet and Waldemarsudde are closed Monday off-season.

Sights to See

👆 ㉘ **Biologiska Museet** (Biological Museum). The Biological Museum, in the shadow of Skansen, exhibits real stuffed animals in various simulated environments. ⊠ *Hazeliusporten*, ☎ *08/4428215*. ☑ *SKr 20.* ☉ *Apr.–Sept., daily 10–4; Oct.–Mar., Tues.–Sun. 10–3.*

NEED A   On Hazeliusbacken, the **Cirkus Theater** (⊠ Djurgårdsslätten, ☎ 08/
BREAK?   58798750) has a lovely terrace café. Or, for terrace dining, head to
           Hasselbacken Hotel (⊠ Hazeliusbacken 20, ☎ 08/6705000).

👆 ㉕ **Gröna Lund Tivoli.** On a smaller scale than Copenhagen's Tivoli and Göteborg's Liseberg, the amusement park Gröna Lund Tivoli is a clean, well-organized pleasure garden with a wide range of rides, attractions, and restaurants. If you're feeling especially daring, try the Power Tower. At 80 meters tall, it's Europe's tallest free-fall amusement-park ride. Concerts are held here all summer long, drawing top performers from Sweden and around the world. ⊠ *Allmänna Gränd 9*, ☎ *08/58750100.* ☑ *SKr 45, not including coupons or passes for rides.* ☉ *May–Sept., daily. Hours vary, call ahead for information.*

★ ☾ ㉓ **Junibacken.** In this fairy-tale house, you travel in small carriages through the storybook world of children's book writer Astrid Lindgren, creator of the irrepressible character Pippi Longstocking. Each of Lindgren's tales is explained as various scenes are revealed. It's perfect for children ages 5 and up. ⊠ *Galärvarsv.,* ☎ *08/58723000.* ☉ *June–Aug., daily 9–6; Sept.–May, Wed.–Sun. 10–5.*

☾ ㉔ **Nordiska Museet** (Nordic Museum). In this elegant late-Victorian structure you'll find peasant costumes from every region of the country and exhibits on the Sami (pronounced *sah*-mee)—Lapps, formerly seminomadic reindeer herders who inhabit the far north. Families with children should visit the delightful "village-life" play area on the ground floor. ⊠ *Djurgårdsv. 616,* ☎ *08/51956000.* ☒ *SKr 60.* ☉ *Tues.–Sun. 10–9.*

㉙ **Rosendals Trädgårder** (Rosendall's Gardens). This gorgeous slice of greenery is a perfect place to spend a few hours on a late summer afternoon. When the weather's nice, families and couples flock to the garden café, which is in one of the greenhouses, to enjoy salads made from the locally grown vegetables and incredibly tasty pastries. Pick your own flowers from the vast flower beds (paying by weight). ⊠ *Rosendalsterassen 12,* ☎ *08/6622814.* ☒ *Free.* ☉ *May–Sept., daily 11–6; Oct.–Apr., call ahead for hours.*

★ ☾ ㉖ **Skansen.** The world's first open-air museum, Skansen was founded in 1891 by philologist and ethnographer Artur Hazelius, who is buried here. He preserved examples of traditional Swedish architecture, including farmhouses, windmills, barns, a working glassblower's hut, and churches, brought from all parts of the country. Not only is Skansen a delightful trip out of time in the center of a modern city, it also provides insight into the life and culture of Sweden's various regions. In addition, the park has a zoo, carnival area, aquarium, theater, and cafés. ⊠ *Djurgårdsslätten 4951,* ☎ *08/4428000.* ☒ *Park and zoo SKr 30, Historical buildings SKr 60, Aquarium SKr 50.* ☉ *June and Aug., weekdays 10–6, weekends 10–7; July, daily 10–8; Sept.–May, weekdays 10–4, weekends 10–5.*

....

NEED A BREAK? For a snack with a view at Skansen, try the **Solliden Restaurant** (☎ 08/6601055) near the front of the park, overlooking the city. The cozy **Bredablick Tower Café** (☎ 08/6634778) is at the back of Skansen, next to the children's circus.

....

★ ㉒ **Vasa Museet.** The warship *Vasa* sank on its maiden voyage in 1628, was forgotten for three centuries, located in 1956, and raised from the seabed in 1961. Its hull was found to be largely intact, because the Baltic's brackish waters do not support the worms that can eat through ships' timbers. Now largely restored to her former glory (however short-lived it may have been), the man-of-war resides in a handsome new museum. Daily tours are available year-round. ⊠ *Galärvarvet, Djurgården,* ☎ *08/6664800.* ☒ *SKr 60.* ☉ *Mid-June–Aug., daily 9:30–7; Sept.–mid-June, daily 10–5.*

㉗ **Waldemarsudde.** This estate, Djurgården's gem, was bequeathed to the Swedish people by Prince Eugen on his death in 1947. It maintains an important collection of Nordic paintings from 1880 to 1940, in addition to the prince's own works. ⊠ *Prins Eugens väg 6,* ☎ *08/54583700.* ☒ *SKr 60.* ☉ *June–Aug., Wed. and Fri.–Sun. 11–5, Tues. and Thurs. 7 AM–9 PM; Sept.–May, Tues.–Sun. 11–4.*

Östermalm and Kaknästornet

Marked by waterfront rows of Renaissance buildings with palatial rooftops and ornamentation, Östermalm is a quiet, residential section of central Stockholm, its elegant streets lined with museums and fine shopping. On Strandvägen, or Beach Way, the boulevard that follows the harbor's edge from the busy downtown area to the staid diplomatic quarter, you can choose one of the three routes. The waterside walk, with its splendid views of the city harbor, bustles with tour boats and sailboats. The inside walk skirts upscale shops and exclusive restaurants. On the tree-shaded paths down the middle you just might meet the occasional horseback rider, properly attired in helmet, jacket, and high polished boots.

A Good Walk

Walk east from the Kungliga Dramatiska Teatern in Nybroplan along Strandvägen until you get to Djurgårdsbron, an ornate little bridge that leads to the park. Resist going to the park and instead turn left up Narvavägen and walk along the right-hand side until you reach Oscars Kyrka. Cross the street and continue up the left side of the street until you reach the **Historiska Museet** ㉚. From here it's only a short walk to Karlaplan, a pleasant, circular park with a fountain. Go across or around the park to find Karlavägen, a long boulevard lined with small shops and galleries. At Nybrogatan, turn left and be sure and take some time to check out the exclusive furniture stores on your way down to **Östermalmstorg** ㉛, where you'll find the Saluhall, an excellent indoor food market. Cut across the square and take a right down Sibyllegatan to the **Musik Museet** ㉜, installed in the city's oldest industrial building. Then go back to Nybroplan, where you can catch Bus 69 going east to **Kaknästornet** ㉝ for a spectacular view of Stockholm from the tallest tower in Scandinavia.

TIMING

This tour requires a little more than a half day. You'll want to spend around an hour in each of the museums. The bus ride from Nybroplan to Kaknästornet takes about 15 minutes, and the tower merits another half hour. Note the Historiska Museet and Musik Museet are closed Monday, and the Millesgården is closed Monday off-season.

Sights to See

㉚ **Historiska Museet** (Museum of National Antiquities). Viking treasures and the Gold Room are the main draw here, but well-presented changing exhibitions also cover various periods of Swedish history, and an excellent shop sells books and gifts. ⊠ *Narvav. 1317,* ☎ *08/7839400.* ⊡ *SKr 60.* ☉ *Tues.–Sun. 11–5, Thurs. until 8.*

NEED A BREAK?	For great coffee and a quick snack, the bistro **Cassi** (⊠ Narvav. 30, just off Karlaplan) is just up the street from the museum.

OFF THE BEATEN PATH	**MILLESGÅRDEN** – This gallery and sculpture garden north of the city is dedicated to the former owner of the property, the American-Swedish sculptor Carl Milles (1875–1955). On display are Milles's own works as well as his private collection. The setting is exquisite: Sculptures top columns on terraces in a magical garden high above the harbor and the city. Millesgården can be easily reached via subway to Ropsten, where you catch the Lidingö train and get off at Torsvik. The trip takes about 30 minutes. ⊠ *Carl Milles väg 2, Lidingö,* ☎ *08/4467590.* ⊡ *SKr 60.* ☉ *May–Sept., daily 10–5; Oct.–Apr., Tues.–Sun. noon–4.*

③ **Kaknästornet** (Kaknäs TV Tower). The 511-ft-high Kaknäs radio and television tower, completed in 1967, is the tallest building in Scandinavia. Surrounded by an impressive array of satellite dishes, it is also used as a linkup station for a number of Swedish satellite TV channels and radio stations. Eat a meal in a restaurant 426 ft above the ground and enjoy panoramic views of the city and the archipelago. ✉ *Mörkakroken, off Djurgårdsbrunsv.,* ☎ *08/7892435.* ☐ *SKr 25.* ☉ *May–Aug., daily 9 AM–10 PM; Sept.–Apr., daily 10–9.*

☺ ㉜ **Musik Museet.** The Music Museum presents a history of music and instruments in its displays. Children are invited to touch and play some of the instruments, and a motion-sensitive "Sound Room" allows visitors to produce musical effects simply by gesturing and moving around. ✉ *Sibylleg. 2,* ☎ *08/6664530.* ☐ *SKr 30.* ☉ *Tues.–Sun. 11–4.*

㉛ **Östermalmstorg.** The market square and its neighboring streets represent old, established Stockholm. **Saluhall** is more like a collection of boutiques than an indoor food market; the fish displays can be especially intriguing. At the other end of the square, **Hedvig Eleonora Kyrka,** a church with characteristically Swedish faux-marble painting throughout its wooden interior, is the site of frequent lunchtime concerts in spring and summer. ✉ *Nybrog at Humlegårdsg.*

NEED A BREAK? | The little restaurants inside the **Saluhall** (✉ Östermalmstorg) offer everything from take-out coffee to sit-down meals.

DINING

The Stockholm restaurant scene has evolved of late, with more upscale restaurants offering good value and inexpensive restaurants appearing on the scene. Local chefs are trying their hand at innovation, fusing traditional Swedish dishes with culinary specialties from around the globe. Among Swedish dishes, the best bets are fish, particularly salmon, and the smörgåsbord buffet, which usually offers variety at a good price. Reservations are often necessary on weekends.

Downtown Stockholm and Beyond

$$$$ ✗ **Operakällaren.** Open since 1787, the haughty grande dame of Stockholm is more a Swedish institution than a seat of gastronomic distinction. Thick Oriental carpeting, shiny polished brass, handsome carved-wood chairs and tables, and a decidedly stuffy atmosphere fill the room. The crystal chandeliers are said to be Sweden's finest, and the high windows on the south side face magnificent views of the Royal Palace. The restaurant is famed for its seasonal smörgåsbord, offered from early June through Christmas. Coveted selections include pickled herring, *rollmops* (rolled herring), reindeer and elk in season, and ice cream with cloudberry sauce. In summer, the veranda opens as the Operabryggan Café, facing Kungsträdgården and the waterfront. ✉ *Operahuset, Jakobs Torg 2,* ☎ *08/6765800. Reservations essential. Jacket and tie. AE, DC, MC, V. Main dining room closed in July.*

$$$$ ✗ **Ulriksdals Wärdshus.** The lunchtime smörgåsbord proffered in this
★ country inn cannot be beat. Built in the park of an 18th-century palace in 1868, the traditionally decorated inn overlooks orchards and a peaceful lake. This restaurant is arguably one of the most expensive in Stockholm, but the impeccable service and outstanding cuisine make a splurge here worthwhile. ✉ *Ulriksdals Slottspark, Solna,* ☎ *08/ 850815. Reservations essential. Jacket required. AE, DC, MC, V. No dinner Sun.*

$$$ ✕ **Chiaro.** This elegant, modern restaurant is a short walk from Sture-plan. The upstairs dining room, with a large circular central bar, is typically filled with a blend of businesspersons in suits and young hipsters. Downstairs is the Form Bar, where DJs mix the latest releases and up-and-coming artists show their newest works. The menu offers a combination of Swedish, French, and Asian dishes, from baked salmon to spring rolls. ✉ *Birger Jarlsg. 24,* ☎ *08/6780009. AE, DC, MC, V. Closed Sun.*

$$$ ✕ **East.** Just off of Stureplan, East is one of the city's culinary hot spots, offering enticing contemporary pan-Asian fare from Thailand, Japan, Korea, and Vietnam—served in colorful vibrant digs. Order a selection of appetizers to truly get a sampling of this cross-cultural cooking. East is a perfect spot to have dinner before a night on the town. ✉ *Stureplan 13,* ☎ *08/6114959. AE, DC, MC, V.*

$$$ ✕ **Edsbacka Krog.** In 1626, Edsbacka, just outside town, became Stockholm's first licensed inn. Its exposed rough hewn beams, plaster walls, and open fireplaces still give it the feel of a country inn for the gentry. The Continental-Swedish cuisine is reliably superb. The owner, Christer Lindström, is an award-winning chef; his tarragon chicken with winter vegetables is worth the occasional long wait. ✉ *Sollentunav. 220, Sollentuna,* ☎ *08/963300. AE, DC, MC, V. Closed Sun. and Mon.*

$$$ ✕ **Fredsgatan 12.** The government crowd files into this elegant, funky
★   restaurant at lunch, the rest of us come at night. In one corner is a group of rainbow-colored lounge chairs that contrast nicely with the dark hardwood floors and beautiful table settings. The menu offers creative combinations, such as rabbit *taquitos* with goat cheese and melon or asparagus Ceasar salad with scallops and tiger prawns. When ordering a cocktail, choose a flavor like mint and sugar or lemon-cherry, and then an alcohol of your choice to mix it with. The restaurant's innovative menu and atmosphere have made it one of the most popular spots in town. And from the bar, you can get a nice view into the kitchen—always a good sign of an unabashed chef. ✉ *Fredsg. 12,* ☎ *08/248052. AE, DC, MC, V. Closed Sun.*

$$$ ✕ **Gåsen.** This is a classic Östermalm restaurant: very classy, cozy, and costly. The Swedish-French menu is excellent, including such dishes as smoked breast of goose with apple chutney, grilled turbot with fresh beet root and spinach, and Arctic raspberry ice cream with blue curaçao sauce. The service is usually impeccable. ✉ *Karlav. 28,* ☎ *08/ 6110269. Jacket and tie. AE, DC, MC, V. Closed weekends May–Aug., Sun. Sept.–Apr., and July.*

$$$ ✕ **Greitz.** Home-style Swedish cuisine is served in this classy and comfortable restaurant. Try the *sotare* (grilled Baltic herring with parsley and butter) or perch and salmon roe with sautéed white beets. The decor is revamped café style, with the once-stained wood paneling around the room painted burgundy red. ✉ *Vasag. 50,* ☎ *08/234820. AE, DC, MC, V. Closed Sun. and July.*

$$$ ✕ **Stallmästaregården.** A historic old inn with an attractive courtyard and garden, Stallmästaregården is in the Haga Park, just north of Norrtull, about 15 minutes by car or bus from the city center. Fine summer meals are served in the courtyard overlooking the waters of Brunnsviken. Specialties include *anka roti* (charcoal-grilled duck kebab). ✉ *Norrtull, near Haga; take bus 52 to Stallmästaregården,* ☎ *08/ 6101300. AE, DC, MC, V. Closed Sun.*

$$$ ✕ **Sturehof.** Sturehof isn't only a restaurant and two huge bars, it's a complete social, architectural, and dining experience. Recently remodeled with wood paneling, leather chairs and sofas, and distinctive lighting fixtures, Sturehof offers a variety of eating and drinking options. There's a bar directly facing Stureplan where you can sit on a summer night and watch Stockholmers gather at the nearby Svampen, a large concrete structure that looks a bit like a mushroom. Inside is an elegant dining room serving fine Swedish cuisine and upstairs in the back is the O-Bar, a dark and smoky boite filled with young people listening to loud music well into the night. ⊠ *Stureplan 2,* ☎ *08/ 4405730. AE, DC, MC, V.*

$$$ ✗ **Wedholms Fisk.** Noted for its fresh seafood dishes, Wedholms Fisk
★ is appropriately set by a bay in Stockholm center, on Berzelii Park. High ceilings, large windows, and tasteful modern paintings from the owner's personal collection create a spacious, sophisticated atmosphere. The traditional Swedish cuisine, which consists almost exclusively of seafood, is simple but outstanding. Try the poached sole in lobster-and-champagne sauce or the Pilgrim mussels Provençale. ⊠ *Nybrokajen 17,* ☎ *08/6117874. AE, DC, MC, V. Closed Sun. and July.*

$$ ✗ **Halv trappa plus gård.** This super-hip restaurant is exactly what its name suggests, two half floors, plus a courtyard. Owned by the same two guys who run Halv Grek Plus Turk (Half a Greek plus a Turk), the retro ambience harkens back to the '70s. The menu is fish-dominant, most of it with a Mediterranean flare. The staff is good-hearted and professional. ⊠ *Lästmakarg. 3,* ☎ *08/6110277. AE, DC, MC, V.*

$$ ✗ **Kjellsons.** Kjellsons is a bar first and restaurant second, but this doesn't mean the menu is short on high-caliber dishes (to say nothing of fine drinks). Appetizers include an excellent pea soup (a Swedish tradition) and a delicious avocado and smoked ham salad—most of the fare is traditional Swedish. And be sure and ask for a basket of cracker bread—it comes with a tube of the famous caviar. In summer there's outdoor seating. ⊠ *Birger Jarlsg. 36,* ☎ *08/6110045. AE, DC, MC, V.*

$$ ✗ **Rolfs Kök.** Small and modern, Rolfs combines an informal atmosphere with excellent Swedish-French cuisine, serving three meals a day at reasonable prices. The lamb is usually a good bet, as are the stir-fried Asian dishes. ⊠ *Tegnérg. 41,* ☎ *08/101696. AE, DC, MC, V. No lunch weekends.*

$$ ✗ **Saigon Bar.** With time-warp speed you are whisked from Stockholm to an American G.I. bar in Saigon, '70s trappings and all. Unusual dishes include Indonesian-style fish served on sweet and spicy potato hash and lamb cutlets with eggplant and bamboo shoot gratin. You'll never go wrong with the wok special. ⊠ *Tegnérg. 19–21, From Rådmandsg. T-banan, east along Tegnérg.* ☎ *08/203887. AE, DC, MC, V. No lunch.*

$$ ✗ **Tranan.** A yuppie crowd frequents Tranan for its bar, which often has live music, and for traditional Swedish fare in its unpretentious restaurant. The stark walls and checkered floor date from Tranan's days as a workingman's beer parlor. ⊠ *Karlbergsv. 14,* ☎ *08/300765. AE, DC, MC, V. No lunch Sat. or Sun.*

$–$$ ✗ **Stockholms Matvarufabriken.** Although it's a bit hard to find, tucked away on a side street and down a small set of stairs, "Stockholm's Food Factory" is well worth seeking out. The popular restaurant is packed full on the weekends as guests young and old come to enjoy the exposed-brick, candle-lighted dining room and varied menu: Here omelets are taken to new levels with ingredients like truffles and asparagus. For dessert, try the hot banana and kiwi with melted white chocolate and vanilla ice cream. ⊠ *Idung. 12,* ☎ *08/320407. AE, DC, MC, V.*

$–$$ ✗ **Wasahof.** Across the street from Vasaparken, and just a short walk from Odenplan, Wasahof has an authentic bistro ambience, but the cooking actually mixes Swedish, French, and Italian recipes. The pleasantly rustic atmosphere and good food attracts all kinds of culturati—actors, writers, journalists. Seafood is a specialty here, especially the oysters (the Wasahof's very own oyster club has more than 1,000 enthusiastic members). ⊠ *Dalagatan 46,* ☎ *08/323440. AE, DC, MC, V. Closed Sun.*

$ ✕ **Il Forno.** You might not expect to find it in Sweden, but Il Forno serves some of the best brick-oven pizza north of the Mediterranean. Choose from more than 25 combinations, all of which use only the freshest ingredients and a tasty crunchy dough. The kitchen also churns out a number of pasta dishes and sells many varieties of Italian olives, olive oil, and gourmet goods. Sit outside when possible—the interior can feel a bit stuffy. ✉ *Atlasg. 9,* ☎ *08/319049. AE, DC, MC, V.*

Gamla Stan and Skeppsholmen

$$$$ ✕ **Grands Franska Matsalen.** From this classic French restaurant in the Grand Hotel, you can enjoy an inspiring view of Gamla Stan and the Royal Palace across the inner harbor waters. The menu changes five times a year, but the emphasis is always on Swedish ingredients, used to create such dishes as medallions of deer with shiitake mushrooms in wild-berry cream sauce. The lofty measure of opulence here is commensurate with the bill. ✉ *Grand Hotel, Södra Blasieholmshamnen 8,* ☎ *08/6115214. Reservations essential. Jacket required. AE, DC, MC, V. Closed weekends.*

$$$$ ✕ **Pontus in the Green House.** After working for some time under the
★   guidance of the famous chef Erik Lallerstedt—who owned this exquisite restaurant when it was called Eriks—Pontus has taken over operations. You can still count on traditional Swedish fare of the higher school, with a concentration on meat and fish dishes. Everything is well prepared, delicious, and expensive. For a calmer dining experience, choose a corner table upstairs; the ground floor always bustles. You'll be dining among Sweden's rich and famous. ✉ *Österlångg. 17,* ☎ *08/ 238500. AE, DC, MC, V.*

$$$ ✕ **De Fyras Krog.** The name "Inn of the Four Estates" refers to the four social classes originally represented in the Swedish Riksdag—Nobility, Clergy, Burghers, and Peasants. The theme is carried out with rococo furnishings, church pews, an upper gallery, and a stone-flagged cellar dining room to represent the four lifestyles. Swedish regional specialties await you in this intimate atmosphere. ✉ *Järntorgsg. 5,* ☎ *08/ 241414. AE, DC, MC, V. Closed Sun.*

$$$ ✕ **Den Gyldene Freden.** Sweden's most famous old tavern has been open for business since 1722. Every Thursday, the Swedish Academy meets here in a private room on the second floor. The haunt of bards and barristers, artists and ad people, Freden could probably serve sawdust and still be popular, but the food and staff are worthy of the restaurant's hallowed reputation. The cuisine has a Swedish orientation, but Continental influences are spicing up the menu. Season permitting, try the oven-baked fillets of turbot served with chanterelles and crêpes; the gray hen fried with spruce twigs and dried fruit is another good selection. ✉ *Österlångg. 51,* ☎ *08/109046. AE, DC, MC, V. Closed Sun. No lunch.*

$$$ ✕ **Källaren Aurora.** Extremely elegant, if a little staid, this Gamla Stan cellar restaurant is set in a beautiful 17th-century house. Its largely foreign clientele enjoys top-quality Swedish and international cuisines served in intimate small rooms. Try charcoal-grilled spiced salmon, veal Parmesan, or orange-basted halibut fillet. ✉ *Munkbron 11,* ☎ *08/ 219359. AE, DC, MC, V. No lunch.*

$$ ✕ **Cassi.** This downtown restaurant, with an espresso bar dominating the front room, specializes in French bistro cuisine at reasonable prices. ✉ *Narvav. 30,* ☎ *08/6617461. DC, MC, V. Closed Sat.*

$$ ✕ **Costas.** This small Greek restaurant has been popular almost from
★   the day it opened a few years ago. Its menu, and the fact that it's owned and run by a Greek expatriot, has gained it a reputation for having some of the most authentic Greek food in town. The feta cheese and red pep-

per mix is a great starter and the meat dishes come with notable twists, like the fried chicken livers served with green apple slices. If you're on a budget, take a window seat, order a beer and a Greek farmer's salad, and watch the people move through the streets of Gamla Stan. ⊠ *Lilla Nyg. 21,* ☎ *08/101224. DC, MC, V. Closed Sun.–Mon.*

$$ ✕ Diana Källaren. This atmospheric Gamla Stan cellar dates from the Middle Ages. During the first part of the 18th century the building was used as a warehouse when owned by Jonas Alströmer, Sweden's Sir Walter Raleigh. Today it's a restaurant whose menu draws on the best indigenous ingredients from the Swedish forests and shores. Try the fillet of reindeer with chanterelle mushrooms, gnocchi, and port wine sauce, or the black peppered tournedos of beef with artichokes, beets, and a cognac-pepper sauce. ⊠ *Brunnsgränd 2–4,* ☎ *08/107310. AE, DC, MC, V. Closed Sun.*

$$ ✕ Grill Ruby. This American-style barbecue joint is just a cobblestone's throw away from the St. George-slaying-the-dragon statue on Gamla Stan. Next to Bistro Ruby, its French cousin, Grill Ruby skips the escargot and instead focuses on steaks and fish grills. Try the grilled steak with french fries and bearnaise sauce. ⊠ *Österlånggatan 14,* ☎ *08/205776. AE, DC, MC, V.*

$$ ✕ Mårten Trotzig. This contemporary, functional space is both a dining room and a bar. The short menu demonstrates the chef's imagination, blending multicultural recipes in intriguing ways. Try the yellow- and red-tomato salad with arugula pesto, and move onto the flounder fillet with artichoke hearts, asparagus, and a light grapefruit sauce. In a beautiful plant-lined courtyard, less expensive lunch specials are served. The staff is young, the service professional. ⊠ *Västerlångg. 79,* ☎ *08/240231. AE, DC, MC, V. Closed Sun.*

Östermalm

$$$$ ✕ Paul & Norbert. This quaint, romantic restaurant is rustic but re-
★ fined. It's on the city's most elegant avenue, overlooking one of its most picturesque bays. Indigenous wild game—reindeer, elk, partridge, and grouse—is prepared with a French flair; fish dishes are also a draw. ⊠ *Strandv. 9,* ☎ *08/6638183. Reservations essential. AE, DC, MC, V. Closed Sun.*

$$$ ✕ Il Conte. The attentive staff at this warm Italian restaurant near Strandvägen serves delicious Italian fare and wines. Tasteful decor creates an alluring, refined atmosphere; you can dine alfresco under cast-iron lanterns when the weather cooperates. ⊠ *Grevg. 9,* ☎ *08/6612628. Reservations essential. AE, DC, MC, V. No lunch.*

$$ ✕ Eriks Bakficka. A favorite among locals, Erika's Bakficka is a block from the elegant waterside, a few steps down from street level. The restaurant serves a wide variety of Swedish dishes, and there's a lower-priced menu in the pub section. ⊠ *Fredrikshovsg. 4,* ☎ *08/6601599. AE, DC, MC, V. Closed in July.*

$ ✕ Örtagården. This is a truly delightful vegetarian, no-smoking restau-
★ rant above the Östermalmstorg food market. It offers an attractive buffet of soups, salads, hot dishes, and homemade bread—not to mention the SKr 5 bottomless cup of coffee—in a turn-of-the-century atmosphere. ⊠ *Nybrog. 31,* ☎ *08/6621728. AE, MC, V.*

Södermalm

$$ ✕ Gondolen. Suspended like a long train car under the gangway of the Katerina elevator at Slussen square, Gondolen has a magnificent view over the harbor, Mälaren, and the Baltic. Swedish preparations of lobster and crab head an extensive menu; the bar is ideal if you come for

Stockholm Dining and Lodging

Karlaplan ↗

ÖSTERMALM

Kommendörsgatan

Sibyllegatan

45

46 Narvavägen

Linnégatan

Banérgatan

Karlavägen

N. DJURGÅRDEN

Oxenstiernsgatan

Gärdesgatan

Skarpögatan

Artillerigatan

Skeppargatan

44 Grevgatan

Styrmangatan

Storgatan

Linnégatan

Riddargatan

42 **43**

Strandvägen

47

Djurgårdsbron

Strandvägen

Djurgårdsbrunnsviken

Rosendalsvägen

SKEPPSHOLMEN

73

74 Svensksundsvägen

Alkärret

Djurgårdsvägen

Falkenb G.

Allmänna Gränd

Djurgårds
Slätten

Sirishovsvägen

DJURGÅRDEN

Soffidsbacken

Singelbacken

**KASTELL-
HOLMEN**

Baltic→

Saltsjön

BECKHOLMEN

N

75

	KEY	
AE	American Express Office	
i	Tourist Information	

0 _____ 550 yards

0 _____ 500 meters

drinks and a view. ⊠ *Stadsgården 6,* ☎ *08/6417090. AE, DC, MC, V. Closed Sun.*

$$ ✕ **Hannas Krog.** What started out as an interesting neighborhood spot has become one of Södermalm's trendiest restaurants. Guests are serenaded at 10 minutes before the hour by a mooing cow that emerges from the cuckoo clock just inside the door. The range of flavorful dishes—from Caribbean shrimp to Provençale lamb—can get a touch pricey. Crowds won't slow down the consistent service or detract from the relaxed atmosphere. ⊠ *Skåneg. 80,* ☎ *08/6438225. Reservations essential. AE, DC, MC, V. No lunch on weekends or in July.*

$$ ✕ **Indira.** This busy Indian restaurant about a block off of Göt-gatanhas has an overwhelming 60 meal choices. The food is cheap and delicious and the service fast. Order right when you enter and find a seat at one of the mosaic-coated tables. The honey saffron ice cream is a perfect end to the meal. ⊠ *Bondeg. 3B,* ☎ *08/6414046. AE, DC, MC, V.*

$$ ✕ **La Cucaracha.** If you're dining with a group of friends, La Cucaracha's cheap, tasty tapas are ideal for sharing. The restaurant bustles with people throughout the night and really gets going after 11, when the staff moves the tables out of the room for dancing. ⊠ *Bondeg. 2,* ☎ *08/6443944. AE, DC, MC, V.*

$$ ✕ **Nils Emil.** This bustling restaurant in Södermalm is known for a royal
★   following, delicious Swedish cuisine, and generous helpings at reasonable prices; try the *kåldomar* (ground beef wrapped in cabbage) or the Baltic herring. The paintings of personable owner-chef Nils Emil's island birthplace in the Stockholm archipelago are by a well-known Swedish artist, Gustav Rudberg. ⊠ *Folkungag. 122,* ☎ *08/6407209. Reservations essential. Jacket and tie required. AE, DC, MC, V. Closed Sun. and July. No lunch Sat.*

LODGING

Although Stockholm has a reputation for prohibitively expensive hotels, great deals can be found during the summer, when prices are substantially lower and numerous discounts are available. More than 50 hotels offer the "Stockholm Package," providing accommodation for one night, breakfast, and the *Stockholmskortet,* or Stockholm Card, which entitles the cardholder to free admission to museums and travel on public transport. All rooms in the hotels reviewed below are equipped with shower or bath unless otherwise noted. Details are available from travel agents, tourist bureaus, or **Stockholm Information Service** (⊠ Box 7542, 103 93 Stockholm, ☎ 08/7892400, FAX 08/7892450). Also try **Hotellcentralen** (⊠ Centralstation, 111 20 Stockholm, ☎ 08/7892425, FAX 08/7918666); service is free if you go in person, but a fee applies if you call.

Note that you should book lodging far in advance if you plan to travel during the August Stockholm Water Festival. Some hotels close during the winter holidays; call ahead if you expect to travel during that time.

Downtown Stockholm and Beyond

$$$$ ⊞ **Berns Hotel.** Successfully distinguishing itself from the rest of the
★   crowd, the mid-19th-century Berns opted for an art deco look with the latest renovation. Indirect lighting, modern Italian furniture, and expensive marble, granite, and wood inlays define the public areas and guest rooms. You can breakfast in the Red Room, immortalized by August Strindberg's novel of the same name: This was one of his haunts. Rates include the use of a nearby fitness center with a pool. ⊠ *Näck-strömsg. 8, 111 47,* ☎ *08/56632200, FAX 08/56632201. 65 rooms, 3*

suites. Restaurant, bar, no-smoking rooms, meeting room. AE, DC, MC, V.

$$$$ ☷ **Castle Hotel.** On a back street just off of Birgar Jarlsgatan, this centrally located hotel has been in operation since the 1930s. The owners are devout jazz enthusiasts, and the hotel is known for hosting such jazz greats as Dizzy Gillespie, Chet Baker, and Benny Carter. Rooms are done with art deco furnishings but are on the diminutive side. ⊠ *Riddarg. 14, 114 35, ☎ 08/6795700, ℻ 08/6112022. 50 rooms. Restaurant, meeting rooms. AE, DC, MC, V.*

$$$$ ☷ **Continental.** In city center across from the train station, the Continental is a reliable hotel that's especially popular with American guests. Rooms are equipped with a minibar, trouser press, and satellite television. An extravagant Scandinavian buffet is served in the Gustavian breakfast rooms. ⊠ *Klara Vattugränd 4, 101 22, ☎ 08/244020, ℻ 08/4113695. 268 rooms. Restaurant, bar, no-smoking rooms, sauna, meeting rooms. AE, DC, MC, V.*

$$$$ ☷ **Royal Viking (Radisson SAS).** A few yards from Central Station, the Royal Viking hotel offers convenience, both in location and service, yet its rooms tend to be cramped. Nevertheless, rooms do have attractive natural textiles and artwork, sturdy writing desks, separate seating areas, and plush robes in the large bathrooms. Triple-glazed windows and plenty of insulation keep traffic noise to a minimum. The large atrium lobby is spacious, and the split-level lounge is elegant. There is a business-class SAS check-in counter in the lobby. ⊠ *Vasag. 1, 101 24, ☎ 08/141000, ℻ 08/4488355. 319 rooms. Restaurant, bar, minibars, no-smoking rooms, indoor pool, sauna, convention center. AE, MC, V.*

$$$$ ☷ **Sergel Plaza.** This stainless-steel-paneled hotel has a welcoming lobby, with cane chairs in a pleasantly skylit seating area. Bright rooms are practical but lack the luxury feel the price tag might lead you to expect. The decor is almost disappointing, with run-of-the-mill furnishings and too much gray. It's central, right on the main pedestrian mall, but most windows face only office buildings. In the morning, you can choose between an international buffet or Japanese breakfast; the Anna Rella Restaurant serves innovative Swedish and international dishes. ⊠ *Brunkebergstorg 9, 103 27, ☎ 08/226600, ℻ 08/215070. 406 rooms. Restaurant, bar, no-smoking rooms, sauna, shops, convention center. AE, DC, MC, V.*

$$$$ ☷ **SkyCity Hotel.** This Radisson SAS–run hotel is dead center in the Arlanda Airport's SkyCity complex. The hotel is equipped and furnished in a variety of tasteful styles. If your room faces the runway, you can watch the planes quietly take off and land. ⊠ *SkyCity, 190 45 Stockholm-Arlanda, ☎ 08/59077300, ℻ 08/59378100. 230 rooms. Restaurant, bar, no-smoking rooms, fitness center, conference facilities. AE, DC, MC, V.*

$$$ ☷ **Amaranten.** Although it's a little out of the way on the island of Kungsholmen, this large, modern hotel is just a few minutes' walk from Stockholm's central train station. Rooms are contemporary, with satellite television and complimentary movie channels. Fifty rooms have air-conditioning and soundproofing for an extra charge. Guests can enjoy a brasserie and a piano bar. ⊠ *Kungsholmsg. 31, Box 8054, 104 20, ☎ 08/6541060, ℻ 08/6526248. 410 rooms. Restaurant, piano bar, no-smoking rooms, indoor pool, sauna, meeting rooms. AE, DC, MC, V.*

$$$ ☷ **Birger Jarl.** A short bus ride from the city center, this contemporary, conservative, thickly carpeted venue hosts business travelers and unfussy tourists. You can choose your breakfast from an extensive buffet just off the lobby, but room service is also available. Rooms are not large but are well furnished and have nice touches, such as heated towel racks in the bathrooms; all double rooms have bathtubs. Four family-style rooms have extra floor space and sofa beds. ⊠ *Tuleg. 8, 104 32,*

☎ *08/6741000*, ℻ *08/6737366. 225 rooms. Coffee shop, no-smoking rooms, sauna, meeting rooms. AE, DC, MC, V.*

$$$ ⌷ **Central Hotel.** Less than 300 yards from Central Station, this practical hotel has small rooms that face a pleasant, quiet courtyard; bathrooms have a shower only. ⌧ *Vasag. 38, 101 20,* ☎ *08/56620800,* ℻ *08/247573. 93 rooms. No-smoking rooms, meeting rooms. AE, DC, MC, V.*

$$$ ⌷ **City.** This large, modern-style hotel is near the city center and Hötorget market. It is owned by the Salvation Army, so alcohol is not on the menu. Breakfast is served in the atrium restaurant Winter Garden. ⌧ *Slöjdg. 7, 111 81,* ☎ *08/7237200,* ℻ *08/7237209. 293 rooms with bath. Restaurant, no-smoking rooms, sauna, meeting rooms. AE, DC, MC, V.*

$$$ ⌷ **Claes på Hörnet.** This may be the most exclusive—and smallest—
★   hotel in town, with only 10 rooms in an 18th-century inn that was converted into a small hotel in 1982. The rooms, comfortably furnished with period antiques, go quickly. The restaurant is worth visiting even if you don't spend the night: Its old-fashioned dining room is tucked away on the ground floor of a restored 1739 inn. The Swedish and Continental menu includes outstanding *strömming* (Baltic herring) and cloudberry mousse cake. Restaurant reservations are essential, as are a jacket and tie. ⌧ *Surbrunnsg. 20, 113 48,* ☎ *08/165130,* ℻ *08/ 6125315. 10 rooms. AE, DC, MC, V. Closed July.*

$$$ ⌷ **Lydmar Hotell.** Just opposite Humlegården in the center of Stockholm lies this modern hotel, a 10-minute walk from the downtown hub of Sergels Torg. The lobby lounge is alive on weekends with the latest jazz sounds. ⌧ *Stureg. 10, 114 36,* ☎ *08/56611300,* ℻ *08/56611301. 61 rooms, 5 junior suites. AE, DC, MC, V.*

$$$ ⌷ **Tegnérlunden.** A quiet city park fronts this modern hotel, a 10-minute walk along shop-lined Sveavägen from the downtown hub of Sergels Torg. Although the rooms are small and sparely furnished, they are clean and well maintained. The lobby is bright with marble, brass, and greenery, as is the sunny rooftop breakfast room. ⌧ *Tegnérlunden 8, 113 59,* ☎ *08/349780,* ℻ *08/327818. 103 rooms. Breakfast room, no-smoking rooms, sauna, meeting room. AE, DC, MC, V.*

$$ ⌷ **Arcadia.** On a hilltop near a large waterfront nature preserve, this converted dormitory is within 15 minutes of downtown by bus or subway, or 30 minutes on foot along pleasant shopping streets. Rooms are furnished in a spare, neutral style, with plenty of natural light. The adjoining restaurant serves meals on the terrace in summer. Take Bus 43 to Körsbärsvägen. ⌧ *Körsbärsv. 1, 114 89,* ☎ *08/160195,* ℻ *08/ 166224. 82 rooms. Restaurant. AE, DC, MC, V.*

$$ ⌷ **Stockholm Plaza Hotel.** On one of Stockholm's foremost streets for shopping and entertainment, this hotel is ideal for the traveler who wants a central location. The building dates from the turn of the century and is furnished in an elegant, old-world manner; rooms are reasonably sized. ⌧ *Birger Jarlsg. 29, 103 95,* ☎ *08/56622000,* ℻ *08/56622020. 151 rooms. AE, DC, MC, V.*

$ ⌷ **Bema.** This small hotel is relatively central, on the ground floor of an apartment block near Tegnérlunden. Room decor is Swedish modern, with beechwood furniture. One four-bed family room is available. Breakfast is served in your room. ⌧ *Upplandsg. 13, 111 23,* ☎ *08/ 232675,* ℻ *08/205338. 12 rooms. AE, DC, MC, V.*

Gamla Stan and Skeppsholmen

$$$$ ⌷ **Grand Hotel.** The city's showpiece hotel is an 1874 landmark on the quayside at Blasieholmen, just across the water from the Royal Palace. Visiting political dignitaries, Nobel Prize winners, and movie stars come to enjoy the gracious old-world atmosphere, which extends to the comfortable, well-furnished rooms. One of the hotel's most allur-

Finally, a travel companion that doesn't snore on the plane or eat all your peanuts.

When traveling, your MCI WorldCom Card is the best way to keep in touch. Our operators speak your language, so they'll be able to connect you back home—no matter where your travels take you. Plus, your MCI WorldCom Card is easy to use, and even earns you frequent flyer miles every time you use it. When you add in our great rates, you get something even more valuable: peace-of-mind. So go ahead. Travel the world. MCI WorldCom just brought it a whole lot closer.

You can even sign up today at www.mci.com/worldphone or ask your operator to make a collect call to 1-410-314-2938.

EASY TO CALL WORLDWIDE

1 Just dial the WorldPhone access number of the country you're calling from.
2 Dial or give the operator your MCI WorldCom Card number.
3 Dial or give the number you're calling.

France ✦	0-800-99-0019
Germany	0800-888-8000
Ireland	1-800-55-1001
Italy ✦	172-1022
Spain	900-99-0014
Sweden ✦	020-795-922
Switzerland ✦	0800-89-0222
United Kingdom To call using BT To call using CWC	0800-89-0222 0500-89-0222

For your complete WorldPhone calling guide, dial the WorldPhone access number for the country you're in and ask the operator for Customer Service. In the U.S. call 1-800-431-5402.

✦ Public phones may require deposit of coin or phone card for dial tone.

EARN FREQUENT FLYER MILES

The first thing you need overseas is the one thing you forget to pack.

FOREIGN CURRENCY DELIVERED OVERNIGHT

Chase Currency To Go® delivers foreign currency to your home by the next business day*

It's easy—before you travel, call 1-888-CHASE84 for delivery of any of 75 currencies

Delivery is free with orders of $500 or more

Competitive rates— without exchange fees

You don't have to be a Chase customer—you can pay by Visa® or MasterCard®

 **CHASE**

THE RIGHT RELATIONSHIP IS EVERYTHING.®

1•888•CHASE84
www.chase.com

ing features is a glassed-in veranda overlooking the harbor, where an excellent smörgåsbord buffet is served. Guests have access to the Sture-badet Health Spa nearby. ⊠ *Södra Blasieholmshamnen 8, Box 16424, 103 27,* ☎ *08/6793500,* ℻ *08/6118686. 307 rooms, 20 suites. 2 restaurants, bar, no-smoking rooms, sauna, shops, meeting rooms. AE, DC, MC, V.*

$$$$ ☆ **Lady Hamilton.** As charming as its namesake, Lord Nelson's mis-
★ tress, the Lady Hamilton opened in 1980 as a modern hotel inside a 15th-century building. Swedish antiques accent the light, natural-toned decor in all the guest rooms and common areas. Romney's "Bacchae" portrait of Lady Hamilton hangs in the foyer, where the Lady also supports the ceiling in the form of a large, smiling figurehead from an old ship. The breakfast room, furnished with captain's chairs, looks out onto the lively cobblestone street, and the subterranean sauna rooms, in whitewashed stone, provide a secluded fireplace and a chance to take a dip in the building's original, medieval well. The honeymoon suite is impeccable. ⊠ *Storkyrkobrinken 5, 111 28,* ☎ *08/234680,* ℻ *08/ 4111148. 34 rooms. Bar, breakfast room, no-smoking rooms, sauna, meeting room. AE, DC, MC, V.*

$$$$ ☆ **Lord Nelson.** The owners of the Lady Hamilton and the Victory run this small hotel with a nautical atmosphere right in the middle of Gamla Stan. Rooms are a touch larger than cabins—but service is excellent. Noise from traffic in the pedestrian street outside can be a problem during the summer. ⊠ *Västerlångg. 22, 111 29,* ☎ *08/232390,* ℻ *08/101089. 31 rooms. Café, no-smoking rooms, sauna, meeting room. AE, DC, MC, V.*

$$$$ ☆ **Reisen.** This 17th-century hotel on the waterfront in Gamla Stan has been open since 1819. It has a fine restaurant with a grill, tea and coffee service in the library, and what is reputed to be the best piano bar in town. The swimming pool is built under the medieval arches of the foundations. ⊠ *Skeppsbron 1214, 111 30,* ☎ *08/223260,* ℻ *08/ 201559. 144 rooms. Restaurant, piano bar, no-smoking floor, indoor pool, sauna, meeting rooms. AE, DC, MC, V.*

$$$$ ☆ **Strand (Radisson SAS).** This old-world yellow-brick hotel, built in 1912 for the Stockholm Olympics, has been completely and tastefully modernized. It's on the water right across from the Royal Dramatic Theater. No two of its rooms are alike, but all are furnished with antiques and have such rustic touches as flowers painted on woodwork and furniture. The Piazza restaurant has an outdoor feel to it: Italian cuisine is the specialty, and the wine list is superb. An SAS check-in counter for business-class travelers adjoins the main reception area. ⊠ *Nybrokajen 9, Box 163 96, 103 27,* ☎ *08/6787800,* ℻ *08/6112436. 148 rooms. Restaurant, no-smoking rooms, sauna, meeting rooms. AE, DC, MC, V.*

$$$$ ☆ **Victory.** Slightly larger than its brother and sister hotels, the Lord Nelson and Lady Hamilton (☞ *above*), this extremely atmospheric Gamla Stan building dates from 1640. The decor is nautical, with items from the HMS *Victory* and Swedish antiques. Each room is named after a 19th-century sea captain. The noted Lejontornet restaurant keeps an extensive wine cellar. ⊠ *Lilla Nyg. 5, 111 28,* ☎ *08/143090,* ℻ *08/ 202177. 48 rooms. Restaurant, bar, bistro, no-smoking floor, 2 saunas, meeting rooms. AE, DC, MC, V.*

$$$ ☆ **Gamla Stan.** This quiet, cozy hotel is tucked away in one of the Gamla Stan's 17th-century houses. Each of its 51 rooms is uniquely decorated. ⊠ *Lilla Nyg. 25,* ☎ *08/7237250,* ℻ *08/7237259. 51 rooms. No-smoking floor, meeting rooms. AE, DC, MC, V.*

$$ ☆ **Mälardrottningen.** One of the more unusual establishments in Stockholm, Mälardrottningen, a Sweden Hotels property, was once Barbara Hutton's yacht. Since 1982, it has been a quaint and pleasant hotel,

with a crew as service-conscious as any in Stockholm. Tied up on the freshwater side of Gamla Stan, it is minutes from everything. The small suites are suitably decorated in a navy-blue and maroon nautical theme. Some of the below-deck cabins are a bit stuffy, but in summer you can take your meals out on deck. The ship's chief assets are novelty and absence of traffic noise. ⊠ *Riddarholmen 4, 111 28,* ☎ *08/243600,* FAX *08/4488355. 59 cabins. Restaurant, bar, grill, no-smoking rooms, sauna, meeting rooms. AE, DC, MC, V.*

Östermalm

$$$$ 🏨 **Diplomat.** Within easy walking distance of Djurgården, this elegant hotel is less flashy than most in its price range. The building is a turn-of-the-century town house that housed foreign embassies in the 1930s and was converted into a hotel in 1966. Rooms have thick carpeting and high ceilings; those in the front, facing the water, have magnificent views over Stockholm Harbor. The tea room restaurant and second-floor bar are ideal for a sightseeing break. ⊠ *Strandv. 7C, 104 40,* ☎ *08/6635800,* FAX *08/7836634. 133 rooms. Restaurant, bar, no-smoking rooms, sauna, meeting room. AE, DC, MC, V.*

$$$$ 🏨 **Hotel Esplanade.** Situated directly on the water and just across the street from Stockholm's Royal Dramatic Theater, Hotel Esplanade is a beautiful hotel with a real touch of old Stockholm. Originally a guest house operated by an elderly woman, the inn's current owners have sought to maintain the homey ambience. Rooms are individually decorated and some offer water views. Breakfast is served in the original Art Nouveau–style breakfast room. ⊠ *Strandv. 7A, 114 56,* ☎ *08/6630740,* FAX *08/6625992. 34 rooms. Sauna. AE, DC, MC, V.*

$$$ 🏨 **Mornington.** A quiet, modern Best Western hotel that prides itself on a friendly atmosphere, the Mornington is within easy walking distance of Stureplan and downtown shopping areas—such as the Östermalmstorg, with the irresistable food displays in the Saluhall. Rooms tend to be small; decor is standard Best Western. ⊠ *Nybrog. 53, 102 44,* ☎ *08/6631240,* FAX *08/6622179. 140 rooms. Restaurant, bar, no-smoking rooms, sauna, steam rooms, meeting rooms. AE, DC, MC, V.*

$$ 🏨 **Örnsköld.** Just behind the Royal Dramatic Theater in the heart of ★ the city, this hidden gem has the atmosphere of an old private club, with a brass-and-leather lobby and Victorian-style furniture in the moderately spacious, high-ceilinged rooms. Rooms over the courtyard are quieter, but those facing the street—not a busy one—are sunnier. The hotel is frequented by actors appearing at the Royal Theater. ⊠ *Nybrog. 6, 114 34,* ☎ *08/6670285,* FAX *08/6676991. 30 rooms. AE, MC, V.*

Södermalm

$$$$ 🏨 **Scandic Hotel Slussen.** Working with what appears to be a dubious location (perched on a tunnel above a six-lane highway), the Scandic has pulled a rabbit out of a hat. Built on special noise- and shock-absorbing cushions, the hotel almost lets you forget about the highway. The intriguing labyrinth of levels, separate buildings, and corridors is filled with such unique details as a rounded stairway lighted from between the steps. The guest rooms are exquisitely designed and modern, with plenty of stainless steel and polished wood inlay to accent the maroon color scheme. French dishes are served at the Couronne d'Or; you can sample wines in a cellar whose collection dates back to 1650. The hotel is at Slussen, easily accessible from downtown. ⊠ *Guldgränd 8, 104 65,* ☎ *08/51735300,* FAX *08/51735311. 264 rooms. 2* *restaurants, piano bar, no-smoking rooms, indoor pool, beauty salon, sauna, meeting rooms. AE, DC, MC, V.*

$$$ ☐ **Anno 1647.** Named for the date the building was erected, this
★ small, pleasant hotel is in Södermalm, three stops on the subway from the city center. Rooms vary in shape, but all have original, well-worn pine floors with 17th-century-style appointments. There's no elevator in this four-story building. ☒ *Mariagränd 3, 116 41,* ☎ *08/4421680,* FAX *08/4421647. 42 rooms, 30 with bath. Snack bar. AE, DC, MC, V.*

$$ ☐ **Alexandra.** Situated in the Södermalm area, to the south of Gamla Stan, this economy hotel is a five-minute walk from the subway and only a few stops from the city center. Rooms are clean and fairly big, although the decor is a reminder that most of the renovations here took place during the late '80s. There are a number of cheaper rooms, adjacent to the parking garage, without windows. ☒ *Magnus Ladulåsg. 42, 118 27,* ☎ *08/840320,* FAX *08/7205353. 68 rooms, 5 two-room suites. Breakfast rooms, no-smoking rooms, sauna. AE, DC, MC, V.*

$ ☐ **Gustav af Klint.** A "hotel ship" moored at Stadsgården quay, near Slussen subway station, the *Gustav af Klint* harbors 120 beds in its two sections: a hotel and a hostel. The hostel section has 18 four-bunk cabins and 10 two-bunk cabins; a 14-bunk dormitory is also available from May through mid-September. The hotel section has 4 single-bunk and 3 two-bunk cabins with bedsheets and breakfast included. The hostel rates are SKr 120 per person in a four-bunk room, and SKr 140 per person in a two-bunk room; these do not include bedsheets or breakfast. All guests share common bathrooms and showers. There is a cafeteria and a restaurant, and you can dine on deck in summer. ☒ *Stadsgårdskajen 153, 116 45,* ☎ *08/6404077,* FAX *08/6406416. 7 hotel cabins, 28 hostel cabins, 28 dormitory beds. Restaurant, cafeteria. AE, MC, V.*

Youth Hostels

Don't be put off by the "youth" bit: there's actually no age limit. The standards of cleanliness, comfort, and facilities offered are usually extremely high. Hostels listed are on Skeppsholmen and Södermalm.

$ ☐ **af Chapman.** This circa-1888 sailing ship, permanently moored in Stockholm Harbor just across from the Royal Palace, is a landmark in its own right. Book early—the place is so popular in summer that finding a bed may prove difficult. Breakfast (SKr 45) is not included in the room rate; there are no kitchen facilities. ☒ *Västra Brobänken, Skeppsholmen 111 49,* ☎ *08/4632266,* FAX *08/6119875. 136 beds, 2- to 6-bed cabins. Café* ☉ *June–Aug. DC, MC, V. Closed Dec. 25–Mar.*

$ ☐ **Bosön.** Out of the way on the island of Lidingö, this hostel is part of the Bosön Sports Institute, a national training center pleasantly close to the water. You can rent canoes on the grounds and go out for a paddle. Breakfast is included in the room rate. There are laundry facilities and a kitchen for guest use. ☒ *Bosön, 181 47 Lidingö,* ☎ *08/6056600,* FAX *08/ 7671644. 70 beds. Cafeteria, sauna, coin laundry. MC, V.*

$ ☐ **Långholmen.** This former prison, built in 1724, was converted into a combined hotel and hostel in 1989. The hotel rooms are made available as additional hostel rooms in the summer. Rooms are small and windows are nearly nonexistent—you *are* in a prison—but that hasn't stopped travelers from flocking here. Each room has two to five beds, and all but 10 have bathrooms with shower. The hostel is on the island of Långholmen, which has popular bathing beaches and a Prison Museum. The Inn, next door, serves Swedish home cooking, the Jail Pub offers light snacks, and a garden restaurant operates in the summer. ☒ *Långholmen, Box 9116, 102 72,* ☎ *08/6680500,* FAX *08/*

7208575. 254 beds June–Sept., 26 beds Sept.–May. Cafeteria, restaurant, sauna, beach, coin laundry. AE, DC, MC, V.

$ ☎ **Skeppsholmen.** This former craftsman's workshop in a pleasant and quiet part of the island was converted into a hostel for the overflow from the *af Chapman*, an anchor's throw away. Breakfast (SKr 45) is not included in the room rate. ⊠ *Skeppsholmen, 111 49,* ☎ *08/ 4632266,* FAX *08/6117155. 155 beds, 2- to 6-bed rooms. DC, MC, V.*

Camping

You can camp in the Stockholm area for SKr 80–SKr 130 per night. Try any of the following sites: **Bromma** (⊠ Ängby Camping, 161 55 Bromma, ☎ 08/370420, FAX 08/378226), **Skärholmen** (⊠ Bredäng Camping, 127 31 Skärholmen, ☎ 08/977071, FAX 08/7087262), **Sollentuna** (⊠ Rösjöbadens Camping, 191 56 Sollentuna, ☎ 08/962184, FAX 08/929295).

NIGHTLIFE AND THE ARTS

The hubs of Stockholm's nightlife are the streets Birger Jarlsgatan, Stureplan, and the city end of Kungsträdgården. On weekends, discos and bars are often packed with tourists and locals, and you might have to wait in line. Many establishments will post and enforce a minimum age requirement, which could be anywhere from 18 to 30, depending on the clientele they wish to serve.

The tourist guide *Stockholm This Week* is available free of charge at most hotels and tourist centers. The Friday editions of the daily newspapers *Dagens Nyheter* and *Svenska Dagbladet* carry current listings of events, films, restaurants, and museums in Swedish.

The **Stockholm Water Festival** (☎ 08/4595500) is *the* big event in Stockholm. People from all over Sweden and the rest of the world come to the city for the concerts featuring major acts, races, a fireworks competition, and a week of general partying and good times. According to a recent survey, every third Swede has visited the festival at some point. It's held in the middle of August—call ahead for exact dates.

Nightlife

Bars

If you prefer exploring areas not entirely swamped by crowds, you will find a bar-hopping visit to Södermalm rewarding. Start at **Mosebacke Etablissement** (⊠ Mosebacke Torg 3, ☎ 08/6419020), a combined indoor theater and outdoor café with a spectacular view of the city. The Stureplan's **O-bar** (⊠ Stureplan 2, ☎ 08/4405730) is where the downtown crowd gathers for late-night drinks and music ranging from country to hard rock. If you'd rather be seen dining or dancing to half a century of pop hits amidst Stockholm's well-heeled types, head to **Riche** (⊠ Birger Jarlsg. 4, ☎ 08/6117022). Wander along Götagatan with its lively bars and head for **Snaps/Rangus Tangus** (⊠ Medborgarplatsen, ☎ 08/ 6402868), an eatery and cellar bar with live music in a 300-year-old building. A trendy 20-something crowd props up the long bar at **WC** (⊠ Skåneg. 51, ☎ 08/7022963), with ladies' drink specials.

Stockholm can also appease your need for pub-style intimacy. Guinness, ale, and cider enthusiasts rally in the tartan-clad **Bagpiper's Inn** (⊠ Rörstrandsg. 21, ☎ 08/311855), where you can get a full range of bar food. **The Dubliner** (⊠ Smålandsg. 8, ☎ 08/6797707) serves up pub food and hosts live folk music on stage. As green as a four-leaf clover, **Limerick** (⊠ Tegnérg. 10, ☎ 08/6734398) is another popular

Hibernian watering hole. The very British **Tudor Arms** (✉ Grevg. 31, ☎ 08/6602712) is just as popular as when it opened in 1969.

Casinos

Many hotels and bars have a roulette table and sometimes blackjack; games operate according to Swedish rules that are designed to limit the amount you can lose. The **Monte Carlo** (☎ 08/4110025), at the corner of Kungsgatan and Sveavägen, offers roulette and blackjack 11:30 AM–5 AM daily; there is food service and a bar, and a disco on weekends. Clientele tends to be on the rough side.

Discos and Cabaret

Stockholm's biggest nightclub, **Börsen** (✉ Jakobsg. 6, ☎ 08/7878500), offers high-quality international cabaret shows. Another popular spot is the **Cabaret Club** (✉ Barnhusg. 12, ☎ 08/4110608), where reservations are advised.

Berns' Salonger (✉ Berzelii Park, ☎ 08/6140500), an elegant restaurant and bar in a renovated period building, turns into a lively disco at night; its large balcony faces the Royal Dramatic Theater. **Café Opera** (✉ Operahuset, ☎ 08/4110026), at the waterfront end of Kungsträgården, is a popular meeting place for young and old alike. It has the longest bar in town, plus dining and roulette, and dancing after midnight; the kitchen offers a night menu until 2:30 AM. **Daily's Bar** (✉ Kungsträdgården, ☎ 08/215655), a glitzy disco at the other end of Kungsträdgården, near Sweden House, has a restaurant and is open until 3 AM. **King Creole** (✉ Kungsg. 18, ☎ 08/244700) offers big-band dance music alternating with rock. **Mälarsalen** (✉ Torkel Knutssonsg. 2, ☎ 08/6581300) caters to the nondrinking jitterbug and fox-trot crowd in Södermalm. **Penny Lane** (✉ Birger Jarlsg. 29, ☎ 08/201411) is a soft-disco nightclub specifically for a 30- and 40-something crowd. **Sture Compagniet** (✉ Stureg. 4, ☎ 08/6117800) is a complex of bars, food service, and dance areas on three levels inside the Sture Gallerian shopping mall.

Gay Bars

Pronounced "Hus-et," the upscale **Hus 1** (✉ Sveav. 57, ☎ 08/315533) dance club—with a restaurant, café, bookshop, and disco—has mirrored walls and weekend drag shows. Be prepared for a cover charge of about SKr 80. Another hot gay-popular hangout is in front of the **Chinateatern,** which is close to a number of clubs at Berzelii Park. **Patricia** (✉ Stadsgården, Berth 25, ☎ 08/7430570) is a floating disco and bar right next to Slussen.

Jazz Clubs

The best and most popular jazz venue is **Fasching** (✉ Kungsg. 63, ☎ 08/216267), where international and local bands play year-round. Relatively new to the jazz scene is the lobby bar at the **Lydmar Hotel** (✉ Stureg. 10, ☎ 08/223160), where live jazz can be enjoyed on weekends and some weekdays. The classic club **Nalens** (✉ Regeringsg. 74 ☎ 08/4533434) is back on the scene with major performances throughout the year. **Stampen** (✉ Stora Nyg. 5, ☎ 08/205793) is an overpriced, but atmospheric, club in Gamla Stan with traditional jazz nightly. Get there early for a seat.

Piano Bars

Piano bars are part of Stockholm's nightlife. The **Anglais Bar** at the Hotel Anglais (✉ Humlegårdsg. 23, ☎ 08/6141600) is recommended on weekends. Also try the **Clipper Club** at the Hotel Reisen (✉ Skeppsbron 1214, ☎ 08/223260).

Rock Clubs
Lido (⊠ Hornsg. 92, subway to Zinkensdamm; ☎ 08/6682333) is on Södermalm. Call ahead for reservations. **Krogen Tre Backar** (⊠ Tegnérg. 1214, ☎ 08/6734400) can be found just off Sveavgen.

The Arts

Stockholm's theater and concert season runs from September through May, so you won't find many big-name artists at the height of the tourist season except during the Stockholm Water Festival in August. For a list of events, pick up the free booklet *Stockholm This Week,* available from hotels and tourist information offices. For tickets to theaters and shows try **Biljettdirekt** at Sweden House (☞ Visitor Information *in* Stockholm A to Z, *below*) or any post office.

Classical Music
Free concerts are held in **Kungsträdgården** every summer—for details, contact the tourist office or check *Stockholm This Week.* International orchestras perform at **Konserthuset** (⊠ Hötorget 8, ☎ 08/102110), the main concert hall. The **Music at the Palace** series (☎ 08/102247) runs June through August. Off-season, there are weekly concerts by Sweden's Radio Symphony Orchestra at **Berwaldhallen** (Berwald Concert Hall, ⊠ Strandv. 69, ☎ 08/7841800).

Film
Stockholm has an abundance of cinemas, all listed in the Yellow Pages under *Biografer.* Current billings are listed in evening papers, normally with Swedish titles; call ahead if you're unsure. Foreign movies are subtitled. Most, if not all, cinemas take reservations over the phone. Popular showings can sell out ahead of time. Most cinemas are part of the SF chain (☎ 08/56260000), including the 14-screen **Filmstaden Sergel** (⊠ Hötorget, ☎ 08/56260000); **Biopalatset** and **Filmstaden Söder** (⊠ Medborgarplatsen, ☎ 08/6443100 and 56260000) are on the south side and have many films from which to choose. The **Grand** (⊠ Sveav. 45, ☎ 08/4112400) is said to be the best-quality cinema in town.

Opera
It is said that Queen Lovisa Ulrika began introducing opera to her subjects in 1755. Since then, Sweden has become an opera center of standing, a launchpad for such names as Jenny Lind, Jussi Björling, and Birgit Nilsson. **Operan** (The Royal Opera House, ⊠ Jakobs Torg 2, ☎ 08/248240), dating from 1898, is now the de facto home of Sweden's operatic tradition. **Folkoperan** (⊠ Hornsg. 72, ☎ 08/6160750) is a modern company with its headquarters in Södermalm. Casting traditional presentation and interpretation of the classics to the wind, the company stages productions that are refreshingly new.

Theater
Kungliga Dramatiska Teatern (Royal Dramatic Theater, called Dramaten, ⊠ Nybroplan, ☎ 08/6670680) sometimes stages productions of international interest, in Swedish, of course. Productions by the **English Theatre Company** and the **American Drama Group Europe** are occasionally staged at various venues in Stockholm. See newspapers or contact Stockholm Information Service for details.

OUTDOOR ACTIVITIES AND SPORTS

Beaches

The best bathing places in central Stockholm are on the island of Långholmen and at Rålambshov at the end of Norr Mälarstrand. Both are grassy or rocky lakeside hideaways. Topless sunbathing is virtually de rigueur.

Biking

Stockholm is laced with bike paths, and bicycles can be taken on the commuter trains (except during peak traveling times) for excursions to the suburbs. You can rent a bike for an average of SKr 80 per day or SKr 400 per week. **Cykelfrämjandet** (⊠ Torsg. 31, Box 6027, 102 31, ☎ 08/321680), a local bicyclists' association, publishes an English-language guide to cycling trips. Bikes can be rented from **Cykel & Mopeduthyrning** (⊠ Strandv. at Kajplats 24, ☎ 08/6607959). Also try **Skepp & Hoj** (⊠ Galärvarvsv. 2, ☎ 08/6605757), pronounced "ship ahoy."

Fitness Centers

Health and fitness is a Swedish obsession. The **Sports Club Stockholm** (⊠ City Sports Club, Birger Jarlsg. 6C. ☎ 08/6798310; Atlanta Sports Club, ⊠ St. Eriksg. 34, ☎ 08/6506625) chain has four centers in all, with women's and mixed gym facilities for SKr 90 a day. For a relatively inexpensive massage, try the **Axelsons Gymnastiska Institut** (⊠ Gästrikeg. 1012, ☎ 08/54545900). **Friskis & Svettis** (⊠ St. Eriksg. 54, ☎ 08/4297000) is a local chain of indoor and, in summer, outdoor gyms specializing in aerobics; branches are scattered throughout the Stockholm area. Monday through Thursday at 6 PM, from the end of May into late August, it hosts free sessions in Rålambshovsparken.

Golf

There are numerous golf courses around Stockholm; contact **Stockholms Golfförbund** (⊠ Solkraftsv. 25, 135 70 Stockholm, ☎ 08/7315370) for information. **Lidingö Golfklubb** (⊠ Kyttingev. 2, Lidingö, ☎ 08/7317900) is about a 20-minute drive from the city center. **Ingarö Golfklubb** (⊠ Fogelvik, Ingarö, ☎ 08/57028244) is also about 20 minutes away.

Running

Numerous parks with footpaths dot the central city area, among them **Haga Park** (which also has canoe rentals), **Djurgården,** and the wooded **Liljans Skogen.** A very pleasant public path follows the waterfront across from Djurgården, going east from Djurgårdsbron past some of Stockholm's finest old mansions and the wide-open spaces of Ladugårdsgärdet.

Skiing

The **Excursion Shop** in the Sweden House (⊠ Kungsträdgården, Stockholm, ☎ 08/7892415) has information on skiing as well as other sport and leisure activities and will advise on necessary equipment.

Spectator Sports

The ultramodern, 281-ft **Globen** (⊠ Box 10055, 121 27, Globentorget 2, ☎ 08/7251000), the world's tallest spherical building, hosts sports like ice hockey and equestrian events. It has its own subway station. North of the city lies the open-air **Råsunda Stadion** (⊠ Box 1216, Solnav. 51, 171 23 Solna, ☎ 08/7350935), famous as the home of soccer in Stockholm.

Swimming

In town center, **Centralbadet** (⊠ Drottningg. 88, ☎ 08/242403) has an extra-large indoor pool, whirlpool, steambath, and sauna. **Sture-**

badet (⊠ Sturegallerian, ☎ 08/54501500) offers aquatic aerobics and
a sauna.

Tennis

Former champion Björn Borg once played at **Kungliga Tennishallen**
(Royal Tennis Hall, ⊠ Lidingöv. 75, ☎ 08/4591500). **Tennisstadion**
(⊠ Fiskartorpsv. 20, ☎ 08/215454) also maintains good courts.

SHOPPING

If you like to shop till you drop then charge on down to any one of
the three main department stores in the central city area. For bargains,
peruse the boutiques and galleries in Västerlånggatan, the main street
of Gamla Stan, and the crafts and art shops that line the raised side-
walk at the start of Hornsgatan on Södermalm. Drottninggatan, Birger
Jarlsgatan, and Hamngatan also offer some of the city's best shopping.

Department Stores and Malls

Sweden's leading department store is **NK** (⊠ Hamng. 1820, across the
street from Kungsträdgården, ☎ 08/7628000); the initials, pronounced
enn-koh, stand for *Nordiska Kompaniet.* Prices are high, as is the
quality. Also try **Åhléns** (⊠ Klarabergsg. 50, ☎ 08/6766000). Before
becoming a famous actress, Greta Garbo used to work at the **PUB** (⊠
Drottningg. 63 and Hötorget, ☎ 08/239915), with 42 independent boutiques. Garbo fans will appreciate the small exhibit on level H2—an
array of photographs begins with her employee ID card.

Gallerian (⊠ Hamngatan), in the city center just down the road from
Sergels Torg, is a large indoor mall closely resembling those found in
the United States. Toys, shoes, music, designer clothes, and food are
among the wares. **Sturegallerian** (⊠ Stureplan), the other main shopping mall, is on Stureplan.

Specialty Stores

Auction Houses

There are three principal local auction houses. Perhaps the finest is **Lilla
Bukowski** (⊠ Strandv. 7, ☎ 08/6140800), in its elegant quarters on
the waterfront. **Auktions Kompaniet** (⊠ Regeringsg. 47, ☎ 08/235700)
is next to NK downtown. **Stockholms Auktionsverk** (⊠ Jakobsg. 10,
☎ 08/4536700) is under the Gallerian shopping center.

Books

Hemlins (⊠ Västerlångg. 6, Gamla Stan, ☎ 08/106180) carries foreign titles and antique books.

Crafts

Swedish arts and crafts from all over the country are available at
Svensk Hemslöjd (⊠ Sveav. 44, ☎ 08/232115). Though prices are high
at **Svenskt Hantwerk** (⊠ Kungsg. 55, ☎ 08/214726), so is the quality.
For elegant home furnishings and timeless fabrics, affluent Stockholmers
tend to favor **Svenskt Tenn** (⊠ Strandv. 5A, ☎ 08/6701600), best known
for its selection of designer Josef Franck's furniture and fabrics.

Glass

The **Crystal Art Center** (⊠ Tegelbacken 4, ☎ 08/217169), near Central Station, has a great selection of smaller glass items. **NK** (☞ *above*)
carries a wide, representative line of Swedish glasswork in its Swedish
Shop downstairs. **Nordiska Kristall** (⊠ Kungsg. 9, ☎ 08/104372),
near Sturegallerian, has a small gallery of one-of-a-kind art glass pieces.

Svenskt Glas (⊠ Birger Jarlsg. 8, ☎ 08/6797909) is near the Royal Dramatic Theater.

Men's Clothing

Top men's fashions can be found on the second floor of **NK** (⊠ Hamng. 1820, ☎ 08/7628000), which stocks everything from outdoor gear and evening wear to swimsuits and workout gear. Another great spot for trendy Swedish designs is **Mr. Walker**(⊠ Regeringsg. 42,, ☎ 08/7966096), where Filippa K, one of Sweden's most popular designers of women's clothing, sells her men's collection. The threads here are fabulous, but be prepared to part with some serious crowns—it's hard to walk out empty-handed. For suits and evening suits for both sale and rental, **Hans Allde** (⊠ Birger Jarlsg. 58, ☎ 08/207191) provides good, old-fashioned service. For shirts, try **La Chemise** (⊠ Smålandsg. 11,☎ 08/6111494).

Women's Clothing

There are many boutiques on **Biblioteksgatan** and **Västerlånggatan** in Gamla Stan, including **Champaigne** (⊠ Biblioteksg. 2,☎ 08/6118803), where the best in European and Swedish designs are often discounted. **Flippa K** (⊠ Greve Tureg. 18, ☎ 08/6622015), has quickly become one of Sweden's hottest designers and her stores are filled with young women grabbing the latest fashions. A shop that specializes in lingerie but also carries fashionable clothing is **Twilfit** (⊠ Nybrog. 11, ☎ 08/6623817; Gallerian, ☎ 08/216996; and Gamla Brog. 3638, ☎ 08/201954). **Hennes & Mauritz** (⊠ Hamng. 22; Drottningg. 53 and 56; Sergelg. 1 and 22; and Sergels Torg 12; all ☎ 08/7965500) is one of the few Swedish-owned clothing stores to have achieved international success. **Polarn & Pyret** (⊠ Hamng. 10, ☎ 08/4114140; Gallerian, ☎ 08/4112247; Drottningg. 29, ☎ 08/106790) carries high-quality Swedish children's and women's clothing. One department store with almost every style and type of clothing and apparel is **NK**(⊠ Hamng. 1820, ☎ 08/7628000).

Street Markets

Hötorget is the site of a lively market every day. The **Loppmarknaden** flea market (*loppmarknad*) is held in the parking garage of the Skärholmen shopping center, a 20-minute subway ride from downtown. Market hours are weekdays 11–6, Saturday 9–3, and Sunday 10–3, with an entry fee of SKr 10 on weekends. Beware of pickpockets. The best streets for bric-a-brac and antiques are **Odengatan** and **Roslagsgatan**; take the subway to the Odenplan station.

STOCKHOLM A TO Z

Arriving and Departing

By Bus

All the major bus and coach services, like Wasatrafik and Swebus, arrive at **Cityterminalen** (City Terminal, ⊠ Karabergsviadukten 72), next to the central railway station. Reservations to destinations all over Sweden on **Swebus/Vasatrafik** can be made by calling ☎ 0200/218218.

By Car

You will approach the city by either the **E20** or **E18** highway from the west, or the **E4** from the north or south. The roads are clearly marked and well sanded and plowed during winter. Signs for downtown read CENTRUM.

By Plane

Initially opened in 1960 solely for international flights, Stockholm's **Arlanda International Airport** also contains a domestic terminal. The airport is 42 km (26 mi) from the city center; a freeway links the city and airport.

Between the Airport and City Center: Travel between Arlanda International Airport and Stockholm has been greatly improved with the completion of the Arlanda Express, a **high-speed train** (☎ 08/58889000) service that started running in August 1999. The yellow-nosed train leaves every 15 minutes, travels at a speed of 200 km/hr (125 mi/hr), and completes the trip from the airport to Stockholm's Central Station in just 20 minutes; single tickets cost 120 SKr.

Buses leave both the international and domestic terminals every 10 to 15 minutes from 6:30 AM to 11 PM and run to the Cityterminalen at Klarabergsviadukten, next to the central railway station. The trip costs SKr 60. For more information, call ☎ 08/6001000.

A **bus-taxi combination package** (☎ 08/6701010) is available. The bus lets you off by the taxi stand at Jarva Krog or Cityterminalen and you present your receipt to the taxi driver, who takes you to your final destination. A trip will cost between SKr 160 and SKr 220, depending on your destination.

For **taxis,** the *fast pris* (fixed price) between Arlanda and the city is SKr 435. For information and bookings, call ☎ 08/7973700. The best bets for cabs are **Taxi Stockholm** and **Taxi Kurir.** Watch out for unregistered cabs, which charge high rates.

SAS operates a shared **limousine** service to any point in central Stockholm for SKr 263 per person; the counter is in the arrivals hall, just past customs. If two or more people travel to the same address together in a limousine, only one is charged the full rate; the others pay SKr 140.

By Train

All trains arrive at Stockholm's **Central Station** (Vasag., ☎ 08/7622000) in downtown Stockholm. From here regular commuter trains serve the suburbs, and an underground walkway leads to the central subway station.

Getting Around

The cheapest way to travel around the city by public transport is to purchase the **Stockholmskortet** (Stockholm Card). In addition to unlimited transportation on city subway, bus, and rail services, it offers free admission to more than 60 museums and several sightseeing trips. The card costs SKr 199 for 24 hours, SKr 398 for two days, and SKr 450 for three days; you can purchase the card from the tourist center at Sweden House on Hamngatan, from the Hotellcentralen accommodations bureau at Central Station, and from the tourist center at Kaknäs Tower.

By Boat

Waxholmsbolaget (Waxholm Ferries, ☎ 08/6795830) offers the *Båtluffarkortet* (Inter-Skerries Card), a discount pass for its extensive commuter network of archipelago boats; the price is SKr 250 for 16 days of unlimited travel. The **Strömma Kanalbolaget** (☎ 08/58714000) operates a fleet of archipelago boats that provide excellent sightseeing tours and excursions.

By Bus and Subway

Stockholm has an excellent bus and subway network operated by **SL** (☎ 08/6001000). Tickets for the two networks are interchangeable. The subway system, known as **T-banan** (*Tunnelbanan*, stations marked by a blue-on-white T), is the easiest and fastest way to get around. Servicing over 100 stations and covering more than 96 km (60 mi) of track, trains run frequently between 5 AM and 2 AM. Late-night bus service connects certain stations when trains stop running. The comprehensive bus network serves out-of-town points of interest, such as Waxholm and Gustavsberg.

Maps and timetables for all city transportation networks are available from the SL information desks at Sergels Torg, Central Station, and Slussen.

Bus and subway fares are based on zones, starting at SKr 14, good for travel within one zone, such as downtown, for one hour. You pay more if you travel in more than one zone. Single tickets are available at station ticket counters and on buses, but it's cheaper to buy an **SL Tourist Card** from one of the many Pressbyrån newsstands. There's also a pass called a **Rikskupong,** valid for both subway and buses that costs SKr 95 and is good for approximately 10 trips (depending on how many zones you travel) within the greater Stockholm area during an unlimited period of time. If you plan to travel within the greater Stockholm area extensively during a 24-hour period, you can purchase a one-day pass for SKr 60; a 72-hour pass costs SKr 120. The 24-hour pass includes transportation on the ferries between Djurgården, Nybroplan, and Slussen. The 72-hour pass also entitles the holder to admission to Skansen, Gröna Lund Tivoli, and Kaknäs Tower. People under 18 or over 65 pay SKr 36 for a one-day pass and SKr 72 for a two-day pass.

By Car

Driving in Stockholm is often deliberately frustrated by city planners, who impose many restrictions to keep traffic down. Get a good city map, called a **Trafikkarta,** available at most service stations for around SKr 75.

By Taxi

Stockholm's taxi service is efficient but overpriced. If you call a cab, ask the dispatcher to quote you a *fast pris,* which is usually lower than the meter fare. Reputable cab companies are **Taxi 020** (☎ 020/939393), **Taxi Stockholm** (☎ 08/150000), and **Taxikurir** (☎ 08/300000). **Taxi Stockholm** has an immediate charge of SKr 25 whether you hail a cab or order one by telephone. A trip of 10 km (6 mi) should cost about SKr 97 between 6 AM and 7 PM, SKr 107 at night, and SKr 114 on weekends.

Contacts and Resources

Car Rentals

Rental cars are readily available in Sweden and are relatively inexpensive. Because of the availability and efficiency of public transport, there is little point in using a car within the city limits. If you are traveling elsewhere in Sweden, you'll find that roads are uncongested and well marked but that gasoline is expensive (SKr 8 per liter). All major car-rental firms are represented, including **Avis** (⊠ Ringv. 90, ☎ 08/6449980) and **Hertz** (⊠ Vasag. 26, ☎ 08/240720).

Doctors and Dentists

There is a 24-hour national health-service **emergency number** (☎ 08/4639100). Private care is available via **City Akuten** (☎ 08/4122961). Contact the emergency dental clinic (☎ 08/6541117 or 08/4122900).

Embassies

Australia (✉ Sergels Torg 12, ☎ 08/6132900). **Canada** (✉ Tegelbacken 4, ☎ 08/4533000). **U.K.** (✉ Skarpög. 68, ☎ 08/6719000). **U.S.** (✉ Strandv. 101, ☎ 08/7835300).

Emergencies

Dial ☎ 112 for emergencies—this covers police, fire, ambulance, and medical help, as well as sea and air rescue services.

English-Language Bookstores

Many bookshops stock English-language books. **Akademibokhandeln** (✉ Mäster Samuelsg. 32, near the city center, ☎ 08/6136170) also has a wide selection of English titles, with an emphasis on reference books. **Hedengren's** (✉ Stureplan 4, Sturegallerian shopping complex, ☎ 08/6115132) has the best and most extensive selection of English- and foreign-language books, from fiction to nonfiction, photography to architecture. **NK** (✉ Hamng. 1820, ☎ 08/7628000) has a large bookstore with an extensive English-language selection.

Guided Tours

Boat and Bus Sightseeing Tours: A bus tour in English and Swedish covering all the main points of interest leaves each day at 9:45 AM from the tourist center at **Sweden House** (✉ Hamng. 27, Box 7542, 103 93 Stockholm, ☎ 08/7892490); it costs SKr 250. Other, more comprehensive tours, taking in museums, Gamla Stan, and City Hall, are also available at the tourist center. **Strömma Kanalbolaget and Stockholm Sightseeing** (✉ Skeppsbron 22, ☎ 08/58714000) runs a variety of sightseeing tours of Stockholm. Boats leave from the quays outside the Royal Dramatic Theater, Grand Hotel, and City Hall.

Guided Tours: You can hire your own guide from Stockholm Information Service's **Guide Centralen** (✉ Sweden House, Hamng. 27, Box 7542, 103 93 Stockholm, ☎ 08/7892496, FAX 08/7892496). In summer, be sure to book guides well in advance.

Walking Tours: City Sightseeing (☎ 08/4117023) runs several tours, including the "Romantic Stockholm" tour of the Cathedral and City Hall; the "Royal Stockholm" tour, which features visits to the Royal Palace and the Treasury; and the "Old Town Walkabout," which strolls through Gamla Stan in just over one hour.

Late-Night Pharmacies

C. W. Scheele (✉ Klarabergsg. 64, ☎ 08/4548130) is open around-the-clock.

Travel Agencies

For a complete listing, see the Yellow Pages under *Resor-Resebyråer*.

Contact **American Express** (✉ Birger Jarlsg. 1, ☎ 08/6795200, 020/793211 toll-free). For air travel, contact **SAS** (✉ Klarabergsviadukten 72, accessible from Central Station, ☎ 020/727000). **SJ** (Statens Järnvägar, ✉ Vasag. 1, ☎ 020/757575), the state railway company, has its main ticket office at Central Station.

Visitor Information

City Hall (summer only, ✉ Hantverkarg. 1, ☎ 08/5082900). **Fjäderholmarna** (☎ 08/7180100). **Kaknästornet** (Kaknäs TV Tower, ✉ Ladugårdsgärdet, ☎ 08/7892435). **Stockholm Central Station** (✉ Vasag., ☎ 020/757575). **Stockholm Information Service: Sweden House** (Sverigehuset, ✉ Hamng. 27, Box 7542, 103 93 Stockholm, ☎ 08/7892490).

Swedish Travel and Tourism Council (✉ Box 3030, Kungsg. 36, 103 61 Stockholm, ☎ 08/7255500, FAX 08/7255531).

3 SIDE TRIPS FROM STOCKHOLM

SURROUNDING STOCKHOLM is a latticework of small, historic islands, most of them crowned with castles straight out of a storybook world. Set aside a day for a trip to any of these; half the pleasure of an island outing is a leisurely boat trip to get there. (Note that the castles can all be reached by alternative overland routes, if you prefer the bus or train.) Farther afield is the island of Gotland, whose medieval festival, Viking remains, and wilderness preserves will take you back in time. The university town of Uppsala is another popular day-trip destination; its quiet atmosphere and Gothic cathedral provide an edifying contrast to Stockholm's more energetic character.

Drottningholm

★ ㉞   *1 km (½ mi) west of Stockholm.*

★ Occupying an island in Mälaren (Sweden's third-largest lake) some 45 minutes from Stockholm's center, **Drottningholms Slott** (Queen's Island Castle) is a miniature Versailles dating from the 17th century. The royal family once used this property only as a summer residence, but, tiring of the Royal Palace back in town, they moved permanently to one wing of Drottningholm in the 1980s. Today it remains one of the most delightful of European palaces, embracing all that was best in the art of living practiced by mid-18th-century royalty. The interiors date from the 17th, 18th, and 19th centuries, and most are open to the public. ⊠ *Drottningholm,* ☎ *08/4026280.* ⊑ *SKr 50.* ☉ *May–Aug., daily 10– 4:30; Sept., daily noon–3:30; guided tours in summer only.*

The lakeside gardens of Drottningholms Slott are its most beautiful asset, containing **Drottningholms Slottsteater** (Court Theater), the only complete theater to survive from the 18th century anywhere in the world. Built by Queen Lovisa Ulrika in 1766 as a wedding present for her son Gustav III, the theater fell into disuse after his assassination at a masked ball in 1792 (dramatized in Verdi's opera *Un Ballo in Maschera*). In 1922, the theater was rediscovered; there is now a small theater museum here as well. To get performance tickets, book well in advance at the box office; the season runs from late May to early September. A word of caution: the seats are extremely hard—take a cushion. ⊠ *Drottningholm,* ☎ *08/7590406, 08/6608225 box office.* ⊑ *SKr 50.* ☉ *May–Aug., daily noon–4:30; Sept., daily 1–3:30. Guided tours in English at 12:30, 1:30, 2:30, 3:30, and 4:30. Closed for 10 days at beginning of July.*

Arriving and Departing

Boats bound for Drottningholms Slott leave from Klara Mälarstrand, a quay close to City Hall. Call **Strömma Kanalbolaget** (☎ 08/58714000) for schedules and fares.

Mariefred

㉟   *63 km (39 mi) southwest of Stockholm.*

The most delightful way to experience the true vastness of Mälaren is the trip to Mariefred—an idyllic little town of mostly timber houses— aboard the coal-fired steamer of the same name, built in 1903 and still going strong.

Mariefred's principal attraction is **Gripsholm Slott.** Built in the 1530s, the castle contains fine Renaissance interiors, a superbly atmospheric theater commissioned in 1781 by the ill-fated Gustav III, and Sweden's royal por-

Side Trips from Stockholm

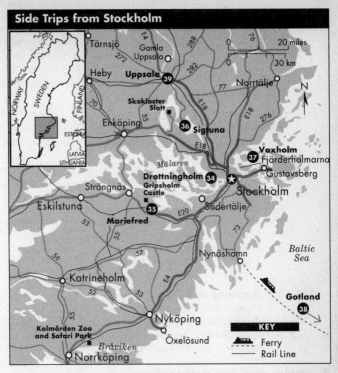

trait collection. ☎ *0159/10194.* ⊠ *SKr 50.* ⊙ *May–Aug., daily 10–4; Sept., Tues.–Sun. 10–3; Oct.–Apr., weekends noon–3; guided tours only.*

The *S.S. Mariefred* departs from Klara Mälarstrand, near Stockholm's City Hall. The journey takes 3½ hours each way, and there is a restaurant on board. ☎ *08/6698850.* ⊠ *SKr 170 round-trip.* ⊙ *Departures at 10 AM May, weekends only; mid-June–late Aug., Tues.–Sun. Return trip departs from Mariefred at 4:30.*

You can also travel by narrow-gauge steam railway from Mariefred to a junction on the main line to Stockholm, returning to the capital by ordinary train. Contact the **Mariefred Tourist Office** (☞ Visitor Information, *below*) for details.

Visitor Information

The **Mariefred Tourist Office** (☎ 0159/29790) is open only in the summer; the rest of the year, call **Mälarturism** (☎ 0152/29690) for information for all of Lake Mälaren.

Sigtuna

③⑥ *48 km (30 mi) northwest of Stockholm.*

An idyllic, picturesque town situated on a northern arm of Lake Mälaren, Sigtuna was the principal trading post of the Svea, the tribe that settled Sweden after the last Ice Age; its Viking history is still apparent in the many runic stones preserved all over town. After it was ransacked by Estonian pirates, its merchants founded Stockholm sometime in the 13th century. Little remains of Sigtuna's former glory, beyond parts of the principal church. The town hall dates from the 18th century, the main part of town from the early 1800s, and there are two houses said to date from the 15th century.

About 20 km (12 mi) northeast of Sigtuna and accessible by the same ferry boat is **Skokloster Slott,** an exquisite Baroque castle. Commissioned in 1654 by a celebrated Swedish soldier, Field Marshal Carl Gustav Wrangel, the castle is furnished with the spoils of Wrangel's successful campaigns in Europe in the 17th century. The castle can be reached by boat from Sigtuna. ⊠ *Bålsta,* ☎ *018/386077.* 🎟 *SKr 60.* ☉ *Daily noon–6.*

Dining and Lodging

$$ ✕🖬 **Sigtuna Stadshotell.** Near the lakeshore, this beautifully restored hotel was built in 1909 and soon after became a central gathering place among locals—despite the fact that at the time it was considered one of the ugliest buildings in all of Sigtuna. In its early days the hotel had Sigtuna's first cinema, and in the cellar the state liquor store operated an inn. Today's hotel rooms have hardwood floors, high ceilings, and interesting little nooks and angles reflecting the building's age. A restaurant offers a great view of the water and is elegantly decorated, with a menu focusing on traditional Swedish cuisine, especially herring. Fresh bread and ice cream are also made on the premises. ⊠ *Stora Nyg. 3, 193 22,* ☎ *08/59250100,* 𝔽𝔸𝕏 *08/59251587. 24 rooms. Restaurant, no-smoking rooms, meeting rooms. AE, DC, MC, V.*

Arriving and Departing

From June to mid-August Sigtuna can be reached by boat from the quay near City Hall (Strömma Kanalbolaget, ☎ 08/58714000); round-trip fare is SKr 140. Another option is to take a commuter train from Stockholm's Central Station to Märsta, where you change to Bus 570 or 575.

Vaxholm and the Archipelago

㊲ *32 km (20 mi) northeast of Stockholm.*

Skärgården (the archipelago) is Stockholm's greatest natural asset: more than 25,000 islands and skerries, many uninhabited, spread across an almost tideless sea of clean, clear water. The islands closer to Stockholm are larger and more lush, with pine tree–covered rock faces and forests. There are also more year-round residents on these islands. But as you move away from the mainland, the islands become smaller and more remote as you encounter rugged, rocky islets. To sail lazily among these islands aboard an old steamboat on a summer's night is a timeless delight, and all throughout the warmer months Swedes flee the chaos of the city for quiet weekends on the waters.

An excellent way to see the archipelago is to purchase an **Inter Skerries Card,** which costs 250 SKr and allows for unlimited travel throughout the islands for 16 days. Use the card for day-trips from Stockolm, or go out for longer excersions and bounce around from island to island. You can also purchase the **See Sea Card,** which costs 440 SKr and allows unlimited travel in Stockholm, Åland, and the Åbo (Finland) archipelago. Both cards are available at the tourist center at the **Stockholm Information Service: Sweden House** (Sverigehuset, ⊠ Hamng. 27, Box 7542, 103 93 Stockholm, ☎ 08/7892490).

For the tourist with limited time, one of the simplest ways to get a taste of the archipelago is the one-hour ferry trip to Vaxholm, an extremely pleasant, though sometimes crowded, mainland seaside town of small, red-painted wooden houses. Guarding what was formerly the main sea route into Stockholm, Vaxholm's fortress now houses the small **Vaxholms Fästnings Museum** (Vaxholm Fortress Museum), which documents the defense of Stockholm over the centuries. You can reach the fortress by taking a small boat from the town landing, in front of the tourist office; a discounted combination ticket includes the boat fare and entrance to the museum. ☎ 08/54172157. 🖾 SKr 30. ☉ Mid-May–Aug., daily noon–4. Group admission at other times by appointment.

An even quicker trip into the archipelago is the 20-minute ferry ride to **Fjäderholmarna** (the Feather Islands), a group of four secluded islands. After 50 years as a military zone, the islands were opened to the public in the early 1980s. Today they are crammed with arts-and-crafts studios, shops, an aquarium, a small petting farm, a boat museum, a large cafeteria, an ingenious "shipwreck" playground, and even a smoked-fish shop.

If you are interested in a longer voyage out into the islands, there are several possibilities. Contact the **Sweden House** (☞ above) and ask for the "Destination Stockholm Archipelago" catalogue, which lists more than 350 holiday homes for rent. For accommodations bookings, contact **Hotellcentralen** ☎ 08/7892456. The representatives at the Sweden House can also help you plan a customized trip.

One of the most popular excursions is to **Sandhamn,** the main town on the island of Sandön—south of Stockholm and home to about 100 permanent residents. The journey takes about three hours by steamship, but there are faster boats available. This is a sailing paradise; the Royal Swedish Yacht Club was founded here 100 years ago. With its fine-sand beaches it's an ideal spot for swimming and you can also give scuba diving a try—introductory lessons are available; ask at the Sweden House for details. Explore the village of Sandhamn and its narrow alleys and wooden houses, or stroll out to the graveyard outside the village where tombstones bear the names of sailors from around the world.

Another popular island is **Utö,** which contains Sweden's oldest iron mine (ca. AD 1100–1200). A number of the miners' homes from the 18th century have been restored. About 200 people live year-round on the island, which has a number of cafés, camping sites, and swimming spots. You can also rent bicycles from a shop near the ferry landing. The boat trip to the island takes about three hours.

A little bit closer to Stockholm is the island of **Grinda,** long a popular recreation spot among Stockholmers. Rental cabins from the '40s have been restored to their original condition; there are about 30 of these available through **Din Skärgård** (☎ 08/54249072). The **Grinda Wärdshus** (☎ 08/54249491), a still-functioning inn from the turn of the century, is one of the largest stone buildings in the archipelago. The island's vegetation is typical of the inner archipelago and a number of walking paths cut through the woods and open fields—it takes just 15 minutes to walk from one end of Grinda to the other so exploring is easy. The trip to the island takes about two hours.

If you'd prefer to stay on board a boat and simply cruise around the islands, seek out the **Blidösund.** A coal-fired steamboat built in 1911 that has remained in almost continuous service, it is now run by a small group of enthusiasts who take parties of around 250 on evening music-and-dinner cruises. The *Blidösund* leaves from a berth close to the Royal Palace in Stockholm. 🖾 Skeppsbron, ☎ 08/4117113. 🖾 SKr 120. ☉ Departures early May–late Sept., Mon.–Thurs. 7 PM (returns at 10:45).

Among the finest of the archipelago steamboats is the **Saltsjön,** which leaves from Nybrokajen, close to the Strand Hotel. Tuesday through Thursday evenings you can take a jazz-and-dinner cruise for SKr 120; Saturday and Sunday from late June to late August, pay SKr 175 to go to Utö, an attractive island known for its bike paths, bakery, and restaurant. In December, there are three daily Julbord cruises, serving a Christmas smörgåsbord. ⊠ *Saltsjön, Strömma Kanalbolaget, Skeppsbron 22,* ☎ *08/58714000.* ☉ *Departures July–early Aug. and Dec.*

Dining

$$$ ✕ **Fjäderholmarnas Krog.** A crackling fire on the hearth in the bar area welcomes the sailors who frequent this place. Lacking your own sailboat, you can time your dinner to end before the last ferry returns to the mainland. The food here is self-consciously Swedish: fresh, light, and beautifully presented; the service is professional, the ambience relaxed. It's a great choice for a quiet, special night out in Stockholm. ⊠ *Fjäderholmarna,* ☎ *08/7183355. AE, DC, MC, V. Closed Oct.–Apr.*

$$$ ✕ **Sandhamns Värdshus.** Built in 1672 as a guest house and restaurant for tired sailors, the bright yellow Sandhamn Inn is now a delightful place to stop for a meal. A terrace provides a view over the colorful sea-side town below, and in the summer there's outdoor seating on a large veranda. The menu is rooted in Swedish traditions with a focus on local seafood. Try the seafood stew spiced with saffron, served with fresh baked bread and aïoli, or the grilled calves' liver served with fried sage and apple chips. ⊠ *Sandhamn,* ☎ *08/57153051. AE, DC, MC, V.*

$ ✕ **Gröna Caféet.** A grassy garden terrace and an appealing selection of fresh open sandwiches on hearty brown bread make this small, old-fashioned Vaxholm café a hit. It's on Rådhusgatan, by the town square. ⊠ *Rådhusg. 26,* ☎ *08/5413151. No credit cards.*

Lodging

Lodging options in the archipelago vary from island to island. The larger more inhabited islands often have at least one decent hotel, if not a few, while some of the smaller more deserted islands have only an inn or two or camping facilities. Hostels are available at low cost on some islands and more and more private homes are renting out rooms and offering bed-and-breakfast accommodations. It's also possible to rent small cabins. Details are available from the **Sweden House** (☞ *above*).

$$$ 🏨 **Sandhamn Hotel and Conference.** Opened in summer 1999 this beautiful hotel is built in the "archipelago" style and overlooks the harbor in Sandhamn. A recreational area comprises an indoor and outdoor pool, plus a gym. Live music is often presented on the grounds in summer. The hotel adjoins the Seglarrestaurangen, which also looks out over the water and serves traditional Swedish cuisine with a French influence. ⊠ *130 30 Sandhamn Island,* ☎ *08/57153170,* 𝖥𝖠𝖷 *08/57450450. 81 rooms, 3 suites. Restaurant, bar, pool, exercise room, sauna, meeting rooms. AE, DC, MC, V.*

$$$ 🏨 **Waxholms Hotell.** Perched directly on Vaxholm's harbor, this excellent little hotel is a stone's throw from where the ferries land. Rooms are clean and bright and most offer a view of the water and the fortress that sits in the harbor. The restaurant and bar are the best in town, also providing great views of the harbor from the wraparound dining room. The varied menu offers everything from Thai spring rolls to Greek salad to clams poached in white wine and garlic. ⊠ *Hamng. 2, 185 21,* ☎ *08/54130150,* 𝖥𝖠𝖷 *08/54131376. 32 rooms. Restaurant, bar, no-smoking rooms, meeting rooms. AE, DC, MC, V.*

$ 🏨 **Gun i Backen.** This enchanting inn is on the main street of Vaxholm on the way down to the harbor and ferry boats, five minutes' walk from the restaurants, shops, and museums in town. The house was built at the turn of the century and was originally used as a meeting house for dances and gatherings. Today it's a lovely and quite affordable lodging alternative. Breakfast, however, is not included. ⊠ *Kungsgatan 14,185 34,* ☎ *08/54131730,* 𝖥𝖠𝖷 *08/54133315. AE, DC, MC, V.*

Vaxholm and the Archipelago A to Z

Regular ferry services to the archipelago depart from Strömkajen, the quayside in front of the Grand Hotel. Cruises on a variety of boats leave from the harbor in front of the Royal Palace or from Nybrokajen, across the road from the Royal Dramatic Theater. Ferries to the Feather Islands run almost constantly all day long in the summer (Apr. 29–Sept. 17), from Slussen, Strömkajen, and Nybroplan. Contact **Strömma Kanalbolaget** (☎ 08/58714000), **Waxholmsbolaget** (☎ 08/6795830), or **Fjäderholmarna** (☎ 08/7180100).

The **Vaxholms Tyristbyrå** (Vaxholm Tourist Office; ⊠ Söderhamnen, 185 83 Vaxholm, ☎ 08/54131480) is in a large kiosk at the bus terminal, adjacent to the marina and ferry landing. Hours are daily 10–5. **Sandhamn Turisbyrå** (Sandhamn Tourist Office; ☎ 08/57153000) is in the town center at Sandhamns Hamnservices. The **Utö Turisbyrå** (Utö Tourist Bureau; ☎ 08/50157410) is near the ferry landing. More information on Grinda is available from the **Sweden House** (☞ *above*).

Gotland

38 *85 km (53 mi) southwest of Stockholm.*

Gotland is Sweden's main holiday island, a place of wide, sandy beaches and wild cliff formations called *raukar.* Measuring 125 km (78 mi) long and 52 km (32 mi) at its widest point, Gotland is where Swedish sheep-farming has its home. In its charming glades, 35 different varieties of wild orchids thrive, attracting botanists from all over the world.

The first record of people living on Gotland dates from around 5000 BC. By the Iron Age, it had become a leading Baltic trading center. When the German marauders arrived in the 13th century, they built most of its churches and established close trading ties with the Hanseatic League in Lübeck. They were followed by the Danes, and Gotland finally became part of Sweden in 1645.

Gotland's capital, **Visby,** is a delightful, hilly town of about 20,000 people. Medieval houses, ruined fortifications, churches, and cottage-lined cobbled lanes lend Visby its fairy-tale atmosphere. Thanks to a very gentle climate, the roses that cover a multitude of the town's facades bloom even in November.

In its heyday Visby was protected by a wall, of which 3 km (2 mi) survive today, along with 44 towers and numerous gateways. It is considered the best-preserved medieval city wall in Europe after that of Carcassonne in southern France. Take a stroll to the north gate for an unsurpassed view of the wall.

Visby's cathedral, **St. Maria Kyrka,** is the only one of the town's 13 medieval churches that is still intact and in use.

Burmeisterska Huset, the home of the Burmeister—or principal German merchant, organizes exhibitions displaying the works of artists from the island and the rest of Sweden. Call the tourist office in Visby (☞ Visitor Information, *below*) to arrange for viewing. ⊠ *Strandg. 9,* ☎ *no phone.* ⊡ *Free.*

Fornsalen (the Fornsal Museum) contains examples of medieval artwork, hoards of silver from Viking times, and impressive picture stones that predate the Viking runic stones. ⊠ *Mellang. 19,* ☎ *0498/292700.*

⊞ *SKr 30.* ⊙ *Mid-May–Sept., daily 11–6; Oct.–mid-May, Tues.–Sun. noon–4.*

The stalactite caves at **Lummelunda,** about 18 km (11 mi) north of Visby on the coastal road, are unique in this part of the world and are worth visiting. A pleasant stop along the way to Lummelunda is the **Krusmyntagården** (☎ 0498/70153), a garden with more than 200 herbs, 8 km (5 mi) north of Visby.

There are approximately 100 old churches on the island that are still in use today, dating from Gotland's great commercial era. **Barlingbo,** from the 13th century, has vault paintings, stained-glass windows, and a remarkable 12th-century font. The exquisite **Dalhem** was constructed in about 1200. **Gothem,** built during the 13th century, has a notable series of paintings of that period. **Grötlingbo** is a 14th-century church with stone sculptures and stained glass (note the 12th-century reliefs on the facade). **Öja,** a medieval church decorated with paintings, houses a famous holy rood from the late 13th century. The massive ruins of a Cistercian monastery founded in 1164 are now called the **Roma Kloster Kyrka** (Roma Cloister Church). **Tingstäde** is a mix of six building periods dating from 1169 to 1300.

Curious rock formations dot the coasts of Gotland, and two **bird sanctuaries, Stora** and **Lilla Karlsö,** stand off the coast south of Visby. The bird population consists mainly of guillemots, which look like penguins. Visits to these sanctuaries are permitted only in the company of a recognized guide. ⊠ *Stora Karlsö,* ☎ *0498/241113; Lilla Karlsö,* ☎ *0498/241139.* ⊞ *SKr 180 for guided tour of one sanctuary.* ⊙ *May– Aug., daily.*

Dining

$$ ✕ Clematis. This campy restaurant is one of the most popular in Visby—guests are thrown back a few centuries to the Middle Ages for an authentic night of food, song, and dance. Here you'll dine from a flat slab of bread instead of a plate, your only utensil a knife. The staff don period attire and are known to break into a tune while delivering food to tables. Traditional Swedish fare is served, with a focus on meats and island ingredients. Drinks are served in stone goblets. ⊠ *Strandg. 20,* ☎ *0498/292727. AE, DC, MC, V.* ⊙ *No lunch.*

$$ ✕ Gutekällaren. Despite the name, which means Gute cellar in Swedish, this restaurant is aboveground in a building that dates from the 12th century. Mediterranean dishes are the draw. ⊠ *Stora Torget 3,* ☎ *0498/210043. DC, MC.*

$$ ✕ Krusmyntagården. This marvelous little garden-café is a must for herb enthusiasts visiting Gotland. Begun in the late '70s and passed down to several owners, the garden today comprises more than 200 kinds of plants and herbs all grown organically and according to tradition, and many used in the traditional Gotland cooking, including tender grilled lamb (served only Tuesday and Thursday nights). ⊠ *Brissund,* ☎ *0498/296900. AE, DC, MC, V.*

$$ ✕ Lindgården. This atmospheric restaurant specializes in both local dishes and French cuisine. ⊠ *Strandg. 26,* ☎ *0498/218700. Reservations essential. AE, DC, MC, V. Closed Sun. No lunch weekends.*

Lodging

$$ ▥ Toftagården. Nestled among the trees near the Gotland coast about 20 km (12 mi) from Visby, this hotel has placid verdant grounds ideal for strolling, lazing about, or reading in the shade. The long sandy beach in Tofta is also nearby, as is the Kronholmen 27-hole golf course. The brightly furnished rooms are all on the ground floor and most have their own terrace. There are also a number of cottages with kitchens—

a two-night minimum stay is required in these. If the seawater at the beach is too cold, take a dip in the outdoor heated pool. The restaurant is well respected and serves very good regional fare. ⊠ *Toftagården, 621 98 Visby,* ☎ *0498/297000,* ℻ *0498/265666. 50 rooms, 15 cottages. Restaurant, pool, sauna. AE, DC, MC, V.*

$ ⊡ **Hotel St. Clemens.** This hotel in Visby's Old Town comprises four buildings, the oldest from the 1600s and the most recent from the 1940s. Rooms are simple and modern with private baths; some have small kitchens. There are two gardens on the property, one shared with the St. Clemens church, one of Visby's oldest. ⊠ *Smedjegatan 3, 621 55 Visby,* ☎ *0498/219000,* ℻ *0498/279443. 32 rooms. Sauna. AE, DC, MC, V.*

$ ⊡ **Kronholmens Gård.** This charming little complex has its own small beach a short walk from Kronholmen's acclaimed 27-hole golf course. There are two cabins, one with four rooms—each with five small beds—and another with a common kitchen and living room, which all the guests share. For families hoping to save a little money and who enjoy cooking for themselves, this is a great spot on the island. Weekly discounts are available. ⊠ *Västergarn, 620 20 Klintehamn,* ☎ *0498/ 245004,* ℻ *0498/245023. 1 4-bedroom cabin. Sauna. AE, DC, MC, V.*

$ ⊡ **Villa Alskog.** A short drive from Ljugarn's sandy beaches—on the
★ southern part of the island—Villa Alskog is a delightful inn surrounded by beautiful open spaces, stones fences, and small groves of trees. The building dates to 1840 and was originally a residence for the local priest. Today its 10 guest rooms have been renovated into bright, simply furnished living spaces with hardwood floors and a cozy atmosphere. Most rooms have their own bath, a few share baths. The location is ideal for bathing, hiking, and horseback riding. ⊠ *620 16 Alskog.* ☎ *0498/ 491188,* ℻ *0498/491120. 10 rooms. Restaurant, café, sauna, meeting room. AE, DC, MC, V.*

Nightlife and the Arts

Medeltidsveckan (Medieval Week), celebrated in Visby during early August, is a city wide festival marking the invasion of the prosperous island by the Danish King Valdemar on July 22, 1361. Celebrations begin with Valdemar's grand entrance parade, and continue with jousts, an open-air market on Strandgatan, and a variety of street-theater performances re-creating the period.

Outdoor Activities and Sports

Bicycles, tents, and camping equipment can be rented from **Gotlands Cykeluthyrning** (⊠ Skeppsbron 8, ☎ 0498/214133). **Gotlandsleden** is a 200-km (120-mi) bicycle route around the island; contact the tourist office (☞ Visitor Information, *below*) for details.

Gotland A to Z

ARRIVING AND DEPARTING

Car ferries sail from Nynäshamn, a small port on the Baltic an hour by car or rail from Stockholm; commuter trains leave regularly from Stockholm's Central Station for Nynäshamn. Ferries depart at 11:30 AM year-round. From June through mid-August there's an additional ferry at 12:30 PM. A fast ferry operates from mid-April until mid-September, departing three times a day. The regular ferry takes about five hours; the fast ferry takes 2½ hours. Boats also leave from Oskarshamn, farther down the Swedish coast and closer to Gotland by about an hour. **Gotland City Travel** (⊠ Kungsg. 57, ☎ 08/4061500; Nynäshamn, ☎ 08/5206400; Visby, ☎ 0498/247065).

GUIDED TOURS

Sightseeing Tours: Guided tours of the island and Visby, the capital, are available in English by arrangement with the tourist office.

VISITOR INFORMATION

The main tourist office is **Gotlands Turistservice** (☎ 0498/203300, FAX 0498/249059), at Österport in Visby. You can also contact **Gotland City AB** in Stockholm for lodging or ferry reservations (☎ 08/4061500).

Uppsala

㊴ *67 km (41 mi) north of Stockholm.*

Sweden's principal university town vies for that position with Lund in the south of the country. August Strindberg, the nation's leading dramatist, studied here—and by all accounts hated the place. Ingmar Bergman, his modern heir, was born here. It is a historic site where pagan (and extremely gory) Viking ceremonies persisted into the 11th century. Uppsala University, one of the oldest and most highly respected institutions in Europe, was established here in 1477 by Archbishop Jakob Ulfson. As late as the 16th century, nationwide *tings* (early parliaments) were convened here. Today it is a quiet home for about 170,000 people, built along the banks of the Fyris River; the town's pleasant jumble of old buildings is dominated by its cathedral, which dates from the early 13th century.

Ideally you should start your visit with a trip to **Gamla Uppsala** (Old Uppsala), 5 km (3 mi) north of the town. Here under three huge mounds lie the graves of the first Swedish kings—Aun, Egil, and Adils—of the 6th-century Ynglinga dynasty. Close by in pagan times was a sacred grove containing a legendary oak from whose branches animal and human sacrifices were hung. By the 10th century, Christianity had eliminated such practices. A small church, which was the seat of Sweden's first archbishop, was built on the site of a former pagan temple. Today the archbishopric is in Uppsala itself, and the church, **Gamla Uppsala Kyrka,** is largely kept up for the benefit of tourists.

To sample a mead brewed from a 14th-century recipe, stop at the **Odinsborg Restaurant** (☎ 018/323525), near the burial mounds of Gamla Uppsala. A small open-air museum in Gamla Uppsala, **Disagården,** features old farm buildings, most of them dating from the 19th century. ▨ *Free.* ☉ *June–Aug., daily 9–5.*

Back in Uppsala, your first visit should be to **Uppsala Domkyrka** (Uppsala Cathedral), whose 362-ft twin towers—whose height equals the length of the nave—dominate the city. Work on the cathedral began in the early 13th century; it was consecrated in 1435 and restored between 1885 and 1893. Still the seat of Sweden's archbishop, the cathedral is also the site of the tomb of Gustav Vasa, the king who established Sweden's independence in the 16th century. Inside is a silver casket containing the bones of Saint Erik, Sweden's patron saint. ☎ *018/187177.* ▨ *Free.* ☉ *Daily 8–6.*

The **Domkyrka Museet** in the north tower has arts and crafts, church vestments, and church vessels on display. ☎ *018/187177.* ▨ *SKr 20.* ☉ *May–Aug., daily 9–5; Sept.–Apr., Sun. 12:30–3.*

Work on **Uppsala Slott** (Uppsala Castle) was started in the 1540s by Gustav Vasa, who intended it to symbolize the dominance of the monarchy over the church. It was completed under Queen Christina nearly a century later. Students gather here every April 30 to celebrate the Feast of Valborg and optimistically greet the arrival of spring. Call the tourist center (☞ Visitor Information, *below*) for information. ▨ *Castle SKr 40.* ☉ *Guided tours of castle mid-Apr.–Sept., daily at 11 and 2 (additional tours late June–mid-Aug., weekends at 10 and 3).*

In the excavated Uppsala Slott ruins, the **Vasa Vignettes,** scenes from the 16th century, are portrayed with effigies, costumes, light, and sound effects. ⚏ *SKr 40.* ⊙ *Mid-Apr.–Aug., daily 11–4; Sept., weekends 10–5.*

One of Uppsala's most famous sons, Carl von Linné, also known as Linnaeus, was a professor of botany at the university during the 1740s and created the Latin nomenclature system for plants and animals. The **Linné Museum** is dedicated to his life and works. ⊠ *Svartbäcksg. 27,* ☎ *018/136540.* ⚏ *SKr 20.* ⊙ *Late May and early Sept., weekends noon–4; June–Aug., Tues.–Sun. 1–4.*

The botanical treasures of Linné's old garden have been re-created and are now on view in **Linnéträdgården.** The garden's orangery houses a pleasant cafeteria and is used for concerts and cultural events. ⊠ *Svartbäcksg. 27,* ☎ *018/109490.* ⚏ *SKr 20.* ⊙ *May–Aug., daily 9–9; rest of yr, daily 9–7.*

Uppsala Universitetet (Uppsala University, ☎ 018/4710000), founded in 1477, is known for its **Carolina Rediviva** (university library), which contains a copy of every book published in Sweden, in addition to a large collection of foreign literature. One of its most interesting exhibits is the *Codex Argentus,* a Bible written in the 6th century.

Completed in 1625, the **Gustavianum,** which served as the university's main building for two centuries, is easy to spot by its remarkable copper cupola, now green with age. The building houses the ancient anatomical theater where lectures on human anatomy and public dissections took place. The Victoria Museum of Egyptian Antiquities and the Museums for Classical and Nordic Archeology are also in the building. ⊠ *Akademig. 3,* ☎ *018/4717571.* ⚏ *SKr 40 (SKr 20 to anatomical theater only).* ⊙ *June–Aug., daily 11–3. Anatomical Theater also Sept.–May, weekends noon–3.*

Dining and Lodging

$$$ ✕ **Domtrappkällaren.** In a 14th-century cellar near the cathedral, Domtrappkällaren serves excellent French and Swedish cuisines. Game is the specialty, and the salmon and reindeer are delectable. ⊠ *Sankt Eriksgränd 15,* ☎ *018/130955. Reservations essential. AE, DC, MC, V.*

$$$$ ▥ **Gillet.** Operated by the Sweden Hotels group, Uppsala's largest hotel was opened in 1971 and renovated most recently in 1999 with the remodeling of the third floor and one of the restaurants. Rooms are bright, with hardwood floors. The hotel is only a short walk from Uppsala's most famous buildings. The lobby is decorated with marble. ⊠ *Dragarbrunnsg. 23, 751 42,* ☎ *018/155360,* 𝖥𝖠𝖷 *018/153380. 160 rooms. 2 restaurants, pool. AE, DC, MC, V.*

$$ ▥ **Grand Hotel Hörnan.** An old-world hotel opened in 1906, the Grand Hotel Hörnan is in the city center near the train station, with a view of the castle and the cathedral. The spacious rooms reflect the hotel's old-world feel with cozy lighting and homey furnishings. ⊠ *Bandgårdsg. 1, 753 20,* ☎ *018/139380,* 𝖥𝖠𝖷 *018/120311. 37 rooms. AE, DC, MC, V.*

Uppsala A to Z

GUIDED TOURS

You can explore Uppsala easily by yourself, but English-language guided group tours can be arranged through the tourist office (☞ Visitor Information, *below*); the guide service number is ☎ 018/274818.

VISITOR INFORMATION

The main **tourist office** (⊠ Fyris Torg 8, ☎ 018/274800) is in the town center; in summer, a **small tourist information office** is also open at Uppsala Castle (☎ 018/554566).

4 GÖTEBORG

IF YOU ARE PASSING THROUGH GÖTEBORG (Gothenburg) on the way to your coastal vacation spot, do try to spend a day or two exploring this attractive port. A quayside jungle of cranes and warehouses attests to the city's industrial might, yet within a 10-minute walk of the waterfront is an elegant, modern city of broad avenues, green parks, and gardens. This is not to slight the harbor along both banks of the Göta Älv (river): It comprises 22 km (14 mi) of quays with warehouses and sheds covering more than 1.5 million square ft, making Göteborg Scandinavia's largest port. The harbor is also the home of Scandinavia's largest corporation, the automobile manufacturer Volvo (which means "I roll" in Latin), as well as of the roller-bearing manufacturer SKF and the world-renowned Hasselblad camera company.

Historically, Göteborg owes its existence to the sea. Tenth-century Vikings sailed from its shores, and a settlement was founded here in the 11th century. Not until 1621, however, did King Gustav II Adolf grant Göteborg a charter to establish a free-trade port on the model of others already thriving on the Continent. The west-coast harbor would also allow Swedish shipping to avoid Danish tolls exacted for passing through Öresund, the stretch of water separating the two countries. Foreigners were recruited to realize these visions: the Dutch were its builders—hence the canals that thread the city—and many Scotsmen worked and settled here, though they have left little trace.

Today Göteborg resists its second-city status by being a leader in attractions and civic structures. The Scandinavium was until recently Europe's largest indoor arena; the Ullevi Stadium stages some of the Nordic area's most important concerts and sporting events; Nordstan is one of Europe's biggest indoor shopping malls; and Liseberg, Scandinavia's largest amusement park in the area, attracts some 2.5 million visitors a year. Over the Göta River is Älvsborgsbron, at 3,060 ft the longest suspension bridge in Sweden, and under a southwestern suburb runs the Gnistäng Tunnel, which at 62 ft claims the distinction of being the world's widest tunnel cut through rock for motor vehicles.

EXPLORING GÖTEBORG

Göteborg is an easy city to explore: Most of the major attractions are within walking distance of one another, and the streetcar network is excellent—in summer you can take a sightseeing trip on an open-air streetcar. The heart of Göteborg is Kungsportsavenyn (more commonly referred to as Avenyn, "the Avenue"), a 60-ft-wide, tree-lined boulevard that bisects the center of the city in a south–north direction. Avenyn links Göteborg's cultural heart, Götaplatsen, at the southern end, with the main commercial area, now dominated by the modern Nordstan shopping center. Beyond lies the waterfront, busy with all the traffic of the port, as well as some of Göteborg's newer cultural developments.

Numbers in the text correspond to numbers in the margin and on the Göteborg map.

Cultural Göteborg

A pleasant stroll will take you from Götaplatsen's modern architecture along the Avenyn—the boulevard Kungsportsavenyn lined with elegant shops, cafés, and restaurants—and across both canals to finish at Kungsportsplats.

56

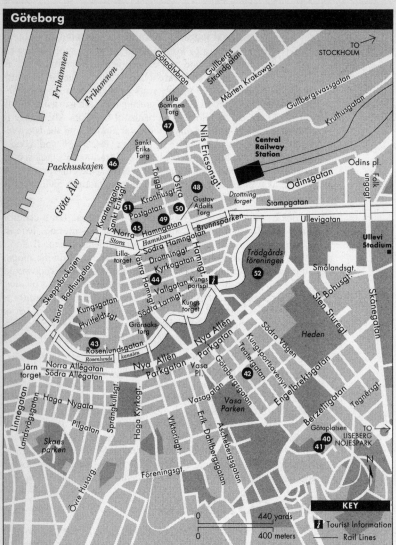

Börshuset, **50**

Domkyrkan, **44**

Feske Körkan, **43**

Götaplatsen, **40**

Konstmuseet, **41**

Kronhuset, **51**

Maritima
Centrum, **47**

Nordstan, **48**

Rådhuset, **49**

Röhsska Museet, **42**

Stadsmuseet, **45**

Utkiken, **46**

Trädgarn, **52**

At the square the street becomes Östra Hamngatan and slopes gently up from the canal and ends at Poseidon's fountain.

A Good Walk

Start your tour in **Götaplatsen** ⑩, a square dominated by a fountain statue of Poseidon; behind him is the **Konstmuseet** ㊶. Stroll downhill past the cafés and restaurants along Avenyn to the intersection with Vasagatan. A short way to the left down Vasagatan, at the junction with Teatergatan, you can visit the **Röhsska Museet** ㊷, the country's only museum of Swedish design.

Continue down Vasagatan to Folkhögskolan, Göteborg Universitet, and, if the weather's good, to the neighboring Vasa Parken, or Vasa Park. Turn right to go north on Viktoriagatan, cross the canal, and then make an immediate left to visit one of the city's most peculiar attractions, **Feske Körkan** ㊸, an archaic spelling of *Fisk Kyrkan,* the Fish Church. It resembles a place of worship but is actually an indoor fish market.

You may now feel inspired to visit the city's principal place of worship, **Domkyrkan** ㊹. Follow the canal eastward from Feske Körkan and turn north onto Västra Hamngatan; walk about four blocks to the church. Continue northward on Västra Hamngatan to the junction with Norra Hamngatan, where you'll find the **Stadsmuseet** ㊺, housed in the 18th-century Swedish East India Company.

TIMING

Depending on how much time you want to spend in each museum, this walk may take anywhere from a couple of hours to the better part of a day. Note that many sites close Monday off-season.

Sights to See

㊹ **Domkyrkan** (Göteborg Cathedral). The cathedral, in neoclassic yellow brick, dates from 1802; though disappointingly plain on the outside, the interior is impressive. ⊠ *Kungsg. 20,* ☎ *031/7316130.* ☉ *Weekdays 8–5, Sat. 8–3, Sun. 10–3.*

㊸ **Feske Körkan** (Fish Church). Built in 1872, this covered fish market gets its nickname from its Gothic-style architectural details. ⊠ *Fisktorget-Rosenlundsg.*

OFF THE
BEATEN PATH

FISKHAMNEN – An excellent view of Älvsborgsbron (Älvsborg Bridge), the longest suspension bridge in Sweden, is available from Fiskhamnen, the Fish Docks west of Stigbergstorget. Built in 1967, the bridge stretches 3,060 ft across the river and is built high so that ocean liners can pass beneath. The government has completed plans to turn this part of the harbor into a scenic walkway with parks and cafés. Also look toward the sea to the large container harbors, Skarvikshamnen, Skandiahamnen (where boats depart for England), and Torshamnen, which welcomes most of the cargo and passengers to the city today.

★ ⑩ **Götaplatsen** (Göta Place). The cultural center of Göteborg was built in 1923 in celebration of the city's 300th anniversary. In the center is the Swedish-American sculptor Carl Milles's fountain statue of Poseidon choking an enormous shark. Behind the statue stands the Konstmuseet, flanked by the **Konserthuset** (Concert Hall) and the **Stadsteatern** (Municipal Theater), three contemporary buildings in which the city celebrates its important contribution to Swedish cultural life. The **Stadsbiblioteket** (Municipal Library) maintains a collection of more than half a million books, many in English.

OFF THE
BEATEN PATH

LISEBERG NÖJESPARK – Göteborg proudly claims Scandinavia's largest amusement park. The city's pride is well earned: Liseberg is one of the best-run, most efficient parks in the world. In addition to a wide selection of carnival rides, Liseberg also has numerous restaurants and theaters, all set amid beautifully tended gardens. It's about a 30-minute walk east from the city center or a 10-minute ride by bus or tram; in summer a vintage open streetcar makes frequent runs to Liseberg from Brunnsparken in the middle of town. ⊠ *Örgrytev.,* ☎ *031/400100.* 💳 *SKr 45.* 🕐 *Late Apr.–June and late Aug., daily 3–11; July–mid-Aug., daily noon–11; Sept., Sat. 11–1, Sun. noon–8.*

㊶ Konstmuseet (Art Museum). This impressive collection of the works of leading Scandinavian painters and sculptors encapsulates some of the moody introspection of the artistic community in this part of the world. One of the recently expanded facilities is the Hasselblad Center, devoted to progress in the art of photography. Among the artists represented are Swedes such as Carl Milles, Johan Tobias Sergel, the Impressionist Anders Zorn, the Victorian idealist Carl Larsson, and Prince Eugen. The 19th- and 20th-century French art collection is the best in Sweden, and there's also a small collection of old masters. ⊠ *Götaplatsen, S412 56,* ☎ *031/612980.* 💳 *SKr 35.* 🕐 *Weekdays 11–4 (Wed. until 9), weekends 11–5. Closed Mon. Sept.–May.*

㊷ Röhsska Museet (Museum of Arts and Crafts). Fine collections of furniture, books and manuscripts, tapestries, and pottery are on view. ⊠ *Vasag. 3739, Box 53178, S400 15,* ☎ *031/613850.* 💳 *SKr 35.* 🕐 *Year-round, weekends noon–5; May–mid-June, weekdays noon–4; mid-June–Aug., Mon. and Wed.–Fri. noon–6, Tues. noon–9; Apr. and Sept., Tues. noon–9, Wed.–Fri. noon–4.*

㊺ Stadsmuseet (City Museum). Once the warehouse and auction rooms of the Swedish East India Company, a major trading firm founded in 1731, this palatial structure dates from 1750. Today it contains exhibits on the Swedish west coast, with a focus on Göteborg's nautical and trading past. One interesting exhibit deals with the East India Company and its ship the *Göteborg,* which in 1745, returning from China, sank just outside the city while members of the crew's families watched from shore. ⊠ *Norra Hamng. 12, S411 14,* ☎ *031/612770.* 💳 *SKr 40.* 🕐 *Weekdays noon–6, weekends 11–4. Closed Mon. Sept.–Apr.*

NEED A
BREAK?

In the cellar of Stadsmuseet, the **Ostindiska Huset Krog & Kafé** (☎ 031/135750) re-creates an 18th-century atmosphere. The *dagenslunch,* priced at SKr 65, is available from 11:30 to 2.

Commercial Göteborg

Explore Göteborg's portside character, both historic and modern, at the waterfront development near town center, where an array of markets and boutiques may keep you busy for hours.

A Good Walk

Begin at the harborside square known as Lilla Bommens Torg, where the **Utkiken** ㊻ offers a bird's-eye view of the city and harbor. The waterfront development here includes the training ship *Viking,* the Opera House, and the **Maritima Centrum** ㊼.

From Lilla Bommens Torg, take the pedestrian bridge across the highway to **Nordstan** ㊽. Leave the mall at the opposite end, which puts you at Brunnsparken, the hub of the city's streetcar network. Turn right and cross the street to Gustav Adolfs Torg, the city's official center, dominated by **Rådhuset** ㊾. On the north side of the square is the **Börshuset** ㊿, built in 1849.

Head north from the square along Östra Hamngatan and turn left onto Postgatan to visit **Kronhuset** (51), the city's oldest secular building, dating from 1643. The **Kronhusbodarna** are carefully restored turn-of-the-century shops and arts and crafts boutiques that surround the entrance to Kronhuset.

Return to Gustaf Adolfs Torg and follow Östra Hamngatan south across the Stora Hamnkanal to Kungsportsplats, where the Saluhall, or Market Hall, has stood since 1888. A number of pedestrian-only shopping streets branch out through this neighborhood on either side of Östra Hamngatan. Crossing the bridge over Rosenlunds Kanalen from Kungsportsplats brings you onto Kungsportsavenyn and the entrance to **Trädgårn** (52).

TIMING

The walk itself will take about two hours; allow extra time to explore the sites and to shop. Note that Kronhuset is always closed weekends, and Utkiken is closed weekdays off-season. The Kronhusbodarna is closed Sunday. Trädgårn is closed Monday off-season.

Sights to See

㊿ **Börshuset** (Stock Exchange). Completed in 1849, the former Stock Exchange building houses city administrative offices as well as facilities for large banquets. ✉ *Gustaf Adolfs Torg 5.*

Kronhusbodarna (Historical Shopping Center). Glassblowing and watchmaking are among the arts and crafts offered in the adjoining Kronhuset; there is also a nice, old-fashioned café. ✉ *Kronhusg. 1D.* ⏲ *Closed Sun.*

(51) **Kronhuset** (Crown House). The city's oldest secular building, dating from 1643, was originally the city's armory. In 1660 Sweden's Parliament met here to arrange the succession for King Karl X Gustav, who died suddenly while visiting the city. ✉ *Postg. 68,* ☎ *031/7117377.* 🎫 *SKr 30.* ⏲ *Weekends 11–4.*

㊼ **Maritima Centrum** (Marine Center). Here modern naval vessels, including a destroyer, submarines, lightship, cargo vessel, and various tugboats, provide an insight into Göteborg's historic role as a major port. ✉ *Packhuskajen, S411 04,* ☎ *031/105950.* 🎫 *SKr 50.* ⏲ *May–June, daily 10–6; July and Aug., daily 10–9; Mar.–Apr. and Sept.–Nov., daily 10–4.*

㊽ **Nordstan.** Sweden's largest indoor shopping mall—open daily—comes replete with a huge parking garage, 24-hour pharmacy, post office, several restaurants, entertainment for children, the department store Åhlens, and a tourist information kiosk. ✉ *Entrances on Köpmansg., Nils Ericsonsg., Kanaltorgsg., and Östra Hamng.*

㊾ **Rådhuset.** Though the Town Hall dates from 1672, when it was designed by Nicodemus Tessin the Elder, its controversial modern extension by Swedish architect Gunnar Asplund dates from 1937. ✉ *Gustaf Adolfs Torg 1.*

(52) **Trädgårn** (Botanic Gardens). The gardens comprises beautiful open green spaces, a magnificent Rose Garden, Butterfly House, and Palm House. ✉ *Just off Kungsportsavenyn.,* ☎ *031/611911 for Butterfly House.* ⏲ *Park 7–8; Palm House 10–4; Butterfly House Oct.–Mar., Tues.–Sun. 10–3; Apr., Tues.–Sun. 10–4; May and Sept., daily 10–4; June–Aug., daily 10–5.*

㊻ **Utkiken** (Lookout Tower). This red-and-white-striped skyscraper towers 282 ft above the waterfront, offering an unparalleled view of the city and skyscrapers. ⊠ *Lilla Bomen.* 🎫 *SKr 25.* ☉ *May–Aug., daily 11–7; Oct.–Apr., weekends 11–4.*

OFF THE
BEATEN PATH

GASVERKSKAJEN – For an interesting tour of the docks, head east from Lilla Bomen about 1½ km (1 mi) along the riverside to the Gas Works Quay, just off Gullbergsstrandgatan. Today, this is the headquarters of a local boating association, its brightly colored pleasure craft contrasting with the old-fashioned working barges either anchored or being repaired at Ringön, just across the river.

NYA ELFSBORGS FÄSTNING – Boats leave regularly from Lilla Bomen to the Elfsborg Fortress, built in 1670 on a harbor island to protect the city from attack. ⊠ *Börjessons, Lilla Bommen, kajskul 205, Box 31084, S400 32,* ☎ *031/609660.* 🎫 *SKr 65.* ☉ *6 departures per day early May–Aug., daily; Sept., weekends.*

Viking – This four-masted schooner, built in 1907, was among the last of Sweden's sailing cargo ships. The Hotel and Restaurant School of Göteborg opened a hotel and restaurant inside the ship in February 1995. Visitors are welcome. ⊠ *Lilla Bommen,* ☎ *031/635800.* 🎫 *SKr 25.*

DINING

You can eat well in Göteborg, but expect to pay dearly for the privilege. Fish dishes are the best bet here. Call ahead to be sure restaurants are open, as many close for a month in summer.

$$$$ ✕ **28+.** Step down from the street into this former wine and cheese cel-
★ lar to find an elegent restaurant owned by two of the best chefs in Göteborg. Finely set tables, flickering candles, and country-style artwork on the walls evoke the mood of a rustic French town. Italian and American flavors blend their ways into the French dishes; choose a five- or seven-course meal, or take your pick à la carte. Note that one of the best wine cellars in Sweden is at your disposal. ⊠ *Götaborgsg. 28,* ☎ *031/202161. Jacket required. AE, DC, MC, V. Closed Sun.*

$$$$ ✕ **Westra Piren Restaurant.** Across the river from central Göteborg lies Eriksberg, where former dockyards mix with modern buildings. Perched at the end of a pier that juts out into the harbor, this restaurant has a main dining hall in an elegant triangular room on the second floor and a less expensive brasserie on the first floor—contemporary French-inspired Swedish fare is presented. In summer food is served on an outdoor patio. Finding the pier by car can prove difficult; consider taking a ferry from the city side of the river. ⊠ *Dockepiren, Eriksberg,* ☎ *031/ 519555. Reservations essential for main dining hall. Jacket and tie. AE, DC, MC, V. Main dining hall closed Sun.*

$$$ ✕ **A Hereford Beefstouw.** Probably as close as you'll come to an American steak house in Sweden, this restaurant has gained popularity in a town controlled by fish restaurants. Chefs grill beef selections in the center of the three dining rooms, one of which is set aside for nonsmokers. Thick wooden tables, pine floors, and landscape paintings lend the place a rustic touch. ⊠ *Linnég. 5,* ☎ *031/7750441. AE, DC, MC, V. No lunch weekends or July.*

$$$ ✕ **Åtta Glas.** This casual, lively restaurant in what was formally a barge offers excellent views of the river and of the Kungsportsbron, a bridge spanning the canal in town center. Swedish-style fish and meat dishes are the focus, and a children's menu is available. The second-floor bar gets crowds on weekends. ⊠ *Kungsportsbron 1,* ☎ *031/136015. AE, DC, MC, V.*

Göteborg Dining & Lodging

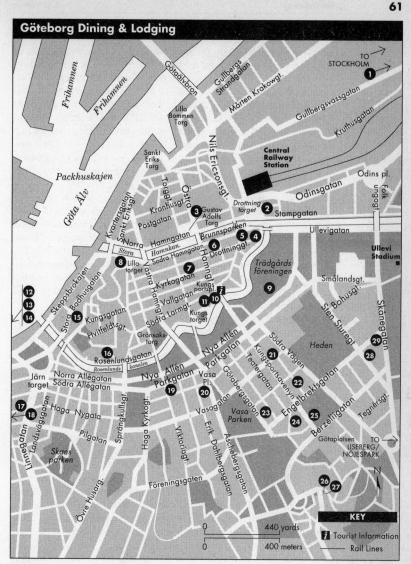

Dining

A Hereford Beefstouw, **17**
Amanda Boman, **11**
Åtta Glas, **10**
Fiskekrogan, **8**
Gabriel, **16**
Kafe Kakel, **7**
Le Village, **18**
Noon, **19**
Palace, **6**
The Place, **24**
Räkan, **22**
Sjömagasinet, **12**
Smaka, **20**
Trägårn, **9**
28+, **23**
Westra Piren Restaurant, **13**

Lodging

Eggers, **2**
Europa, **3**
Göteburgs Vandrarhem, **27**
Liseberg Heden, **29**
Opalen, **28**
Panorama, **26**
Park Avenue (Radisson SAS), **25**
Partille Vandrarhem, **1**
Quality Hotel II, **14**
Riverton, **15**
Royal, **4**
Rubinen, **21**
Sheraton Hotel and Towers, **5**

$$$ ✕ **Le Village.** Ever been to a restaurant with tables and chairs you liked so much that you wished you could take them home? What about the lamps or the paintings on the wall? Well, at Le Village that's exactly what you can do. Everything in this restaurant, and the connected antiques shop (☎ 031/143833), is for sale. The food is exceptional, especially the seasonal meat dishes. Try the smaller dining room if you want to avoid some of the prices in the main dining room. ⊠ *Tredje Läng. 13,* ☎ *031/242003. AE, DC, MC, V. Closed Sun.*

$$$ ✕ **Noon.** Swedish and Asian styles fuse into each other to produce innovative, quality seafood and noodle dishes that are served in a simple, modern setting. Try a few of the smaller, less expensive appetizers or go all out with the flounder in lemon ginger sauce with saffron dumplings. ⊠ *Viktoriag. 2,* ☎ *031/138800. AE, DC, MC, V.*

$$$ ✕ **Palace.** Located in the center of Brunnsparken, the Palace is one of Göteborg's most popular summer spots for eating, dancing, and drinking. Renovations in spring 1999 added 350 seats to the outdoor patio. Live bands and DJs play the '70s and '80s favorites of the well-dressed fortysomethings who frequent both the restaurant and nightclub. The extensive single-malt whiskey collection is known around town: Call ahead to arrange a tasting. The menu of mostly traditional Swedish cuisine is extensive. ⊠ *Brunnsparken,* ☎ *031/802100. AE, DC, MC, V. Closed Sun.*

$$$ ✕ **The Place.** Possibly Göteborg's finest dining establishment, the Place
★ offers a warm, intimate atmosphere created by terra-cotta ceilings, pastel-yellow walls, and white linen tablecloths. A wide selection of exotic dishes, from smoked breast of pigeon to beef tartare with caviar, are prepared with quality ingredients. This is also the home of one of the best wine cellars in Sweden, with Mouton Rothschild wines dating from 1904. An outdoor terrace is open during summer. ⊠ *Arkivg. 7,* ☎ *031/160333. Reservations essential. AE, DC, MC, V.*

$$$ ✕ **Räkan.** This informal and popular place makes the most of an unusual gimmick: the tables are arranged around a long tank, and if you order shrimp, the house specialty, they arrive at your table in radio-controlled boats you navigate yourself. ⊠ *Lorensbergsg. 16,* ☎ *031/ 169839. Reservations essential. AE, DC, MC, V. No lunch weekends.*

$$$ ✕ **Sjömagasinet.** Seafood is the obvious specialty at this waterfront restaurant. In a 200-year-old renovated shipping warehouse, the dining room has views of the harbor and suspension bridge. An outdoor terrace opens up in summer. ⊠ *Klippans Kulturreservat,* ☎ *031/ 7755920. Reservations essential. AE, DC, MC, V.*

$$$ ✕ **Smaka.** Deep-blue walls and ambient music create Smaka's mellow mood, a perfect backdrop for sampling what the chef calls "modernized" Swedish cuisine. Göteborg's younger crowd tends to stay here for a few extra drinks after eating. ⊠ *Vasaplatsen 3,* ☎ *031/132247. AE, DC, MC, V.*

$$$ ✕ **Trägårn.** Spicy, Asian-influenced cuisine stands out against linen tablecloths in this earth-tone restaurant; the vegetarian menu is extensive. A wall of glass in the two-story dining hall affords a view of Göteborg's famous Trägårnpark; another wall is covered in blond wood paneling, contrasting sharply with the black slate floor. ⊠ *Nya Allén,* ☎ *031/ 102080. AE, DC, MC, V. Closed Sun.*

$$ ✕ **Fiskekrogen.** Its name means Fish Inn, and it has more than 30 fish and seafood dishes from which to choose. Lunches are particularly good, ideal if you're coming from the Stadsmuseet across the canal. ⊠ *Lilla Torget 1,* ☎ *031/101005. AE, DC, MC, V. Closed Sun.*

$$ ✕ **Kafe Kakel.** Inside a late-18th-century building, this café is perfect for a relaxing, inexpensive lunch or a drink. It's centered around a bright indoor courtyard that is filled with buffet tables offering soups, salads, and sandwiches. ⊠ *Kyrkog. 33,* ☎ *031/7115920. MC, V. No dinner Sun.*

In case you want to see the world.

At American Express, we're here to make your journey a smooth one. So we have over 1,700 travel service locations in over 130 countries ready to help. What else would you expect from the world's largest travel agency?

do more   **AMERICAN EXPRESS**

Travel

Call 1 800 AXP-3429 or visit
www.americanexpress.com/travel

In case you want to be welcomed there.

We're here to see that you're always welcomed at establishments everywhere. That's why millions of people carry the American Express® Card – for peace of mind, confidence, and security, around the world or just around the corner.

do more

Cards

In case you're running low.

We're here to help with more than 190,000 Express Cash locations around the world. In order to enroll, just call American Express at 1 800 CASH-NOW before you start your vacation.

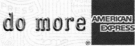

do more

AMERICAN EXPRESS

Express Cash

And in case you'd rather be safe than sorry.

We're here with American Express® Travelers Cheques. They're the safe way to carry money on your vacation, because if they're ever lost or stolen you can get a refund, practically anywhere or anytime. To find the nearest place to buy Travelers Cheques, call 1 800 495-1153. Another way we help you do more.

do more

Travelers Cheques

$ ✕ **Amanda Boman.** This little restaurant in one corner of the market hall at Kungsportsplats keeps early hours, so unless you eat an afternoon dinner, plan on lunch instead. The cuisine is primarily Swedish, including fish soup and gravlax (marinated salmon). ⊠ *Saluhallen,* ☎ *031/137676. AE, DC, MC, V. Closed Sun. No dinner.*

$ ✕ **Gabriel.** A buffet of fresh shellfish and the fish dish of the day draw crowds to this restaurant on a balcony above the fish hall. You can watch all the trading as you eat lunch. ⊠ *Feske Körkan,* ☎ *031/ 139051. AE, DC, MC, V. Closed Sun. and Mon. No dinner.*

LODGING

$$$$ 🏨 **Park Avenue (Radisson SAS).** Though this modern luxury hotel sorely lacks ambience, all the facilities are in place, including an SAS check-in counter. The well-equipped rooms are decorated in earth tones and have good views of the city. ⊠ *Kungsportsavenyn 3638, Box 53233, S400 16,* ☎ *031/176520,* ℻ *031/169568. 318 rooms. 2 restaurants, bar, 2 no-smoking floors, indoor pool, sauna, meeting room. AE, DC, MC, V.*

$$$$ 🏨 **Sheraton Hotel and Towers.** Opened in 1986 across Drottningtorget from the picturesque central train station, the Sheraton Hotel and Towers is Göteborg's most modern and spectacular international-style hotel. The attractive atrium lobby is home to two restaurants: Frascati, which serves international cuisine, and the Atrium piano bar with a lighter menu. Rooms are large and luxurious and decorated in pastels. Guests receive a 20% discount at the well-appointed health club on the premises. ⊠ *Södra Hamng. 5965, S401 24,* ☎ *031/806000,* ℻ *031/159888. 344 rooms. Restaurant, piano bar, no-smoking rooms, beauty salon, health club, shops, casino, convention center, travel services. AE, DC, MC, V.*

$$$ 🏨 **Eggers.** Dating from 1859, Best Western's Eggers has more old-world
★ character than any other hotel in the city. It is a minute's walk from the train station and was probably the last port of call in Sweden for many emigrants to the United States. Rooms vary in size, and all are beautifully appointed, often with antiques. Only breakfast is served. ⊠ *Drottningtorget, Box 323, S401 25,* ☎ *031/806070,* ℻ *031/154243. 65 rooms. No-smoking rooms, meeting rooms. AE, DC, MC, V.*

$$$ 🏨 **Europa.** Large and comfortable, this hotel is part of the Nordstan
★ mall complex, very close to the central train station. The rooms are airy and colorful with a very modern feel and renovations in 1998 gave rooms either new carpeting or wood floors. There are also special rooms with Internet hook-ups. Service throughout is deft and courtly. ⊠ *Köpmansg. 38, S401 24,* ☎ *031/801280,* ℻ *031/154755. 475 rooms, 5 suites. Restaurant, piano bar, no-smoking floors, indoor pool, sauna, convention center, parking. AE, DC, MC, V.*

$$$ 🏨 **Liseberg Heden.** Not far from the famous Liseberg Amusement Park, Liseberg Heden is a popular family hotel. Each of the modern rooms has light-color walls, a satellite television, a minibar, a large desk, and most have wood floors. Perks include a sauna and a very good restaurant. ⊠ *Sten Stureg., S411 38,* ☎ *031/7506900,* ℻ *031/7506930. 160 rooms. Restaurant, minibars, no-smoking rooms, sauna, meeting rooms. AE, DC, MC, V.*

$$$ 🏨 **Opalen.** If you are attending an event at the Scandinavium stadium, or if you have children and are heading for the Liseberg Amusement Park, this RESO hotel is ideally located. Rooms are bright and modern. ⊠ *Engelbrektsg. 73, Box 5106, S402 23,* ☎ *031/7515300,* ℻ *031/ 7515311. 241 rooms. Restaurant, bar, 2 no-smoking floors, sauna. AE, DC, MC, V.*

$$$ **☎ Panorama.** Within reach of all downtown attractions and close to Liseberg, this Best Western hotel succeeds in providing a quiet, relaxing atmosphere. ⊠ *Eklandag. 5153, Box 24037, S400 22,* ☎ *031/7677000,* FAX *031/7677070. 339 rooms. Restaurant, no-smoking floors, hot tub, sauna, nightclub, meeting rooms, free parking. AE, DC, MC, V.*

$$$ **☎ Quality Hotel 11.** Situated on the water's edge in Eriksberg, Hotel 11 combines the warehouse style of the old waterfront with a modern interior of multitiered terraces. Commonly used by large companies for business conferences, the hotel also welcomes families who want to stay across the harbor from downtown Göteborg. The rooms are clean, bright, and modern; some offer panoramic views of the harbor. Next door is Eriksbergshallen, a theater and conference hall that hosts international performances. ⊠ *Masking. 11, 417 64,* ☎ *031/7791111,* FAX *031/7791110. 133 rooms. Restaurant, bar, no-smoking rooms, sauna, meeting rooms. AE, DC, MC, V.*

$$$ **☎ Riverton.** Convenient for people arriving in the city by ferry, this hotel is close to the European terminals and overlooks the harbor. Built in 1985, it has a glossy marble floor and reflective ceiling in the lobby. Rooms are decorated with abstract-pattern textiles and whimsical prints. ⊠ *Stora Badhusg. 26, S411 21,* ☎ *031/101200,* FAX *031/130866. 190 rooms. Restaurant, bar, no-smoking rooms, hot tub, sauna, meeting rooms, free parking. AE, DC, MC, V.*

$$$ **☎ Royal.** Göteborg's oldest hotel, built in 1852, is small, family-
★   owned, and traditional. Rooms, most with new parquet floors, are individually decorated with reproductions of elegant Swedish traditional furniture. The Royal is located in the city center a few blocks from the central train station. ⊠ *Drottningg. 67, S411 07,* ☎ *031/806100,* FAX *031/156246. 82 rooms. Breakfast room, no-smoking floor. AE, DC, MC, V.*

$$$ **☎ Rubinen.** The central location on Avenyn is a plus, but this Scandic hotel can be noisy in summer. Rooms aren't especially notable but the location of this hotel makes it a great spot if you want to be in the middle of the action. ⊠ *Kungsportsavenyn 24, Box 53097, S400 14,* ☎ *031/7515400,* FAX *031/7515400. 185 rooms. Restaurant, bar, no-smoking rooms, meeting rooms. AE, DC, MC, V.*

$ **☎ Göteborgs Vandrarhem.** This hostel is 5 km (3 mi) from the train station, in a modern apartment block. Rooms are contemporary, with Swedish-designed furnishings. Breakfast (SKr 40) is not included in the rates. ⊠ *Mejerig. 2, S412 76,* ☎ *031/401050,* FAX *031/401151. 250 beds, 6- to 8-bed apartments. MC, V. Closed Sept.–May.*

$ **☎ Partille Vandrarhem.** This hostel is in a pleasant old house 15 km (9 mi) outside the city, next to a lake for swimming. You can order meals or prepare them yourself in the guest kitchen. ⊠ *Landvetterv., Box 214, S433 24, Partille,* ☎ *031/446501,* FAX *031/446163. 120 beds, 2- to 6-bed rooms. No credit cards.*

Camping

You'll find fine camping sites at Uddevalla (**Hafstens Camping,** ☎ 0522/644117), Göteborg (**Kärralund,** ☎ 031/840200, FAX 031/840500), and Askim (**Askim Strand,** ☎ 031/286261, FAX 031/681335).

NIGHTLIFE AND THE ARTS

Music, Opera, and Theater

Home of the highly acclaimed Göteborg Symphony Orchestra, **Konserthuset** (⊠ Götaplatsen, S412 56, ☎ 031/615310) features a mural by Sweden's Prince Eugen in the lobby. **Operan** (⊠ Packhuskajen, ☎ 031/131300), home of the Göteborg's Opera Company, was completed in 1994 and incorporates a 1,250-seat auditorium with a glassed-in dining area overlooking the harbor. **Stadsteatern** (✉ Götaplatsen, Box 5094, S402 22, ☎ 031/615050 tickets, 031/615100 information) has a good reputation in Sweden. The vast majority of its productions are in Swedish.

OUTDOOR ACTIVITIES AND SPORTS

Beaches

There are several excellent local beaches. The two most popular—though you'll be unlikely to find them crowded—are Näset and Askim.

Fishing

Mackerel fishing is popular here. Among the boats that take expeditions into the archipelago is the **M.S. Daisy** (☎ 031/963018 or 010/2358017), which leaves from Hjuvik on the Hisingen side of the Göta River.

SHOPPING

Department Stores

Åhléns (☎ 031/800200) is in the Nordstan mall (☞ *above*). Try the local branch of **NK** (✉ Östra Hamng. 42 ☎ 031/107000).

Specialty Stores

Antiques
Antikhallarna (Antiques Halls, ✉ Västra Hamng. 6, ☎ 031/7111324) has one of Scandinavia's largest antiques selections. You'll find Sweden's leading auction house, **Bukowskis** (✉ Kungsportsavenyn 43, ☎ 031/200360), on Avenyn.

Crafts
Excellent examples of local arts and crafts can also be bought at **Bohusslöjden** (✉ Kungsportsavenyn 25, ☎ 031/160072). If you are looking to buy Swedish arts and crafts and glassware in a suitably atmospheric setting then visit the various shops in **Kronhusbodarna** (✉ Kronhusg. 1D).

Men's Clothing
The fashions at **Gillblads** (✉ Kungsg. 44, ☎ 031/108846) suit a younger, somewhat trendier customer. **Ströms** (✉ Kungsg. 2729, ☎ 031/177100) has occupied its street corner location for two generations, offering clothing of high quality and good taste.

Women's Clothing
Gillblads (✉ Kungsg. 44, ☎ 031/108846) has the most current fashions. **Hennes & Mauritz** (✉ Kungsg. 5557, ☎ 031/7110011) sells clothes roughly comparable to the standard choices at Sears or Marks & Spencer. **Ströms** (✉ Kungsg. 2729, ☎ 031/177100) offers clothing of high quality and mildly conservative style.

GÖTEBORG A TO Z

Arriving and Departing

By Bus
All buses arrive in the central city area and the principal bus company is **Swebus** (☎ 0200/218218).

By Car

Göteborg is reached by car either via the E20 or the E4 highway from Stockholm (495 km/307 mi) and the east, or on the E6/E20 coastal highway from the south (Malmö is 290 km/180 mi away). Markings are excellent, and roads are well sanded and plowed in winter.

By Plane

Landvetter airport (☏ 031/941100) is approximately 26 km (16 mi) from the city. Among the airlines operating from the airport are **Air France** (☏ 031/941180), **British Airways** (☏ 020/781144), **Lufthansa** (☏ 031/941325 or 020/228800), and **SAS** (☏ 031/942000 or 020/727000).

Between the Airport and City Center: Landvetter is linked to Göteborg by freeway. Buses leave Landvetter every 15 to 30 minutes and arrive 30 minutes later at Nils Ericsonsplatsen by the central train station, with stops at Lisebergsstationen, Korsvägen, the Park Avenue (Radisson SAS), and Kungsportsplatsen; weekend schedules include some nonstop departures. The price of the trip is SKr 50. For more information, call **GL** (Göteborg Bus and Tram, ☏ 031/801235).

The **taxi** ride to the city center should cost no more than SKr 250. A shared **SAS limousine** for up to four people to the same address costs SKr 215 (SAS Limousine Service, ☏ 031/7942424).

By Train

There is regular service from Stockholm, taking a little over 4½ hours, as well as frequent high-speed (X2000) train service, which takes about three hours. All trains arrive at the **central train station** (☏ 031/805000) in Drottningtorget, downtown Göteborg. For schedules, call **SJ** (☏ 031/104445 or 020/757575). Streetcars and buses leave from here for the suburbs, but the hub for all streetcar traffic is a block down Norra Hamngatan, at Brunnsparken.

Getting Around

By Boat

Traveling the entire length of the Göta Canal by passenger boat to Stockholm takes between four and six days. For details, contact the **Göta Canal Steamship Company** (✉ Hotellplatsen 2, Box 272, S401 24, Göteborg, ☏ 031/806315; ✉ N. Riddarholshamnen 5, 111 28, Stockholm, ☏ 08/202728). For information about sailing your own boat on the Göta Canal, contact **AB Göta Kanalbolaget** (☏ 0141/53510).

By Bus and Tram

Stadstrafiken is the name of Göteborg's excellent transit service. Transit brochures, which are available in English, explain the various discount passes and procedures; you can pick one up at a TidPunkten office (✉ Drottningtorget, Brunnsparken, Nils Ericsonsplatsen, and Folkungabron, ☏ 031/801235).

The best bet for the tourist is the **Göteborg Card,** which covers free use of public transport, various sightseeing trips, and admission to Liseberg and local museums, among other benefits. The card costs SKr 75 for one day, SKr 125 for two days, and SKr 225 for three days; there are lower rates for children younger than 18 years from mid-June to mid-September. You can buy the Göteborg Card as well as regular tram and bus passes at Pressbyrån shops, camping sites, and the tourist information offices.

By Car
Avis has offices at the airport (☎ 031/946030) and the central railway station (☎ 031/805780). Also try **Hertz** (✉ Spannmålsg. 16, ☎ 031/946020).

By Taxi
To order a taxi, call **Taxi Göteborg** (☎ 031/650000); for advance bookings, call ☎ 031/500504.

Contacts and Resources

Doctors and Dentists
Dial ☎ 031/7031500 day or night for information on medical services. Emergencies are handled by the **Mölndalssjukhuset** (☎ 031/861000), **Östrasjukhuset** (☎ 031/374000), and **Sahlgrenska Hospital** (☎ 031/601000). There is a private medical service at **City Akuten** weekdays 8–6 (✉ Drottningg. 45, ☎ 031/101010). There is a 24-hour children's emergency service at Östrasjukhuset as well.

The national dental-service emergency number is ☎ 031/807800; the private dental-service emergency number is ☎ 031/800500. Both are available 8 AM–9 PM only; for emergencies after hours, call ☎ 031/7031500.

Embassies and Consulates
Canadian Consulate (✉ Sydatlanten, Scandiahamnen, ☎ 031/645580). **U.K. Consulate** (✉ Drottningg. 63, ☎ 031/131327).

Emergencies
Dial ☎ 112.

English-Language Bookstores
Nearly all bookshops stock English-language books. The broadest selection is at **Eckersteins Akademibokhandeln** (✉ Södra Larmg. 11, ☎ 031/171100).

Guided Tours
Boat and Bus Sightseeing Tours: A 90-minute bus tour and a two-hour combination boat-and-bus tour of the chief points of interest leave from outside the main tourist office at Kungsportsplatsen every day from mid-May through August and on Saturday in April, September, and October. Call the tourist office for schedules.

For a view of the city from the water and an expert commentary on its sights and history in English and German, take one of the **Paddan** sightseeing boats. *Paddan* means "toad" in Swedish, an apt commentary on the vessels' squat appearance. The boats pass under 20 bridges and take in both the canals and part of the Göta River. ✉ *Kungsportsbron*, ☎ *031/133000.* ⊞ *SKr 70.* ☉ *Late Apr.–late June and mid-Aug.–early Sept., daily 10–5; late June–mid-Aug., daily 10–9; early Sept.–Oct. 1, daily noon–3.*

Late-Night Pharmacy
Vasen (✉ Götg. 12, ☎ 031/804410), in the Nordstan shopping mall, is open 24 hours.

Travel Agencies
See the Yellow Pages under *Resor-Resebyråer.* **STF** (✉ Drottningtorget 6, Box 305, S401 24, ☎ 031/150930). **Ticket Travel Agency** (✉ Östra Hamng. 35, ☎ 031/176860).

Visitor Information
The main tourist office is **Göteborg's Turistbyrå** (✉ Kungsportsplatsen 2, S411 10 Göteborg, ☎ 031/612500, ℻ 031/132184). There are

also offices at the **Nordstan shopping center** (✉ Nordstadstorget, S411 05 Göteborg, ☎ 031/615371) and in front of the central train station at Drottningtorget.

A free visitor's guide called *Göteborgarn* is available in English during the summer; you can pick it up at tourist offices, shopping centers, and some restaurants, as well as on the streetcars.

The Friday edition of the principal morning newspaper, *Göteborgs Posten,* includes a weekly supplement called "Aveny"—it's in Swedish but is reasonably easy to decipher.

5 SIDE TRIPS FROM GÖTEBORG

BOHUSLÄN

The Bohuslän coastal region north of Göteborg, with its indented, rocky coastline, provides a foretaste of Norway's fjords farther north. It was from these rugged shores that the 9th- and 10th-century Vikings sailed southward on their epic voyages. Today small towns and attractive fishing villages nestle among the distinctively rounded granite rocks and the thousands of skerries and islands that form Sweden's western archipelago, best described by Prince Vilhelm, brother of the late King Gustav V, as "an archipelago formed of gneiss and granite and water that eternally stretches foamy arms after life." The ideal way to explore the area is by drifting slowly north of Göteborg, taking full advantage of the uncluttered beaches and small, picturesque fishing villages. Painters and sailors haunt the region in summer.

Kungälv

53 *15 km (9 mi) north of Göteborg.*

Strategically placed at the confluence of the two arms of the Göta River, Kungälv was an important battleground in ancient times. Though today it is something of a bedroom suburb for Göteborg, the town still has several ancient sights, including a white wooden church dating from 1679, with an unusual Baroque interior.

For a sense of Kungälv's military past, visit the ruins of **Bohus Fästning,** a fortress built by the Norwegians in 1308; it was the site of many battles between Swedish, Norwegian, and Danish armies. ⊠ *Kungälv.* ☎ *0303/99200.* ⊡ *SKr 25.* ☉ *May–June and Aug., daily 10–7; July, daily 10–8; Sept., weekends 11–5.*

Outdoor Activities and Sports

Skärhamn on the island of Tjörn offers excellent **deep-sea fishing**; mackerel is the prized catch. You can drive over the road bridge from Stenungsund.

Uddevalla

54 *64 km (40 mi) north of Kungälv, 79 km (49 mi) north of Göteborg.*

A former shipbuilding town located at the head of a picturesque fjord, Kungälv is best known in history for a battle in which heavy rains doused musketeers' tinderboxes, effectively ending hostilities.

En Route   Lysekil, off the E6 highway on a promontory at the head of the Gullmarn Fjord, has been one of Sweden's most popular summer resorts since the 19th century. It specializes in boat excursions to neighboring islands and deep-sea fishing trips. The best bathing is at Pinnevik Cove. A little to the north lies the Sotenäs Peninsula and the attractive island of **Smögen,** which can be reached by road bridge. It is renowned locally for its shrimp.

Before the E6 highway reaches Strömstad, stop at **Tanumshede** to see Europe's largest single collection of Bronze Age rock carvings at **Vitlycke.** They cover 673 square ft of rock and depict battles, hunting, and fishing. The carvings are close to the main road and are well marked.

Strömstad

55 *90 km (56 mi) northwest of Uddevalla, 169 km (105 mi) north of Göteborg.*

This popular Swedish resort claims to have more summer sunshine than any other town north of the Alps. Formerly Norwegian, it has been

Side Trips from Göteborg

NORWAY

Torsby

62

242

Örre Fryken

45

Uddeholm

Åmotfors

Sunne 68

Rottneros

241

Sunnemo

Munkfors

Mårbacka

Arvika

172

Glafs
fjorden

61

Klarälven

63

Filipstad

Foxen

Årjäng

237

64

Halden

Grums

E18

Karlstad 67

Kristinehamn

E18

64

Karlskoga

Bengtsfors

Säffle

Åmål

Ed

Strömstad 55

Koster

Vänern

Sjötorp 64

Laxå

E20

Askersund

49

Tanumshede

165

172

Mellerud

Mariestad

Viken

TO:
STOCKHOLM

Smögen

Vänersborg 63

62

Lidköping

E20

Tibro

Motala 66

Lysekil

Gullmarn

54

Skara

49

Skövde

Vadstena 65

E4

Uddevalla

61

Trollhättan

Vara

47

48

Vättern

Stenungsund

E20

Floby

Falköping

Tjörn

E6

45

Lödöse

Hakefjord

Göta Canal

Herrljunga

Gränna

Tranås

Kungälv 53

Älvsfjord

Alingsås

Borås

Ulricehamn

40

Jönköping

31

Göteborg

E20

40

Nässjö

33

Kungsbacka 56

Viskan

41

Svenljunga

26

27

Vaggeryd

30

31

Skillingaryd

Sävsjö

Tjolöholm

E6/E20

Veddige

Læsø

Ätran

Varberg 57

Värnamo

E4

Kattegat

Hyltebruk

26

Nissan

Bolmen

Moheda

Alvesta

Falkenberg 58

Oskarström

25

Växjö

Halmstad 59

Traryd

23

DENMARK

Laholms
bukten

Åsen

Grenå

Båstad 60

Laholm

E6/E20

Markaryd

E4

Älmhult

Skälder
viken

Ängelholm

N

0   20 miles

0   30 km

KEY
— Rail Lines
🚢 Ferry

the site of many battles between warring Danes, Norwegians, and Swedes. A short trip over the Norwegian border takes you to Halden, where Sweden's warrior king, Karl XII, died in 1718.

OFF THE   **KOSTER ISLANDS** – There are regular ferry boats from Strömstad to the
BEATEN PATH   Koster Islands, a favorite holiday spot, with uncluttered beaches and
                 trips to catch prawn and lobster.

Bohuslän A to Z

Arriving and Departing

Buses leave from behind the central train station in Göteborg; the main bus lines are **Bohus Trafiken** (☎ 0522/14030) and **GL** (☎ 031/801235). The trip to Strömstad takes between two and three hours.

Getting Around

BY CAR

The best way to explore Bohuslän is by car. The E6 highway runs the length of the coast from Göteborg north to Strömstad, close to the Norwegian border, and for campers there are numerous well-equipped and uncluttered camping sites along the coast's entire length.

BY TRAIN

Regular service along the coast connects all the major towns of Bohuslän. The trip from Göteborg to Strömstad takes about two hours, and there are several trains each day. For schedules, call **SJ** (⊠ Göteborg, ☎ 031/103000 or 020/757575).

Visitor Information

REGIONAL TOURIST OFFICE

Göteborg Turistbyrå (☞ Göteborg A to Z *in* Chapter 4).

LOCAL TOURIST OFFICE

Kungälv (⊠ Fästningsholmen, ☎ 0303/99200). **Kungshamn** (⊠ Hamng. 6, ☎ 0523/37150). **Öckerö** (⊠ Stranden 2, ☎ 031/965080). **Strömstad** (⊠ Tullhuset, Norra Hamnen, ☎ 0526/62330). **Uddevalla** (⊠ Kampenhof, ☎ 0522/97700).

SWEDISH RIVIERA

The coastal region south of Göteborg, Halland—locally dubbed the Swedish Riviera—is the closest that mainland Sweden comes to having a resort area. Fine beaches abound, and there are plenty of opportunities for many sporting activities. The region stretches down to Båstad in the country's southernmost province, Skåne.

Kungsbacka

⑤ *25 km (15 mi) south of Göteborg.*

This bedroom suburb of Göteborg holds a market on the first Thursday of every month. A break in a high ridge to the west, the **Fjärås Crack,** offers a fine view of the coast. On the slopes of the ridge are Iron Age and Viking graves.

En Route   At Tjolöholm, 12 km (7 mi) down the E6/E20 highway from Kungsbacka, you'll encounter **Tjolöholms Slott** (Tjolöholm Castle), a manor house built by a Scotsman at the beginning of this century in mock English Tudor style. ⊠ *S430 33 Fjärås,* ☎ *0300/544200.* ☑ *SKr 50.* ☉ *June–Aug., daily 11–4; Apr.–May and Sept., weekends 11–4; Oct., Sun. 11–4.*

Near Tjolöholm is the tiny 18th-century village of Äskhult, the site of an open-air museum, the **Gamla By.** ☎ *0300/542159.* 🎫 *SKr 20.* ☉ *May–Aug., daily 10–6; Sept., weekends 10–6.*

Varberg

57 *40 km (25 mi) south of Kungsbacka, 65 km (40 mi) south of Göteborg.*

Varberg is a busy port with connections to Grenå in Denmark. The town boasts some good beaches but is best known for a suit of medieval clothing preserved in the museum in the 13th-century **Varbergs Fästning** (Varberg Fortress). The suit belonged to a man who was murdered and thrown into a peat bog. The peat preserved his body, and his clothes are the only suit of ordinary medieval clothing in existence. The museum also contains a silver bullet said to be the one that killed Karl XII. ☎ *0340/18520.* 🎫 *SKr 30.* ☉ *Weekdays 10–4, weekends noon–4. Hourly guided tours mid-June–mid-Aug., daily 10–7; May–mid-June and mid-Aug.–Sept., Sun. 10–7.*

Falkenberg

58 *29 km (18 mi) south of Varberg, 94 km (58 mi) south of Göteborg.*

With its fine beaches and plentiful salmon in the Ätran River, Falkenberg is one of Sweden's most attractive resorts. Its Gamla Stan (Old Town) is full of narrow, cobblestone streets and quaint old wooden houses.

Shopping
Here you'll find the pottery shop **Törngren's** (✉ Krukmakareg. 4, ☎ 0346/16920, ☎ 0346/10354 pottery); probably the oldest still operating in Scandinavia, it is owned and run by the seventh generation of the founding family. It's open normal business hours, but you might have to call ahead to view pottery.

Halmstad

59 *40 km (25 mi) south of Falkenberg, 143 km (89 mi) south of Göteborg.*

With a population of 50,000, including Per Gestle of the rock group Roxette, Halmstad is the largest seaside resort on the west coast. The Norreport town gate, all that remains of the town's original fortifications, dates from 1605. The modern Town Hall has interior decorations by the so-called Halmstad Group of painters, formed here in 1929. A 14th-century church in the main square contains fragments of medieval murals and a 17th-century pulpit.

Båstad

60 *35 km (22 mi) south of Halmstad, 178 km (111 mi) south of Göteborg.*

In the southernmost province of Skåne, Båstad is regarded by locals to be Sweden's most fashionable resort, where ambassadors and local captains of industry have their summer houses. Aside from this, it is best known for its tennis. In addition to the **Båstad Open**, a Grand Prix tournament in late summer, there is the annual **Donald Duck Cup** in July for children ages 11 to 15; it was the very first trophy won by Björn Borg, who later took the Wimbledon men's singles title an unprecedented five times in a row. Spurred on by Borg and other Swedish champions, such as Stefan Edberg and Mats Wilander, thousands of youngsters take part in the Donald Duck Cup each year. For details, contact the

Svenska Tennisförbundet (Swedish Tennis Association, ⊠ Lidingöv. 75, Stockholm, ☎ 08/6679770).

Norrviken Gardens, 3 km (2 mi) northwest of Båstad, are beautifully laid out in different styles, with a restaurant, shop, and pottery studio. ☎ 0431/369040. ⊠ SKr 35. ⊙ Early June–mid-Aug., daily 10–6; late Aug.–May, daily 10:30–5.

Swedish Riviera A to Z

Arriving and Departing

BY BUS

Buses leave from behind Göteborg's central train station.

BY CAR

Simply follow the E6/E20 highway south from Göteborg. It runs parallel to the coast.

BY TRAIN

Regular train services connect Göteborg's central station with all major towns. Contact **SJ** (⊠ Göteborg, ☎ 031/103000 or 020/757575).

Visitor Information

Båstad (⊠ Stortorget 1, ☎ 0431/75045). **Falkenberg** (⊠ Stortorget, ☎ 0346/17410). **Halmstad** (⊠ Lilla Torg, ☎ 035/109345). **Kungsbacka** (⊠ Storg. 41, ☎ 0300/34595). **Laholm** (⊠ Rådhuset, ☎ 0430/15216 or 0430/15450). **Varberg** (⊠ Brunnsparken, ☎ 0340/88770).

GÖTA CANAL

Stretching 614 km (382 mi) between Stockholm and Göteborg, the Göta Canal is actually a series of interconnected canals, rivers, lakes, and even a stretch of sea. Bishop Hans Brask of Linköping in the 16th century was the first to suggest linking the bodies of water; in 1718, King Karl XII ordered the canal to be built, but work was abandoned when he was killed in battle the same year. Not until 1810 was the idea again taken up in earnest. The driving force was a Swedish nobleman, Count Baltzar Bogislaus von Platen (1766–1829), and his motive was commercial. Von Platen saw in the canal a way of beating Danish tolls on shipping that passed through the Öresund and of enhancing the importance of Göteborg by linking the port with Stockholm on the east coast. At a time when Swedish fortunes were at a low ebb, the canal was also envisaged as a means of reestablishing faith in the future and boosting national morale.

The building of the canal took 22 years and involved a total of 58,000 men. The linking of the various stretches of water required 87 km (54 mi) of man-made cuts through soil and rock, and the building of 58 locks, 47 bridges, 27 culverts, and 3 dry docks. Unfortunately, the canal never achieved the financial success hoped for by von Platen. By 1857 the Danes had removed shipping tolls, and in the following decade the linking of Göteborg with Stockholm by rail effectively ended the canal's commercial potential. The canal has nevertheless come into its own as a modern-day tourist attraction.

You may have trouble conceiving of the canal's industrial origins as your boat drifts lazily down this lovely series of waterways, across the enormous lakes, Vänern and Vättern, and through a microcosm of all that is best about Sweden: abundant fresh air; clear, clean water; pristine nature; well-tended farmland. A bicycle path runs parallel to the canal, offering another means of touring the country.

En Route The trip from Göteborg takes you first along the Göta Älv, a wide waterway that 10,000 years ago, when the ice cap melted, was a great fjord. Some 30 minutes into the voyage the boat passes below a rocky escarpment, topped by the remains of **Bohus Fästning** (Bohus Castle), distinguished by two round towers known as Father's Hat and Mother's Bonnet. It dates from the 14th century and was once the mightiest fortress in western Scandinavia, commanding the confluence of the Göta and Nordre rivers. It was strengthened and enlarged in the 16th century and successfully survived 14 sieges. From 1678 onward, the castle began to lose its strategic and military importance; it fell into decay until 1838, when King Karl XIV passed by on a river journey, admired the old fortress, and ordered its preservation.

Just north of Kungälv along the Göta Canal, you'll come to the quiet village of **Lödöse,** once a major trading settlement and a predecessor of Göteborg. From here, the countryside becomes wilder, with pines and oaks clustered thickly on either bank between cliffs of lichen-clad granite.

Trollhättan

61 *70 km (43 mi) north of Göteborg.*

In this pleasant industrial town of about 50,000 inhabitants, a spectacular waterfall was rechanneled in 1906 to become Sweden's first hydroelectric plant. In most years, on specific days the waters are allowed to follow their natural course, a fall of 106 ft in six torrents. This sight is well worth seeing. The other main point of interest is the area between what were the falls and the series of locks that allowed the canal to bypass them. Here are disused locks from 1800 and 1844 and a strange Ice Age grotto where members of the Swedish royal family have carved their names since the 18th century. Trollhättan also has a fine, wide marketplace and pleasant waterside parks.

En Route Soon after leaving Trollhättan, the Göta Canal takes you past Hunneberg and Halleberg, two flat-topped hills, both more than 500 ft high; the woods surrounding them are extraordinarily rich in elk, legend, and Viking burial mounds. The canal then proceeds through **Karls Grav,** the oldest part of the canal, begun early in the 18th century; its purpose was to bypass the Ronnum Falls on the Göta River, which have been harnessed to power a hydroelectric project.

Vänersborg

62 *15 km (9 mi) north of Trollhättan, 85 km (53 mi) north of Göteborg.*

Eventually, the canal enters **Vänern,** Sweden's largest and Europe's third-largest lake: 3,424 square km (1,322 square mi) of water, 145 km (90 mi) long and 81 km (50 mi) wide at one point.

At the southern tip of the lake is Vänersborg, a town of about 30,000 inhabitants that was founded in the mid-17th century. The church and the governor's residence date from the 18th century, but the rest of the town was destroyed by fire in 1834. Vänersborg is distinguished by its fine lakeside park, the trees of which act as a windbreak for the gusts that sweep in from Vänern.

Lidköping

63 *55 km (34 mi) east of Vänersborg, 140 km (87 mi) northeast of Göteborg.*

On an inlet at the southernmost point of Vänern's eastern arm lies the town of Lidköping, which received its charter in 1446 and is said to have the largest town square in Sweden.

OFF THE
BEATEN PATH

LÄCKÖ SLOTT – Lying 24 km (15 mi) to the north of Lidköping, on an island off the point dividing the eastern arm of Vänern from the western, is Läckö Castle, one of Sweden's finest 17th-century Renaissance palaces. Its 250 rooms were once the home of Magnus Gabriel de la Gardie, a great favorite of Queen Christina. Only the Royal Palace in Stockholm is larger. In 1681 Karl XI confiscated it to curtail the power of the nobility, and in 1830 all its furnishings were auctioned. Many of them have since been restored to the palace.

En Route   On a peninsula to the east of Lidköping, the landscape is dominated by the great hill of **Kinnekulle,** towering 900 ft above the lake. The hill is rich in colorful vegetation and wildlife and was a favorite hike for the botanist Linnaeus.

Sjötorp

64 *67 km (42 mi) northeast of Lidköping, 207 km (129 mi) northeast of Göteborg.*

At the lakeside port of Sjötorp, the Göta Canal proper begins: a cut through earth and granite with a series of locks raising the steamer to Lanthöjden, at 304 ft above sea level the highest point on the canal. The boat next enters the narrow, twisting lakes of Viken and Bottensjön and continues to Forsvik through the canal's oldest lock, built in 1813. It then sails out into **Vättern,** Sweden's second-largest lake, nearly 129 km (80 mi) from north to south and 31 km (19 mi) across at its widest point. Its waters are so clear that in some parts the bottom is visible at a depth of 50 ft. The lake is subject to sudden storms that can whip its normally placid waters into choppy waves.

Vadstena

65 *249 km (155 mi) northeast of Göteborg (via Jönköping).*

This little-known historic gem of a town grew up around the monastery founded by Saint Birgitta, or Bridget (1303–73), who wrote in her *Revelations* that she had a vision of Christ in which he revealed the rules of the religious order she went on to establish. These rules seem to have been a precursor for the Swedish ideal of sexual equality, with both nuns and monks sharing a common church. Her order spread rapidly after her death, and at one time there were 80 Bridgetine monasteries in Europe. Little remains of the Vadstena monastery, however; in 1545 King Gustav Vasa ordered its demolition, and its stones were used to build **Vadstena Slott** (Vadstena Castle), the huge fortress dominating the lake. Swedish royalty held court here until 1715. It then fell into decay and was used as a granary. Today it houses part of the National Archives and is also the site of an annual summer opera festival. ☎ *0143/15123.* ☒ *SKr 40.* ☉ *Mid-May–June and late Aug., daily noon–4; July–mid-Aug., daily 11–4. Guided tours mid-May–mid-Aug. at 12:30 and 1:30, late Aug. also at 2:30.*

Also worth a visit is **Vadstena Kyrka.** The triptych altarpiece on the south wall of the church features Saint Birgitta presenting her book of revelations to a group of kneeling cardinals. There is also a fine wood carving of the Madonna and Child from 1500.

Lodging

$$ ☒ **Kungs-Starby Wärdshus.** This functional guest house, reached via Route 50, adjoins a renovated manor house and restaurant, surrounded by a park on the outskirts of town. ☒ *S592 01 Vadstena,* ☎ *0143/75100,* ☒ *0143/75170. 61 rooms. Restaurant, no-smoking rooms, indoor pool, sauna, meeting rooms. AE, DC, MC, V.*

$$ ⊡ **Vadstena Klosterhotel.** This hotel is housed in Sweden's oldest secular building, parts of which date from the 13th century. Rooms are modern and well appointed, and there are three comfortable lounges. ⊠ *Klosterområdet, off Lasarettsg., S592 30 Vadstena,* ☎ *0143/31520,* FAX *0143/13648. 29 rooms. Restaurant, no-smoking rooms, meeting rooms. AE, DC, MC, V.*

Motala

66 *13 km (8 mi) north of Vadstena, 262 km (163 mi) northeast of Göteborg.*

Before reaching Stockholm, the canal passes through Motala, where Baltzar von Platen is buried close to the canal. He had envisaged the establishment of four new towns along the waterway, but only Motala rose according to plan. He designed the town himself, and his statue is in the main square.

En Route At Borenshult a series of locks take the boat down to **Boren,** a lake in the province of Östergötland. On the southern shore of the next lake, Roxen, lies the city of **Linköping,** capital of the province and home of Saab, the aircraft and automotive company. Once out of the lake, you follow a new stretch of canal past the sleepy town of **Söderköping.** A few miles east, at the hamlet of Mem, the canal's last lock lowers the boat into Slätbaken, a Baltic fjord presided over by the **Stegeborg Slottsruin,** the ancient ruins of the Stegeborg Fortress. The boat then steams north along the coastline until it enters **Mälaren** through the Södertälje Canal and finally anchors in the capital at Riddarholmen.

Göta Canal A to Z

Arriving and Departing

BY BOAT

For details about cruises along the Göta Canal, *see* Getting Around *in* Göteborg A to Z *in* Chapter 4.

BY CAR

From Stockholm, follow E18 west; from Göteborg, take Route 45 north to E18.

BY TRAIN

Call **SJ** (Göteberg, ☎ 031/103000) for information about service.

Visitor Information

REGIONAL TOURIST OFFICES

Skövde (Västergötlands Turistråd, ⊠ Kyrkog. 11, ☎ 0500/418050). **Uddevalla** (Bohusturist, ⊠ Skansg. 3, ☎ 0522/14055).

LOCAL TOURIST OFFICES

Karlsborg (⊠ N. Kanalg. 2, ☎ 0505/17350). **Vadstena** (⊠ Rådhustorget, ☎ 0143/15125).

VÄRMLAND

Close to the Norwegian border on the north shores of Vänern, the province of Värmland is rich in folklore. It was also the home of Alfred Nobel and the birthplace of other famous Swedes, among them the Nobel Prize–winning novelist Selma Lagerlöf, the poet Gustaf Fröding, former prime minister Tage Erlander, and present-day opera star Håkan Hagegård. Värmland's forested, lake-dotted landscape attracts artists seeking refuge and Swedes on holiday.

Karlstad

🚇 *255 km (158 mi) northeast of Göteborg.*

Värmland's principal city (population 74,000) is situated on Klarälven (Klara River) at the point where it empties into Vänern. Founded in 1684, when it was known as Tingvalla, the city was totally rebuilt after a fire in 1865. Its name was later changed to honor King Karl IX—Karlstad, meaning Karl's Town. In **Stortorget,** the main square, there is a statue of Karl IX by the local sculptor Christian Eriksson.

The **Värmlands Museum** has rooms dedicated to both Eriksson and the poet Fröding. ⊠ *Sandgrun, Box 335, S651 08, Karlstad,* ☎ *054/ 143100.* 🎫 *SKr 30.* ⏱ *Thurs.–Tues. noon–4, Wed. noon–8.*

The **Marieberg Skogspark** (Marieberg Forest Park) is worth visiting. A delight for the whole family, the park has restaurants and an outdoor theater. ⏱ *Early June–late Aug., Thurs.–Tues. 11–5, Wed. 11–8; late Aug.–early June, Tues.–Sun. noon–4, Wed. noon–8.*

Karlstad is the site of the **Emigrant Registret** (Emigrant Registry), which maintains detailed records of the Swedes' emigration to America. Visitors of Swedish extraction can trace their ancestors at the center's research facility. ⊠ *Norra Strandg. 4, Box 331, S651 08, Karlstad,* ☎ *054/107727.* 🎫 *Free.* ⏱ *May–Sept., daily 8–4; Oct.–Apr., Tues.–Sun. 8–4:30, Mon. 8–7.*

Dining and Lodging

$$$ ✕ **Inn Alstern.** Overlooking Lake Alstern, this elegant restaurant offers Swedish and Continental cuisine, with fish dishes as the specialty. Reservations are advised. ⊠ *Morgonv. 4,* ☎ *054/834900. AE, MC, V.*

$$$ 🏨 **Stadshotellet.** On the banks of Klarälven (Klara River), this hotel built in 1870 is steeped in tradition. All of the rooms are decorated differently, some in modern Swedish style, others evoking their original look. You can dine at the gourmet Matsalon or in the more casual atmosphere of the Cafeet Statt. ⊠ *Kungsg. 22, S651 08,* ☎ *054/ 293000,* 🆅 *054/188211. 143 rooms. Restaurant, pub, no-smoking rooms, sauna, nightclub, meeting rooms. AE, DC, MC, V.*

$$ 🏨 **Gösta Berling.** In the town center, this small hotel, named for the hero of the Selma Lagerlöf novel, offers nondescript common rooms but inviting, plushly carpeted guest rooms. ⊠ *Drottningg. 1, S652 24,* ☎ *054/150190,* 🆅 *054/154826. 66 rooms. No-smoking rooms, sauna, meeting rooms. AE, DC, MC, V.*

En Route   Värmland is, above all, a rural experience. Drive along the **Kläräalven,** through the beautiful Fryken Valley, to Ransater, where author Erik Gustaf Geijer was born in 1783 and where Erlander, the former prime minister, also grew up. The rural idyll ends in **Munkfors,** where some of the best-quality steel in Europe is manufactured.

OFF THE   **SUNNEMO AND UDDEHOLM** – Ten kilometers (6 mi) north of Munkfors lies
BEATEN PATH the little village of **Sunnemo,** with its beautiful wooden church. At the
northern end of Lake Råda, the town of **Uddeholm** is home of the Uddeholm Corporation, which produces iron and steel, forestry products, and chemicals.

Sunne

🚇 *63 km (39 mi) north of Karlstad, 318 km (198 mi) northeast of Göteborg.*

Straddling the long, narrow Fryken Lake, Sunne is best known as a jumping-off point for **Mårbacka,** a stone's throw southeast. Here the estate where Nobel Prize winner Selma Lagerlöf was born in 1858 has been kept much as she left it at the time of her death in 1940; it can be seen by guided tour. ✉ *Östra Ämtervik, S686 26 Sunne,* ☎ *0565/ 31027.* 🎫 *SKr 40.* ☉ *Mid-May–June and Aug.–early Sept., daily 10– 5, tours every hr; July, daily 9:30–5, tours every half hr.*

OFF THE
BEATEN PATH

ROTTNEROS HERRGARDS PARK – On the western shore of Fryken Lake, 5 km (3 mi) south of Sunne, you'll find Rottneros Manor, the inspiration for Ekeby, the fictional estate in Lagerlöf's *Gösta Berlings Saga* (*The Tale of Gösta Berling*). The house is privately owned, but visitors are invited to admire its park, with its fine collection of Scandinavian sculpture—including works by Carl Milles, Norwegian artist Gustav Vigeland, and Wäinö Aaltonen of Finland. The entrance fee covers both the sculpture park and the Nils Holgerssons Adventure Park, an elaborate playground for children. ✉ *S686 02 Rottneros,* ☎ *0565/60295.* 🎫 *SKr 50.* ☉ *Mid-May–early June and late Aug., weekdays 10–4, weekends 10–6; rest of June, weekdays 10–5, weekends 10–6; July–Aug., daily 10–6.*

Värmland A to Z

Arriving and Departing

BY CAR
From Stockholm, follow E18 west; from Göteborg, take Route 45 north to E18.

BY TRAIN
There is regular service to Karlstad from Stockholm and Göteborg on **SJ** (Göteborg, ☎ 031/103000 or 020/757575).

Visitor Information

REGIONAL TOURIST OFFICE
Värmlands Turistbyrå (✉ Tage Erlanderg. 10, Karlstad, ☎ 054/222550).

LOCAL TOURIST OFFICE
Karlstad (Karlstad Conference Center, ☎ 054/222140). **Sunne** (Turistbyrå, ✉ Mejerig. 2, ☎ 0565/16400).

6 THE SOUTH AND THE KINGDOM OF GLASS

SOUTHERN SWEDEN is a world of its own, clearly distinguished from the rest of the country by its geography, culture, and history. Skåne (pronounced *skoh*-neh), the southernmost province, is known as the granary of Sweden. It is a comparatively small province of beautifully fertile plains, sand beaches, thriving farms, medieval churches, and summer resorts. These gently rolling hills and fields are broken every few miles by lovely castles, chronologically and architecturally diverse, that have given this part of Sweden the name Château Country; often they are surrounded by beautiful grounds and moats. A significant number of the estates has remained in the hands of the original families; many are still inhabited.

The two other southern provinces, Blekinge and Halland, are also fertile and rolling and edged by seashores. Historically, these three provinces are distinct from the rest of Sweden: They were the last to be incorporated into the country, having been ruled by Denmark until 1658. They retain the influences of the continental culture in their architecture, language, and cuisine, viewing the rest of Sweden—especially Stockholm—with some disdain. Skåne even has its own independence movement, and the dialect here is so akin to Danish that many Swedes from other parts of the country have trouble understanding it.

Småland, to the north, is larger than the other provinces, with a harsh countryside of stone and woods, the so-called Kingdom of Glass. It is an area of small glassblowing firms, such as Kosta Boda and Orrefors, that are world renowned for the quality of their products. In addition to visiting these works (and perhaps finding some bargains), you will gain insight into a poorer, bleaker way of life that led thousands of peasants to emigrate from Småland to the United States in search of a better life. Those who stayed behind developed a reputation for their inventiveness in setting up small industries to circumvent the region's traditional poverty and are also notorious for being extremely careful—if not downright mean—with money.

Your itinerary should follow the coast from the western city of Helsingborg around the southern loop and up the eastern shore, taking a side trip to the Baltic island province of Öland before heading inland to finish at Växjö. The entire route can be followed by train, with the exception of Öland and most of the glassworks in Småland—the Orrefors factory is the only one on the railway line. It's easy to continue your trip in any direction from Växjö, as it lies at a main crossroads for both highways and railway lines.

Helsingborg

69 *221 km (137 mi) south of Göteborg, 186 km (116 mi) southwest of Växjö, 64 km (40 mi) north of Malmö.*

Helsingborg (still sometimes spelled the old way, Hälsingborg), with a population of 120,000, may seem to the first-time visitor little more than a small town with a modern ferry terminal (it has connections to Denmark, Norway, and Germany). Actually, it has a rich history, having first been mentioned in 10th-century sagas; later it was the site of many battles between the Danes and the Swedes. Together with its twin town, Helsingør (Elsinore in William Shakespeare's *Hamlet*), across the Öresund, it controlled shipping traffic in and out of the Baltic for centuries. Helsingborg was officially incorporated into Sweden in 1658 and totally destroyed in a battle with the Danes in 1710. It was then

The South and the Kingdom of Glass

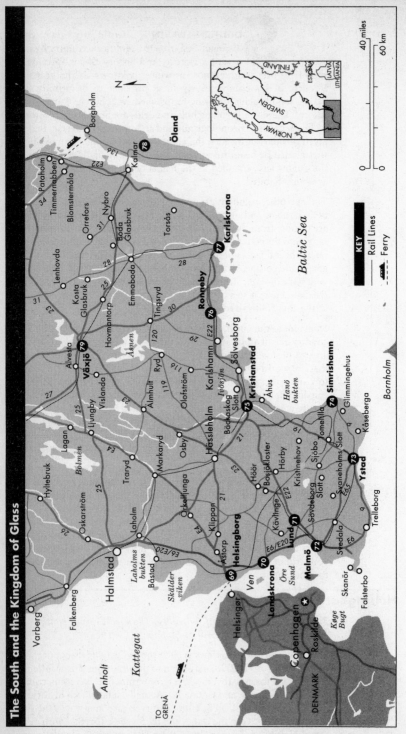

N

40 miles

60 km

FINLAND

ESTONIA

LATVIA

LITHUANIA

SWEDEN

NORWAY

KEY

Rail Lines

Ferry

Baltic Sea

Bornholm

Öland

Borgholm

Pataholm

Timmernabben

Blomstermåla

Kalmar

78

136

E22

34

Orrefors

Boda Glasbruk

Nybro

31

Blomsterfors

Karlskrona

77

Torsås

28

Lenhovda

28

Kosta Glasbruk

25

Emmaboda

Ronneby

76

23

31

Hovmantorp

Tingsryd

30

E22

Alvesta

Växjö

79

120

Ryd

Karlshamn

Sölvesborg

29

Kristianstad

75

Simrishamn

74

27

25

Vislanda

Almhult

116

Olofström

Åhus

Glimmingehus

Ljungby

23

119

Markaryd

Osby

Hässleholm

Bäckaskog Slott

Hanö bukten

Käseberga

Lagan

Bölmen

E4

Traryd

Laholm

Klippan

Örkelljunga

21

Höör

Bosjökloster

Hörby

Kristinehov

Sjöbo

Tomelilla

Svaneholms Slott

Ystad

73

Hyltebruk

Oskarström

25

24

Örkelljunga

21

23

Markaryd

Bjärröd

Höör

Kävlinge

E22

Sövdeborg Slott

E65

Trelleborg

9

Halmstad

Laholms bukten

Båstad

Skälderviken

Åstorp

Helsingborg

Klippan

F4

Lund

71

Malmö

72

Sturup

E6/E20

E6

Falkenberg

Varberg

69

70

Landskrona

Ven

Öre Sund

Skanör

Falsterbo

Trelleborg

Helsingør

Köge Bugt

Copenhagen

Roskilde

DENMARK

Kattegat

Anholt

TO GRENÅ

rebuilt, and Jean-Baptiste Bernadotte, founder of the present Swedish royal dynasty, landed here in 1810.

The Helsingborg **Stadshuset** (Town Hall) has a small museum of exhibits on the city and the region. ⊠ *Södra Storg. 31,* ☎ *042/105963.* 🖾 *SKr 30.* ⊙ *May–Aug., Tues.–Sun. noon–5; Sept.–Apr., Tues.–Sun. noon–4.*

All that remains of Helsingborg's castle is **Kärnan** (The Keep). The surviving center tower, built to provide living quarters and defend the medieval castle, is the most remarkable relic of its kind in the north. The interior is divided into several floors, where you'll see a chapel, kitchen, and other medieval fittings. It stands in a park and offers fine views over the Öresund from the top. ⊠ *Slottshagen,* ☎ *042/105991.* 🖾 *SKr 30.* ⊙ *June–Aug., daily 10–7; Apr.–May and Sept., daily 9–4; Oct.– Mar., daily 10–2.*

★ In 1864 **Sofiero Slott** (Sofiero Castle) was built in the Dutch Renaissance style by Prince Oscar and his wife, Sofia, as a summer home. Half a century later Oscar II gave the castle to his grandson, Gustav Adolf, and his wife, Margareta, as a wedding gift. Since the estate is now owned by the city of Helsingborg, you can gain access to Sofiero's park, a haven for more than 300 kinds of rhododendron, various statues donated by international artists, and a large English garden; nearby greenhouses have a number of plant exhibits. A café and fine restaurant are on the grounds. ⊠ *Sofierov. (on the road to Laröd),* ☎ *042/137400.* 🖾 *SKr 40.* ⊙ *Mid-May–mid-Sept., daily 10–6; guided tours only. Park open year-round. Restaurant and café open Mar.–Dec.* ☎ *042/140440.*

Dining

$$$ ✕ **Gastro.** A long leather booth divides this dining room into two halves: One is packed with small tables for groups of two or three, the other with tables for five or six. Larger parties sit in the more formal back of the restaurant, but everyone orders from the same menu of Swedish-based international fare. Fish and seafood are the stars. ⊠ *Södra Storgatan 11-13,* ☎ *042/243470. AE, DC, MC, V. Closed Sun.*

$$$ ✕ **Oscar's Trapp.** Oscar's Trapp is housed in two towers that were built
★ in 1904 to resemble Kärnan (The Keep), which sits at the top of the hill overlooking the town. In one tower is the dining area; in the other are a bar and lounge. The brick arches, antique furnishings, and the portraits and torches on the wall create an authentic, rustic setting: You have entered the knight's keep. Guests can choose a three- or five-course menu; no à la carte is available. ⊠ *Stortorget,* ☎ *042/146044. AE, DC, MC, V. Closed Sun. and parts of July.*

$$ ✕ **Pälsjö Krog.** Right on the water, beside the pier that leads out to the
★ Pälsjö Bath House, this restaurant offers a beautiful view of the channel between Sweden and Denmark. Over the last few years the owners have been working to restore the restaurant to the original 1930s style—note the antique sofa in the lounge and the art on the walls. Seafood is the specialty during summer months; in winter it's the game of the season. ⊠ *Drottningg. 151,* ☎ *042/149730. Reservations essential in summer. AE, DC, MC, V.*

Lodging

$$$ 🏨 **Grand Hotel.** One of Sweden's oldest hotels has been completely ren-
★ ovated, maintaining its long-standing reputation for excellence. Antiques and fresh flowers fill the hotel, and the well-equipped guest rooms have cable TV, a hair dryer, minibar, and trouser press. The hotel is conveniently close to the railway station and ferry terminals. The bar offers a good selection of wines at reasonable prices. ⊠ *Stortorget 812, S251 11,* ☎ *042/120170,* 🖾 *042/118833. 117 rooms. Restaurant, bar, no-smoking rooms, sauna, meeting rooms. AE, DC, MC, V.*

$$$ 🏨 **Hotel Mollberg.** In the center of town, only a short walk from the central station, Hotel Mollberg has spacious rooms with hardwood floors and large windows, cable TV, minibar, and trouser press. Corner rooms have balconies that overlook a cobblestone square. The restaurant offers great dining at reasonable prices, everything from nachos and club sandwiches to grilled tuna with an avocado vinaigrette. ✉ *Stortorget 18, 251 14,* 📞 *042/373700,* 📠 *042/373737. 97 rooms. Restaurant, minibar, sauna. AE, DC, MC, V.*

$$$ 🏨 **Marina Plaza.** This modern hotel, with its enormous central glass
★   atrium, is right next to the Knutpunkten ferry, rail, and bus terminal. Relaxing and stylish, the Marina Plaza has spacious, elegantly decorated rooms with air-conditioning, minibars, trouser presses, and cable TV. ✉ *Kungstorget 6, S251 11,* 📞 *042/192100,* 📠 *042/149616. 190 rooms. Restaurant, bar, no-smoking rooms, sauna, meeting rooms. AE, DC, MC, V.*

$$ 🏨 **Hotel Högvakten.** This hotel on the main square has bright, fresh rooms with a mix of modern and antique furniture. Rooms can be a bit small, but the hotel is close to the main shopping street and the central station. ✉ *Stortorget 14, 251 10,* 📞 *042/120390,* 📠 *042/120095. 40 rooms. Sauna, meeting rooms. AE, DC, MC, V.*

$ 🏨 **Villa Thalassa.** This youth hostel has fine views over Öresund. One large building contains 140 bunks in two-, four-, and six-bunk rooms. There are also 12 cottages near the water, each with two bedrooms (with double bed and bunk bed), bathroom with shower, and kitchen. The SKr 40 breakfast is not included. ✉ *Dag Hammarskjölds väg, 254 33,* 📞 *042/210384,* 📠 *042/128792. 140 beds, 4- to 6-bed rooms (in winter 2-bed rooms also available). Meeting rooms. No credit cards.*

Outdoor Activities and Sports

Consider relaxing and taking a dip in the sound at the late-19th-century **Pälsjö Baden** (Pälsjö Bath House) just north of town. The Helsingborg tradition of sweating in a sauna and then jumping into the cool waters of the channel—even in the winter months—might also appeal to you. A long pier extends out into the water, separating the men from the women. After an evening sauna, why not go for a bite at nearby Pälsjö Krog (☞ Dining, *above*)? ✉ *Drottningg. 151,* 📞 *042/149707.* 💳 *Single visit SKr 25, multiple visit cards available.* ☉ *June–Aug., Mon, Wed., Thurs. 9–7:30, Tues. 6:45–9, Fri. 6:45–7, weekends 8–5; Sept.–May, Tues. and Thurs. 2–8, Fri. 2–7, weekends 9–5.*

Ramlösa Brunnspark (📞 042/105888) is the source of the famous Ramlösa spring water, which contains healthful minerals and salts; it is served in restaurants and cafés throughout the world. Since it opened in 1707, the park has attracted summertime croquet players and those eager to taste the water (but an outdoor café also serves beer and wine). Nearby is the Ramlösa Wärdshus (📞 042/296257), which has been serving authentic Swedish cuisine since 1830. To reach the park by bus, take bus 5 going south from central station.

Landskrona

⑦⓪   *26 km (16 mi) south of Helsingborg (via E6/E20), 41 km (25 mi) north of Malmö, 204 km (127 mi) southwest of Växjö.*

The 17th-century Dutch-style fortifications of Landskrona are among the best preserved of their kind in Europe. Though it appears to be just another modern town, Landskrona actually dates from 1413, when it received its charter. In 1888, author Selma Lagerlöf worked at Landskrona's elementary school, where she began her novel *Gösta Berlings Saga.*

Landskrona's **Citadellet** (castle) was built under orders of the Danish King Christian III in 1549 and is all that remains of the original town, which was razed in 1747 by decree of the Swedish Parliament to make way for extended fortifications. The new town was then built on land reclaimed from the sea. ⊠ *Slottsg.,* ☎ *0418/473000.* ⊠ *SKr 30.* ☉ *Early June–late Aug., daily 11–4.*

OFF THE BEATEN PATH

VEN – From Landskrona Harbor there are regular 25-minute boat trips to the island of Ven (⊠ SKr 60 round-trip; boats depart every 90 minutes 6 AM–9 PM). The Danish astronomer Tycho Brahe conducted his pioneering research here from 1576 to 1597. The foundations of his Renaissance castle, **Uranienborg,** can be visited, as can Stjärneborg, his reconstructed observatory. The small **Tycho Brahe Museet** is dedicated to Brahe and his work. ⊠ *Landsv., Ven,* ☎ *0418/473121.* ⊠ *SKr 30.* ☉ *May–Sept., daily 10–4:30.*

Outdoor Activities and Sports

Three kilometers (2 mi) north of Landskrona lies the **Borstahusen recreation area** (⊠ 261 61 Landskrona, ☎ 0418/10837), with long stretches of beach, a marina, and a holiday village with 74 summer chalets. Ven is ideal for **camping;** check with the local tourist office. There are special paths across Ven for **bicycling;** rentals are available from Bäckviken, the small harbor.

Lund

71 *34 km (21 mi) southeast of Landskrona (via E6/E20 and Route 16), 25 km (15 mi) northeast of Malmö, 183 km (113 mi) southwest of Växjö.*

One of the oldest towns in Europe, Lund was founded in 990. In 1103 Lund became the religious capital of Scandinavia and at one time had 27 churches and eight monasteries—until King Christian III of Denmark ordered most of them razed to use their stones for the construction of Malmöhus Castle in Malmö. Lund lost its importance until 1666, when its university was established. It is now one of Sweden's two chief university towns and one of the nicest of Swedish towns, having managed to preserve its historic character.

Lund's **Domkyrkan,** a monumental gray stone Romanesque cathedral, is the oldest in Scandinavia, consecrated in 1145. Its crypt features 23 finely carved pillars, but its main attraction is an astrological clock, *Horologum Mirabile Lundense* (miraculous Lund clock), dating from 1380 and restored in 1923. It depicts an amazing pageant of knights jousting on horseback, trumpets blowing a medieval fanfare, and the Magi walking in procession past the Virgin and Child as the organ plays *In Dulci Jubilo.* The clock plays at noon and 3 PM on weekdays and at 1 and 3 PM on Sunday.

One block east of the cathedral is the **Botaniska Trädgården** (Botanical Gardens), which contains 7,500 specimens of plants from all over the world—very pleasant on a summer's day. ⊠ *Östra Vallg. 20,* ☎ *046/ 2227320.* ⊠ *Free.* ☉ *Gardens daily 6 AM–8 PM, greenhouses noon–3.*

Also just a short walk from the cathedral is the **Skissernas Museum** (Sketches Museum). Founded in 1934 in connection with Lund University, it houses one of the world's largest collections of sketches and first drafts by major artists. The international collection contains the early ideas of artists such as Matisse, Picasso, Léger and many others. ⊠ *Finng. 2,* ☎ *046/2227283.* ⊠ *SKr 30.* ☉ *Tues.–Sat. 12–4., Wed. 6:30–8:30, Sun. 1–5.*

Esaias Tegnér, the Swedish poet, lived from 1813 to 1826 in a little house immediately behind the cathedral. The house has since been turned into the **Tegnér Museet,** providing insight into his life and works. ✉ *Gråbrödersg.,* ☎ *046/350400.* 🎫 *SKr 10.* ☉ *First Sun. each month noon–3.*

On the southern side of the main square is **Drottens Kyrkoruin** (the Church Ruins of Drotten), an "underground" museum showing life as it was in Lund in the Middle Ages. The foundations of three Catholic churches are here: The first and oldest was built of wood in approximately AD 1000. It was torn down to make room for one of stone around 1100; this was replaced by a second stone church built around 1300. ✉ *Kattensund 6,* ☎ *046/141328.* 🎫 *SKr 10.* ☉ *Tues.–Fri. and Sun. noon–4, Sat. 10–2.*

☾ **Kulturen** (the Museum of Cultural History) is both an outdoor and an indoor museum, including 20 old cottages, farms, and manor houses from southern Sweden plus an excellent collection of ceramics, textiles, weapons, and furniture. ✉ *Karolinsplats,* ☎ *046/350400.* 🎫 *SKr 30.* ☉ *May–Sept., Fri.–Wed. 11–5, Thurs. 11–9; Oct.–Apr., Tues.–Sun. noon–4.*

On the corner of Måtenstorget is **Lund Konsthallen** (Lund Art Gallery). The all-brick building may have a rather forboding iron entrance and few windows, but skylights allow ample sunlight into the large exhibit room inside. Despite its small-town location, the gallery has hosted some major works. ✉ *Måtenstorget 3,* ☎ *046/355000.* 🎫 *Free.* ☉ *Mon.–Wed., Fri. 12–5, Thurs. 12–8, Sat. 10–5, Sun. 12–6.*

Dining and Lodging

$$$ ✕ **Barntorget 9.** The restaurant-bar inside this 18th-century building
★ seems stuck in time: Note the restored woodwork and paintings on the ceilings, the antique flowerpots and candleholders, and the classical statues in the corners of the room. The menu offers traditional Swedish dishes plus some more intriguing twists like smoked duck breast with a mushroom and endive salad and an orange vinaigrette. Fillet of sole cooked in butter and served with beets and pesto is another favorite. Barntorget 9 is a short walk from Lund's central train station. ✉ *Barntorget 9,* ☎ *046/320200. AE, DC, MC, V. Closed Sun.*

$$ ✕ **Ebbas Brödbar.** Just across the central station, Ebba's "Bread Bar" serves a number of excellent sandwiches on bagels, baguettes, or ciabattas. The spot is run by two brothers, who create a mellow mood— perfect for a quick sightseeing break and some people-watching. ✉ *Bang. 8,* ☎ *046/127127. AE, DC, MC, V.*

$$ ✕ **Godset.** Inside an old railroad warehouse right on the tracks near central station, Godset's modern tables and chairs stand on the more rustic wooden floors between brick walls. On one wall hangs a large 1950s clock taken from Mariakyrkan (Maria Church) in nearby Ystad. The menu offers excellent seafood from the grill and a number of meat dishes. The roasted venison poached in a cream sauce with raspberry vinaigrette is delicious as is the smoked turkey breast with shrimp in an avocado cream–and–coconut curry dressing. ✉ *Bang. 3,* ☎ *046/ 121610. AE, DC, MC, V. Closed Sun.*

$$ ✕ **Petri Backficka Bar & Restaurant.** With large, black-leather booths and a long bar with red barstools, Petri Backficka's modern look is tempered with a 1950s touch. The food is delicious and well-presented—start with the salmon and halibut appetizer served with a cauliflower sauce and smoked mushrooms and move on to the baked cod with cilantro and a fennel-dill butter. ✉ *St. Petri Kyrkog. 7,* ☎ *046/135515. AE, DC, MC, V.*

$$ ✕ **Restaurang Café Finn.** Connected to the Lund Konsthallen, Café Finn is an excellent option for lunch or dinner. The asparagus soup with mussels is perfect if you're not overly hungry, but to satisfy more substantial hunger pangs go for the fried breast of pheasant served with goose liver pâté and port-wine gravy. Take some time to look at the extensive collection of museum exhibit posters from the 60s, 70s, and 80s. Just outside the restaurant is the Krognoshuset; built in the 1300s, it is Lund's best-kept medieval residence. ⊠ *Mårtenstorget 3,* ☎ *046/ 157646. AE, DC, MC, V.*

$$$ ☶ **Djingis Khan.** This English colonial-style Best Western hotel caters to business travelers but is also a great place for families or couples seeking a quiet location. The hotel's unusual name comes from a comedy show that has been performed at Lund University since 1954. With squash, tennis, and badminton courts nearby, along with a large swimming pool, it's ideal if you're looking to keep in shape. ⊠ *Margarethev. 7, S222 40,* ☎ *046/140060,* ⊞ *046/143626. 55 rooms. No-smoking rooms, hot tub, sauna, exercise room, bicycles, meeting rooms. AE, DC, MC, V. Closed July.*

$$$ ☶ **Grand.** This elegant red-stone hotel is in the heart of the city, close to the railway station on a pleasant square. Renovated rooms have vintage turn-of-the-century decor and charm. The fine restaurant offers an alternative vegetarian menu. ⊠ *Bantorget 1, S221 04,* ☎ *046/ 2806100,* ⊞ *046/2806150. 80 rooms. Restaurant, no-smoking rooms, hot tub, meeting rooms. AE, DC, MC, V.*

$$$ ☶ **Hotel Lundia.** Only 330 ft from the train station, Hotel Lundia is ideal for those who want to be within walking distance of the city center. Built in 1968, the modern, four-story square building has transparent glass walls on the ground floor. Rooms are decorated with Scandinavian fabrics and lithographs. ⊠ *Knut den Stores torg 2, Box 1136, S221 04,* ☎ *046/2806500,* ⊞ *046/2806510. 97 rooms. Restaurant, no-smoking rooms, nightclub, meeting rooms. AE, DC, MC, V.*

$$ ☶ **Concordia.** This city-center Sweden Hotel property is in an elegant former mansion built in 1890. A 1990 renovation gave the rooms a modern and clean, if somewhat colorless, look. ⊠ *Stålbrog. 1, S222 24,* ☎ *046/135050,* ⊞ *046/137422. 49 rooms. No-smoking rooms, sauna, meeting rooms. AE, DC, MC, V.*

$ ☶ **STF Vandrarhem Tåget.** So named because of its proximity to the train station (*tåget* means "train"), this youth hostel faces a park in central Lund. ⊠ *Bjerredsparken, Vävareg. 22, S222 37 Lund,* ☎ *046/ 142820. 108 beds. No credit cards.*

OFF THE BEATEN PATH	**BOSJÖKLOSTER –** About 30 km (19 mi) northeast of Lund via E22 and Route 23, Bosjökloster is an 11th-century, white Gothic castle with lovely grounds on Ringsjön, the second-largest lake in southern Skåne. The castle's original owner donated the estate to the church, which turned it over to the Benedictine order of nuns. They founded a convent school for the daughters of Scandinavian nobility, no longer in existence, and built the convent church with its tower made of sandstone. The 300-acre castle grounds, with a 1,000-year-old oak tree, a network of pathways, a children's park, a rose garden, and an indoor-outdoor restaurant, are ideal for an afternoon outdoors. ⊠ Höör, ☎ 0413/25048. ▨ SKr 40. ☉ Castle grounds May–Oct., daily 8–8, restaurant and exhibition halls May–Sept., Tues.–Sun. 10–6.

Malmö

🅰 *25 km (15 mi) southwest of Lund (via E22), 198 km (123 mi) southwest of Växjö.*

Capital of the province of Skåne, with a population of about 250,000, Malmö is Sweden's third-largest city. With the completion of the nearly 8-km-long bridge from Malmö to Copenhagen in July 2000, the city and much of southern Sweden are geared up for a new era in commercial shipping and leisure travel. Eight years in the making, the multibillion-dollar project provides drivers with an alternative to ferry travel between Sweden and Denmark; it also allows trains to connect Malmö and Copenhagen. If you're in the region after the bridge is completed, you'll be able to move easily between the two countries.

The city's castle, **Malmöhus,** completed in 1542, was for many years used as a prison (James Bothwell, husband of Mary, Queen of Scots, was one of its notable inmates). Today it houses a variety of museums, including the City Museum, the Museum of Natural History, and the Art Museum with a collection of Nordic art. Across the street you will find the Science and Technology Museum, the Maritime Museum, and a toy museum. ⊠ *Malmöhusv.,* ☎ *040/341000.* ☎ *SKr 40.* ☉ *June–Aug., daily 10–4; Sept.–May, Tues.–Sun. noon–4.*

On the far side of the castle grounds from Malmöhus, **Aq-va-kul** is a water park that offers a wide variety of bathing experiences for children and their parents, from water slides to bubble baths. ⊠ *Regementsg. 24,* ☎ *040/300540.* ☎ *SKr 60 adults.* ☉ *Weekdays 9–9, weekends 9–6; Mon. and Wed. evening adult sessions 7–9:30.*

In the same park is the recently completed **Malmö Stadsbibliotek** (Malmö City Library), designed by the famous Danish architect Henning Larsen. Take a walk through the colossal main room where you'll find a four-story wall of glass that allows the library's interior to change with the seasons. ⊠ *Regementsg. 3,* ☎ *040/6608500.*

There's a clutch of tiny red-painted shacks called the **Fiskehodderna** (Fish Shacks), adjoining a dock where the fishing boats come in every morning to unload their catch. The piers, dock, and huts were restored in 1991 and are now a government-protected district. You can buy fresh fish directly from the fishermen Tuesday through Saturday mornings.

In Gamla Staden, the Old Town, look for the **St. Petri Church** on Kalendegatan; dating from the 14th century, it is an impressive example of the Baltic Gothic style, with its distinctive stepped gables. Inside there is a fine Renaissance altar.

★ You can learn about Scandinavian art and design at the **Form/Design Centre** just off Lilla Torg. The center is run by SvenskForm, a nonprofit association that promotes top-quality design in Sweden; Swedish and other Scandinavian art are on display throughout the center. You can buy objects from the shop or read the latest design magazines in the café. ⊠ *Lilla Torg,* ☎ *040/103610.* ☉ *Aug.–June, Tues., Wed., Fri. 11–5, Thurs. 11–6, Sat. 11–4, Sun. 12–4; July, Tues.–Fri. 11–5, Sat. 10–4.*

Rådhuset (Town Hall), dating from 1546, dominates Stortorget, a huge, cobbled market square in Gamla Staden, and makes an impressive spectacle when illuminated at night. In the center of the square stands an equestrian statue of Karl X, the king who united this part of the country with Sweden in 1658. Off the southeast corner of Stortorget is Lilla Torg, an attractive, small cobblestone square surrounded by restored buildings from the 17th and 18th centuries.

The **Idrottsmuseum** (Museum of Sport) occupies **Baltiska Hallen,** next to Malmö Stadium. It traces the history of sports, including soccer and wrestling, from antiquity to the present. ☎ *040/342688.* ☎ *Free.* ☉ *Weekdays 8–4.*

Also downtown, the **Rooseum,** in a turn-of-the-century brick building that was once a power plant, is one of Sweden's most outstanding art museums, with exhibitions of contemporary art and a quality selection of Nordic art. ✉ *Gasverksg. 22,* ☎ *040/121716.* ✉ *SKr 30.* ☉ *Tues.–Sun. 11–5. Guided tours weekends at 2.*

If you're still searching for more contemporary art, go to the free **Malmö Konsthall** (Malmö Art Gallery). Founded in 1975, the gallery is one of the largest in Europe, with a huge single room that has a floor space of more than 2,000 square m. It arranges about 10 exhibitions a year, ranging from the classics of modern art to present-day experiments. Other activities at the gallery include theater performances, film presentations, and poetry readings. There is a bookstore and an exceptional café. ✉ *St. Johannesg. 7,* ☎ *040/341286.* ☉ *Daily 11–5, Wed. 11–10.*

Dining and Lodging

$$$ ✕ **Årstiderna i Kockska Huset.** Marie and Wilhelm Pieplow's former
★ Årstiderna has merged with the Kockska Krogen. The new spot still has a pleasant, intimate atmosphere and serves large portions from a good, medium-price bistro menu and wine list. The business crowd comes in regularly. ✉ *Stortorget,* ☎ *040/230910. AE, DC, MC, V.*

$$$ ✕ **Hipp.** This bar-restaurant first opened its doors in 1899; today you can still marvel at the ornate columns that support a high ceiling painted with decorative flower patterns. If you sip your drink at the dark wood bar in the center of the restaurant, look up to see the heavy chandeliers hanging over you. Hipp's hearty fare is the perfect cap to a night at the city theater next door. If the huge blue mussels served with white wine and garlic don't fill you up, try a few of the many French cheeses available. Dry martinis are a specialty from the bar, and there's also a short but well-chosen wine list. ✉ *Kalendegatan 12,* ☎ *040/974030. AE, DC, MC, V. Closed Sun. and Mon.*

$$$ ✕ **Johan P.** This extremely popular restaurant specializes in seafood and shellfish prepared in Swedish and Continental styles. White walls and crisp white tablecloths give it an elegant air, which contrasts with the generally casual dress of the customers. An outdoor section opens during the summer. ✉ *Saluhallen, Lilla Torg,* ☎ *040/971818. AE, DC, MC, V. Closed Sun.*

$$$ ✕ **Nyströms Gastronomi.** Modern international cuisine with Mediter-
★ ranean hints, an elegent presentation, a courteous, casual staff, and a warm atmosphere have earned this restaurant a sparkling reputation. The wine list is extensive and a cigar lounge is available for an after-dinner smoke. ✉ *St. Pauli Kyrkogata 11,* ☎ *040/305303. AE, DC, MC, V. Closed Sun.*

$$$ ✕ **Spot.** A lively group of regulars flocks to this popular Italian restaurant for reasonable prices and unpretentious food. Lunchtime can get busy—ideal for people-watching, but at night Spot calms down and has a cozy atmosphere. ✉ *Corner of Stora Nyg./Kalendeg.,* ☎ *040/120203. AE, DC, MC, V. Closed Sun.*

$$ ✕ **Anno 1900.** The charming little restaurant sits in a former working-class area of Malmö. It is a popular local luncheon place with a cheerful outdoor garden terrace for summer eating. ✉ *Norra Bulltoftav. 7,* ☎ *040/184747. Reservations essential. AE, MC, V.*

$$ ✕ **B & B.** It stands for *Butik och Bar* (Shop and Bar) because of its location in the market hall in central Malmö. There's always good home cooking, and sometimes even entertainment at the piano. The restaurant is extremely popular with a young crowd on weekday nights; a broad group of regulars comes for good food and perhaps more than just one beer. ✉ *Saluhallen, Lilla Torg,* ☎ *040/127120. AE, DC, MC, V.*

$$ ✕ **Glorias.** This friendly little restaurant usually offers extremely good value. The special menu, *Kvartersmenyn,* is an excellent bet, with a three-course prix fixe for SKr 175. The food is traditional Swedish, with a few American-inspired appetizers thrown in for good measure. Reservations are advised. ✉ *Foreningsg. 37,* ☎ *040/70200. AE, DC, MC, V.*

\$\$ ✕ **Valvet.** This restaurant inside the St. Jörgen hotel may have deem-phasized its wine list, but you can still rely on the Swedish cuisine, pre-pared with a French accent and a focus on grilled meats and fish. ✉ *Stora Nyg. 35,* ☎ *040/77300. AE, DC, MC, V. Closed Sun. and mid-June–mid-Aug.*

\$\$\$\$ 🏨 **Mäster Johan Hotel.** The unpretentious exterior of this Best West-★   ern hotel disguises a plush and meticulously crafted interior. The 1990 top-to-bottom redesign of a 19th-century building, with the focal point an Italianate atrium breakfast room, is unusually personal in tone for a chain hotel. The rooms are impressive, with exposed Dutch brick walls, recessed lighting, oak floors, Oriental carpets, and French cherry-wood furnishings. ✉ *Mäster Johansg. 13, S211 22,* ☎ *040/6646400,* FAX *040/6646401. 68 rooms. Breakfast room, no-smoking rooms, room service, sauna, meeting rooms. AE, DC, MC, V.*

\$\$\$\$ 🏨 **Radisson SAS Hotel.** Only a five-minute walk from the train station, this modern luxury hotel has rooms decorated in several styles: Scan-dinavian, Asian, and Italian. There are even special rooms for guests with pets. Service is impeccable. The restaurant serves Scandinavian and Continental cuisine, and there's a cafeteria for quick meals. ✉ *Österg. 10, S211 25,* ☎ *040/239200,* FAX *040/6112840. 221 rooms. Restaurant, no-smoking rooms, sauna, exercise room, meeting rooms. AE, DC, MC, V.*

\$\$\$\$ 🏨 **Scandic Hotel Triangeln.** Ultramodern, in steel and glass, the Sher-aton is the city's only skyscraper—at a modest 20 floors. It provides excellent views all the way to Copenhagen on a clear day. Rooms are standard Sheraton style. The hotel is connected to the Triangeln shop-ping center. ✉ *Triangeln 2, S200 10,* ☎ *040/6934700,* FAX *040/6934711. 214 rooms. Restaurant, bar, no-smoking rooms, sauna, exercise room, meeting rooms. AE, DC, MC, V.*

\$\$ 🏨 **Baltzar.** This turn-of-the-century house in central Malmö was con-★   verted in 1920 into a small, comfortable hotel. Rooms are modern, with thick carpets. ✉ *Söderg. 20, S211 34,* ☎ *040/72005,* FAX *040/236375. 41 rooms. No-smoking rooms. AE, DC, MC, V.*

\$ 🏨 **Prize Hotel.** In a rejuvenated part of Malmö Harbor, this low-over-head, minimal-service hotel has small but comfortable rooms equipped with satellite TV, telephone, and radio. The large front entrance and lobby atrium are inventively created out of a narrow strip of empty space between two buildings. Though the hotel doesn't add a surcharge to the telephone bill, it also doesn't include the SKr 65 breakfast in the room rate: You get exactly what you pay for. ✉ *Carlsg. 10C, S211 20,* ☎ *040/ 112511,* FAX *040/112310. 109 rooms. Breakfast room. AE, DC, MC, V.*

OFF THE   **FALSTERBO AND SKANÖR –** The idyllic towns of Falsterbo and Skanör are
BEATEN PATH   two popular summer resorts located on a tiny peninsula, 32 km (20 mi) away from Mälmö at the country's southwesternmost corner. Falsterbo is popular among ornithologists who flock there every fall to watch the spectacular migration of hundreds of raptors.

TORUP SLOTT – Built around 1550 near a beautiful beech forest, Torup Castle is a great example of the classic, square fortified stronghold. From Malmö, drive 10 km (6 mi) southeast on E65, then head north for another 6 km (4 mi) to Torup. ✉ *Torup.* 🎫 *SKr 30.* ⏱ *May–June, week-ends 1–4:30. Group tours available at other times through Malmö Turist-byrå,* ☎ *040/341270.*

En Route   One of Skåne's outstanding Renaissance strongholds, **Svaneholms Slott** lies 30 km (19 mi) east of Malmö, on E65. First built in 1530 and rebuilt in 1694, the castle today features a museum occupying four floors with sections depicting the nobility and peasants. On the grounds are a noted restaurant (Gästgiveri, ☎ 0411/40540), walking paths, and a lake for fishing and rowing. ⊠ *Skurup,* ☎ *0411/40012.* ☜ *SKr 25.* ⊙ *May–Aug., Tues.–Sun. 11–5; Sept.–mid-Oct., Wed.–Sun. 11–4.*

Ystad

73 *64 km (40 mi) southeast of Malmö (via E65), 205 km (127 mi) southwest of Växjö.*

A smuggling center during the Napoleonic Wars, Ystad has preserved its medieval character with winding, narrow streets and hundreds of half-timber houses dating from four or five different centuries. The principal ancient monument is **St. Maria Kyrka,** begun shortly after 1220 as a basilica in the Romanesque style but with later additions.

OFF THE BEATEN PATH

SÖVDEBORG SLOTT – Twenty-one kilometers (13 mi) north of Ystad on Route 13 is Sövdeborg Slott (Sövdeborg Castle). Built in the 16th century and restored in the mid-1840s, the castle, now a private home, consists of three two-story brick buildings and a four-story-high crenellated corner tower. The main attraction is the Stensal (Stone Hall), with its impressive stuccowork ceiling. It's open for tours booked in advance for groups of at least 10. ⊠ *Sjöbo,* ☎ *0416/16012.* ☜ *SKr 60.*

En Route   Eighteen kilometers (11 mi) east of Ystad, on the coastal road off Route 9, is the charming fishing village of Kåseberga. On the hill behind it stand the impressive **Ales stenar** (Ale's stones), an intriguing 251-ft arrangement of 58 Viking stones in the shape of a ship. The stones are still something of a puzzle to anthropologists.

About 28 km (17 mi) east of Ystad and 10 km (6 mi) southwest of Simrishamn just off Route 9 lies **Glimmingehus** (Glimminge House), Scandinavia's best-preserved medieval stronghold. Built between 1499 and 1505 to defend the region against invaders, the late-Gothic castle was lived in only briefly. The walls are 8 ft thick at the base, tapering to 6½ ft at the top of the 85-ft-high building. On the grounds are a small museum and a theater. There are concerts and lectures throughout the summer and a medieval festival at the end of August. ⊠ *Hammenhög,* ☎ *0414/18620.* ☜ *SKr 50.* ⊙ *Apr. and Sept., daily 10–4; May–Aug., daily 9–6; Oct., weekends 11–4.*

Simrishamn

74 *41 km (25 mi) northeast of Ystad (via Route 9), 105 km (65 mi) east of Malmö, 190 km (118 mi) southwest of Växjö.*

This bustling fishing village of 25,000 swells to many times that number during the summer. Built in the mid-1100s, the town has cobblestone streets lined with tiny brick houses covered with white stucco. The medieval **St. Nicolai kyrka** (St. Nicolai's Church), which dominates the town's skyline, was once a landmark for local sailors. Inside are models of sailing ships.

The **Frasses Musik Museum** contains an eclectic collection of music oddities, such as self-playing barrel organs, antique accordions, children's gramophones, and the world's most complete collection of Edison phonographs. ⊠ *Peder Mörksv. 5,* ☎ *0414/14520.* ☜ *SKr 10.* ⊙ *Early June–late Aug., Sun. 2–6; July, Sun.–Wed. 2–6.*

En Route   If you're in the area between July 1 and August 10, you might want to stop off at **Kristinehov,** about 8 km (5 mi) west of Brösarp and 35 km (22 mi) north of Simrishamn, via Route 9. A summer wine festival is presented at the castle by a local Swedish wine producer, **Åkersson**

& Sons (☎ 0417/19700). Known as the pink castle, Kristinehov was built in 1740 by Countess Christina Piper in the late Caroline style. Although closed to the public since 1989, the castle is occasionally used for rock concerts and other summer programs.

Kristianstad

73 *73 km (45 mi) north of Simrishamn (via Routes 9/19 and E22), 95 km (59 mi) northeast of Malmö (via E22), 126 km (78 mi) southwest of Växjö.*

Kristianstad was founded by Danish King Christian IV in 1614 as a fortified town to keep the Swedes at bay. Its former ramparts and moats are today wide, tree-lined boulevards.

About 17 km (11 mi) east of Kristianstad is **Bäckaskog Slott** (Bäckaskog Castle), located on a strip of land between two lakes, just north of the E22 highway. Originally founded as a monastery by a French religious order in the 13th century, it was turned into a fortified castle by Danish noblemen during the 16th century and later appropriated by the Swedish government and used as a residence for the cavalry. The castle was a favorite of the Swedish royalty until 1900. ⊠ *Fjälkinge,* ☎ *044/53250.* 🎫 *SKr 30.* ⊘ *May 15–Aug. 15, daily 10–6; open off-season to groups by appointment only.*

Ronneby

76 *86 km (53 mi) east of Kristianstad (via E22), 181 km (112 mi) north-east of Malmö, 86 km (53 mi) southeast of Växjö.*

The spa town of Ronneby has a picturesque waterfall and rapids called **Djupadal,** where a river runs through a cleft in the rock just 5 ft wide but 50 ft deep. There are boat trips on the river each summer.

Karlskrona

77 *111 km (69 mi) east of Kristianstad (via E22), 201 km (125 mi) north-east of Malmö, 107 km (66 mi) southeast of Växjö.*

A small city built on the mainland and five nearby islands, Karlskrona achieved great notoriety in 1981, when a Soviet submarine ran aground a short distance from its naval base. The town dates from 1679, when it was laid out in Baroque style on the orders of Karl XI. In 1790 it was severely damaged by fire.

The **Admiralitetskyrkan** (Admiralty Church) is Sweden's oldest wooden church. Two other churches, **Tre Faldighets kyrkan** (Holy Trinity) and **Frederiks**, were designed by the 17th-century architect Nicodemus Tessin. The **Marinmuseum** (Naval Museum), dating from 1752, is one of the oldest museums in Sweden. ⊠ *Admiralitetsslatten,* ☎ *0455/84000.* 🎫 *SKr 40.* ⊘ *June and Aug., daily 10–4; July, daily 10–6; Sept.–May, daily noon–4.*

Kalmar

77 *91 km (57 mi) northeast of Karlskrona (via E22), 292 km (181 mi) northeast of Malmö, 109 km (68 mi) east of Växjö.*

★ The attractive coastal town of Kalmar, opposite the Baltic island of Öland, is dominated by the imposing **Kalmar Slott,** Sweden's best-preserved Renaissance castle, part of which dates from the 12th century. The living rooms, chapel, and dungeon can be visited. ⊠ *Slottsv.,* ☎ *0480/451490.* 🎫 *SKr 60.* ⊘ *Mid-June–mid-Aug., Mon.–Sat. 10–6, Sun. noon–*

6; *Apr.–mid-June and mid-Aug.–Oct., weekdays 10–4, weekends noon–4; Nov.–Mar., Sun. 1–3.*

The **Kalmar Läns Museum** (Kalmar District Museum), with good archaeological and ethnographic collections, contains the remains of the royal ship *Kronan*, which sank in 1676. Consisting primarily of cannons, wood sculptures, and old coins, they were raised from the seabed in 1980. Another exhibit focuses on Jenny Nystrom, a painter famous for popularizing the *tomte*, a rustic Christmas elf. ⊠ *Skeppsbrog. 51,* ☎ *0480/15350.* ☞ *SKr 40.* ◷ *Mid-June–mid-Aug., Mon.–Sat. 10–6, Sun. noon–6; mid-Aug.–mid-June, weekdays 10–4, Wed. until 8, weekends noon–4.*

Lodging

$$$ ⊞ **Slottshotellet.** Occupying a gracious old house on a quiet street, Slottshotellet faces a waterfront park, a few minutes' walk from both the train station and Kalmar Castle. Guest rooms are charmingly individual, with carved-wood bedsteads, old-fashioned chandeliers, pretty wallpaper, wooden floors, and antique furniture. The bathrooms are spotlessly clean. Only breakfast is served year-round, but in summer, full restaurant service is offered on the terrace. ⊠ *Slottsv. 7, S392 33,* ☎ *0480/88260,* ℻ *0480/88266. 36 rooms. No-smoking rooms, sauna, meeting room. AE, DC, V.*

$$ ⊞ **Stadshotellet.** In city center, Best Western's Stadshotellet is a fairly large hotel with traditional English decor. The main building dates from 1907. Guest rooms are freshly decorated and have hair dryers and radios, among other amenities. There's also a fine restaurant. ⊠ *Stortorget 14, S392 32,* ☎ *0480/15180,* ℻ *0480/15847. 140 rooms. Restaurant, bar, no-smoking rooms, hot tub, sauna, meeting rooms. AE, DC, MC, V.*

Öland

㉘ *8 km (5 mi) east of Kalmar (via the Ölandsbron bridge).*

First settled some 4,000 years ago, the island is fringed with fine sandy beaches and is dotted with old windmills and archaeological remains. **Gråborg,** a 6th-century fortress with massive stone walls measuring 625 ft in diameter, is a must-see. The 5th-century fortified village of **Eketorp** and the medieval **Borgholms Slottsuin** (Borgholm Castle) are also impressive. In spring and fall, Öland is a way station for hundreds of species of migrating birds.

The royal family has a summer home at **Solliden** on the outskirts of Borgholm, the principal town, 25 km (16 mi) north of the bridge via Route 136.

Lodging

$$ ⊞ **Halltorps Gästgiveri.** This manor house dating from the 17th century has modernized duplex rooms decorated in Swedish landscape tones and an excellent restaurant. Drive north from Ölandsbron, and it's on the left-hand side of the road. ⊠ *S387 92 Borgholm,* ☎ *0485/85000,* ℻ *0485/85001. 35 rooms. Restaurant, no-smoking rooms, 2 saunas, meeting rooms. AE, DC, MC, V.*

OFF THE
BEATEN PATH

PATAHOLM AND TIMMERNABBEN – On the mainland coast opposite Öland, along E22, numerous picturesque seaside towns dot the coastline, such as **Pataholm,** with its cobblestone main square, and **Timmernabbe,** which is famous for its caramel factory and from which the Borgholm-bound car ferries depart. Miles of clean, attractive, and easily accessible—if windy—beaches line this coastal strip.

The Kingdom of Glass

Stretching roughly 109 km (68 mi) between Kalmar and Växjö.

Scattered among the rocky woodlands of Småland province are isolated villages whose names are synonymous with quality in crystal glassware. In the streets of Kosta, Orrefors, Boda, and Strömbergshyttan, red-painted cottages surround the actual factories, which resemble large barns. The region is the home of 16 major glassworks, and you may see glass being blown and crystal being etched by skilled craftspeople. *Hyttsil* evenings are also arranged, a revival of an old tradition in which Baltic herring (*sil*) is cooked in the glass furnaces of the *hytt* (literally "hut," but meaning the works). Most glassworks also have shops selling quality firsts and not-so-perfect seconds at a discount. The larger establishments have restrooms and cafeterias.

Fifteen kilometers (9 mi) north of Route 25 on Route 28 is **Kosta Glasburk,** the oldest works, dating from 1742 and named for its founders, Anders Koskull and Georg Bogislaus Stael von Holstein, two former generals. Faced with a dearth of local talent, they initially imported glassblowers from Bohemia. The Kosta works pioneered the production of crystal (to qualify for that label, glass must contain at least 24% lead oxide). You can see glassblowing off-season (August 18–June 6) between 9 and 3. To get to Kosta from Kalmar, drive 49 km (30 mi) west on Route 25, then 14 km (9 mi) north on Route 28. ☎ *0478/ 34500.* ☉ *Late June–early Aug., weekdays 9–6, Sat. 9–4, Sun. 11–4; early Aug.–late June, weekdays 9–6, Sat. 10–4, Sun. noon–4.*

On Route 31, about 18 km (11 mi) east of Kosta, is **Orrefors,** one of the best known of the glass companies. Orrefors arrived on the scene late—in 1898—but set particularly high artistic standards. The skilled workers in Orrefors dance a slow, delicate minuet as they carry the pieces of red-hot glass back and forth, passing them on rods from hand to hand, blowing and shaping them. The basic procedures and tools are ancient, and the finished product is the result of unusual teamwork, from designer to craftsman to finisher. One of Orrefors's special attractions is a magnificent display of pieces made during the 19th century; you can appease bored children in the cafeteria and playground. In summer, June 7– August 17, you can watch glassblowing at 9–10 and 11–3. ☎ *0481/34000.* ☉ *Aug.–May, weekdays 10–6; June and July, weekdays 9–4, Sat. 10–4, Sun. 11–4.*

Boda Glasbruk, part of the Kosta Boda Company, is just off Route 25, 42 km (26 mi) west of Kalmar. ☎ *0481/42400.* ☉ *Daily 9–4.*

Växjö

79 *109 km (68 mi) northwest of Kalmar (via Rte. 25), 198 km (123 mi) northeast of Malmö, 228 km (142 mi) southeast of Göteborg, 446 km (277 mi) southwest of Stockholm.*

Some 10,000 Americans visit this town every year, for it was from this area that their Swedish ancestors set sail in the 19th century. On the second Sunday in August, Växjö celebrates "Minnesota Day": Swedes and Swedish-Americans come together to commemorate their common heritage with American-style square dancing and other festivities. The **Utvandrarnas Hus** (Emigrants' House) in the town center tells the story of the migration, when more than a million Swedes—one quarter of the population—departed for the promised land. The museum exhibits provide a vivid sense of the rigorous journey, and an archive room and research center allow American visitors to trace their ancestry.

Ever see someone

waiting for the sun to come out

while trying to photograph

a charging rhino?

New!
Kodak Max film:

*Now with better color,
Kodak's maximum
versatility film gives
you great pictures in
sunlight, low light,
action or still.*

It's all you need
to know about film.

www.kodak.com

Distinctive guides packed with up-to-date expert advice and smart choices for every type of traveler.

Fodor's. For the world of ways you travel.

✉ *Museum Park, Box 201, S351 04,* ☎ *0470/20120.* ☜ *Free.* ☉ *June–Aug., weekdays 9–5, Sat. 11–3, Sun. 1–5; Sept.–May, weekdays 9–4.*

The **Småland Museum** has the largest glass collection in northern Europe; it was reopened in summer 1996 after extensive renovation. ✉ *Södra Jarn-vägsg. 2, S351 04,* ☎ *0470/45145.* ☜ *SKr 40.* ☉ *Call for hrs.*

OFF THE BEATEN PATH   **KRONOBERGS SLOTT** – About 5 km (3 mi) north of Växjö, this 14th-century castle ruin lies on the edge of the Helgasjön (Holy Lake). The Småland freedom fighter Nils Dacke used the castle as a base for his attacks against the Danish occupiers during the mid-1500s; now it's an idyllic destination. In summer, you can eat waffles from the café under the shade of birch trees or take a lunch or sightseeing cruise around the lake on the toylike *Thor,* Sweden's oldest steamboat. ☎ *0470/45145 Castle, 0470/63000 Boat tours.* ☉ *Tours offered late June–late Aug.* ⊛ *Lunch cruise SKr 280, 2½-hr canal trip to Årby SKr 120, 1-hr around-the-lake trip SKr 85.*

Lodging

$$$ ⊞ **Hotel Statt.** Now a Best Western hotel, this conveniently located, traditional property is popular with tour groups. The building dates from 1853, but the rooms themselves are modern. The hotel has a cozy pub, nightclub, bistro, and café. ✉ *Kungsg. 6, S-351 04,* ☎ *0470/13400,* FAX *0470/44837. 130 rooms. Restaurant, café, pub, no-smoking rooms, sauna, exercise room, meeting rooms. AE, DC, MC, V.*

$ ⊞ **Esplanad.** In town center, the Esplanad is a small, family hotel offering basic amenities. ⊞ *Norra Esplanaden 21A, S-351 04,* ☎ *0470/22580,* FAX *0470/26226. 27 rooms. No-smoking rooms. MC, V.*

The South and the Kingdom of Glass A to Z

Arriving and Departing

BY BOAT

Until the Malmö–Copenhagen bridge opens in July 2000, the most common way to get to southern Sweden is still by boat. Several regular services run from Copenhagen to Malmö, including hovercraft that make the trip in less than an hour, and a bus-ferry service from Copenhagen Station, which also goes to Lund. There are also regular ferry connections to Denmark, Germany, and Poland from such ports as Malmö, Helsingborg, Landskrona, Trelleborg, and Ystad. **Stena Line** (✉ Kungsg. 12–14, Stockholm, ☎ 08/141475; ✉ Danmarksterminalen, Göteborg, ☎ 031/858000) is one of the major Swedish carriers.

Day-trippers can pick up tickets at Malmö Harbor and catch one of the hourly Copenhagen-bound hovercraft operated by the following ferry lines: **Flygbåtarna** (☎ 040/103930), **Pilen** (☎ 040/234411), and **Shopping Linje** (☎ 040/110099). SFL Skandlines (☎ 040/362000) runs the only car-ferry service between Dragör, Denmark, and Limhamn, Sweden, a town that adjoins Malmö's southern edge.

BY CAR

Malmö is 620 km (386 mi) from Stockholm. Take the E4 freeway to Helsingborg, then the E6/E20 to Malmö and Lund. From Göteborg, take the E6/E20. If you are approaching from Copenhagen, take the bridge across the sound to Malmö.

BY PLANE

Malmö's airport, **Sturup** (☎ 040/6131100), is approximately 30 km (19 mi) from Malmö and 25 km (15 mi) from Lund. **KLM** (☎ 040/500530), **Malmö Aviation** (☎ 040/502900), and **SAS** (☎ 040/357200 or 020/727000) serve the airport. SAS offers discounts on trips to Malmö year-round; ask for the "Jackpot" discount package.

Between the Airport and City Center: Buses for Malmö and Lund meet all flights at Sturup Airport. The price of the trip is SKr 60 to either destination. For more information on bus schedules, routes, and fares, call ☎ 020/616161 or the airport at ☎ 040/6131100. A **taxi** from the airport to Malmö or Lund costs about SKr 250. For SAS **limousine service,** call ☎ 040/500600.

BY TRAIN

There is regular service from Stockholm to Helsingborg, Lund, and Malmö. Each trip takes about 6½ hours, and about 4½ hours by high-speed (X2000) train. All three railway stations are central.

Getting Around

A special 48-hour *Öresund Runt* (Around Öresund) pass is available from the Malmö Tourist Office: at SKr 149, the ticket covers a train from Malmö to Helsingborg, a ferry to Helsingør, a train to Copenhagen, and a ferry back to Malmö.

The *Malmökortet* (Malmö Card), entitles the holder to, among other benefits, free travel on the city buses, free parking, discounts on tours, and free admission or discounts to most museums, concert halls, nightclubs, theaters, the Royal Cab company, and many shops and restaurants. A one-day card costs SKr 150, two-day card SKr 275, and a three-day card SKr 400. Cards are available from the tourist office in Malmö.

BY CAR

Roads are well marked and well maintained. Traveling around the coast counterclockwise from Helsingborg, you take the E6/E20 to Landskrona, Malmö, and Lund, then the E6/E22 to Trelleborg; Route 9 follows the south coast from there to Simrishamn and north until just before Kristianstad, where you pick up E22 all the way through Karlshamn, Ronneby, Karlskrona, and up the east coast to Kalmar. From Kalmar, Route 25 goes almost directly west through Växjö to Halmstad, on the west coast between Helsingborg and Göteborg.

BY TRAIN

The major towns of the south are all connected by rail.

Contacts and Resources

CAR RENTALS

If you are coming from Denmark and want to rent a car as soon as you arrive, several rental companies have locations at Malmö Harbor, including **Avis** (☎ 040/77830), **Hertz** (☎ 040/74955), and **Europcar/InterRent** (☎ 040/71640). Hertz car rentals are available for less than SKr 600 a day on weekends (less during the summer) if you book an SAS (☎ 040/357200 or 020/727000) flight.

EMERGENCIES

As elsewhere in Sweden, call ☎ 112 for emergencies.

VISITOR INFORMATION

Regional Tourist Offices: Jönköping (⊠ Västra Storg. 18A, ☎ 036/199570). **Skånes Turistråd** (Skåne Tourist Council, ⊠ Skifferv. 38, Lund, ☎ 046/124350).

Local Tourist Offices: Helsingborg (⊠ Knutpunkten terminal, ☎ 042/120310). **Kalmar** (⊠ Larmg. 6, ☎ 0480/15350). **Karlskrona** (⊠ Borgnästoreg. 68, ☎ 0455/303490). **Kristianstad** (⊠ Stora Torg, ☎ 044/121988). **Landskrona** (⊠ Rådhusg. 3, ☎ 0418/473000; ⊠ Landsv. 2, ☎ 0418/72420). **Lund** (⊠ Kyrkog. 11, ☎ 046/355040). **Malmö** (⊠ Skeppsbron at the Central Station, ☎ 040/300150). **Ronneby** (⊠ Kallingev. 3, ☎ 0457/18090). **Växjö** (⊠ Kronobergsg. 8, ☎ 0470/41410). **Ystad** (⊠ St. Knuts Torg, ☎ 0411/77681).

7 DALARNA: THE FOLKLORE DISTRICT

DALARNA IS CONSIDERED the most typically Swedish of all the country's 24 provinces, a place of forests, mountains, and red-painted wooden farmhouses and cottages by the shores of pristine, sun-dappled lakes. It is the favorite site for Midsummer Day celebrations, in which Swedes don folk costumes and dance to fiddle and accordion music around maypoles garlanded with wildflowers.

Dalarna played a key role in the history of the nation. It was from here that Gustav Vasa recruited the army that freed the country from Danish domination during the 16th century. The region is also important artistically, both for its tradition of naive religious decoration and for producing two of the nation's best-loved painters, Anders Zorn (1860–1920) and Carl Larsson (1853–1915), and one of its favorite poets, the melancholy, mystical Dan Andersson, who sought inspiration in the remote camps of the old charcoal burners deep in the forest.

As for dining and lodging, do not expect too much in Dalarna. Traditionally, visitors to the area—many from elsewhere in Scandinavia or from Germany—make use either of the region's many well-equipped campsites or of *stugbyar* (small villages of log cabins, with cooking facilities), usually set near lakesides or in forest clearings.

Our itinerary circles Lake Siljan, the largest of the 6,000 lakes in the province and the center of Dalarna's folklore, then crosses east to the coastal town of Gävle. The main points can all be reached by train, except for the southern side of Lake Siljan.

En Route   On the route from Stockholm to Dalarna, 158 km (98 mi) from Stockholm and just south of Avesta on Route 70, stands the world's biggest *Dalahäst* (Dala horse), 43 ft tall. The bright orange-red painted monument marks a modern roadside rest stop with a spacious cafeteria and a helpful tourist information center.

Falun

⑧⓪   *224 km (139 mi) northwest of Stockholm (via E18 and Rte. 70).*

Falun is the traditional capital of Dalarna, though in recent years the nondescript railway town of Borlänge has grown in importance. Falun's history has always been very much bound to its copper mine, worked since 1230 by Stora Kopparbergs Bergslags AB (today just *Stora*), which claims to be the oldest limited company in the world. Its greatest period of prosperity was the 17th century, when it financed Sweden's "Age of Greatness," and the country became the dominant Baltic power. In 1650, Stora produced a record 3,067 tons of copper; probably as a result of such rapid extraction, 37 years later its mine shafts caved in. Fortunately, the accident was on Midsummer's Day, when most of the miners were off duty, and as a result no one was killed. Today the major part of the mine is an enormous hole in the ground that has become Falun's principal tourist attraction, with its own museum, **Stora Museum.** ☎ 023/711475. ⊠ *Mine SKr 60, museum free with mine tour.* ☼ *Mine May–Aug., daily 10–4:30; Sept.–mid-Nov. and Mar.–Apr., weekends 12:30–4:30; museum May–Aug., daily 10–4:30; Sept.–Apr., daily 12:30–4:30.*

Lodging

$$$ 🏨 **Grand.** Part of the First Hotel chain, this conventional, modern hotel is close to town center. The bright rooms are decorated with Chippendale-style furniture, and most have minibars. ⊠ *Trotzg. 911, S791 71,* ☎ *023/18700,* FAX *023/14143. 183 rooms. Restaurant, bar, minibars, no-*

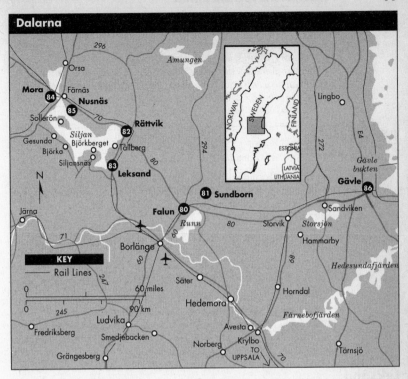

Dalarna

smoking rooms, indoor pool, sauna, exercise room, convention center, parking. AE, DC, MC, V.

$$$ ⊞ **Hotel Winn.** This small, cozy hotel in town center is built in tradi-
★ tional Dalarna style and filled with antique furnishings. Some rooms
share bathrooms. ⊠ *Bergskolegränd 7, S791 26,* ☎ *023/63600,* FAX *023/
22524. 88 rooms. Restaurant, no-smoking rooms, hot tub, sauna,
meeting room. AE, DC, MC, V.*

$$$ ⊞ **Scandic.** This ultramodern, Legolike hotel is in the expanded Lugnet
sports and recreation center outside Falun, where the 1993 World Ski-
ing Championships took place. The comfortable rooms have good views.
⊠ *Svärdsjög. 51, S791 31 Falun,* ☎ *023/22160,* FAX *023/12845. 135
rooms. Restaurant, pub, snack bar, no-smoking rooms, indoor pool,
sauna, meeting rooms, parking. AE, DC, MC, V.*

$$ ⊞ **Hotel Falun.** Rolf Carlsson runs this small, friendly, but bland-look-
ing hotel just 1,300 ft from the railway station. The 12 rooms that share
baths are offered at a lower rate. The front desk closes at 9 PM. ⊠ *Cen-
trumhuset, Trotzg. 16, S791 30,* ☎ *023/29180,* FAX *023/13006. 27 rooms,
15 with bath. No-smoking rooms, meeting rooms. AE, DC, MC, V.*

$ ⊞ **Birgittagården.** This small hotel, 8 km (5 mi) out of town, is run
by the religious order Stiftelsen Dalarnas Birgitta Systrar (the Dalarna
Sisters of Birgitta). It's smoke-free and alcohol-free, and set in a fine
park. There are no telephones or televisions in the rooms. ⊠ *Ud-
dnäsv., S791 46,* ☎ *023/32147,* FAX *023/32471. 25 rooms. No-smok-
ing rooms, meeting rooms. No credit cards.*

Sundborn

③ *10 km (6 mi) northeast of Falun (off Rte. 80).*

In this small village you can visit **Carl Larsson Gården,** the lakeside home
of the Swedish artist Carl Larsson. Larsson was an excellent textile de-

signer and draftsman who painted scenes from his family's busy, domestic life. The house itself was creatively painted and decorated by Larsson's wife, Karin, also trained as an artist. Their home's turn-of-the-century fittings and furnishings have been carefully preserved; their great-grandchildren still use the house on occasion. Lines for guided tours can take two hours in summer. ☎ 023/60053 in summer, ☎ 023/60069 in winter. ◻ Guided tours only, SKr 65. ☉ May–Sept., daily 10–5; Oct.–Apr., Tues. 11. Off-season visits by advance reservation.

Rättvik

82 48 km (30 mi) northwest of Falun (via Rte. 80).

Surrounded by wooded slopes, Rättvik is a pleasant town of timbered houses on the eastern tip of Lake Siljan. A center for local folklore, the town has several shops that sell handmade articles and produce from the surrounding region.

Every year in June, hundreds of people wearing traditional costumes arrive in longboats to attend Midsummer services at the town's 14th-century church, **Rättvik Kyrka**, which stands on a promontory stretching into the lake. Its interior contains some fine examples of local naive religious art.

The open-air museum **Rättvik Gammalgård** reconstructs peasant lifestyles of bygone days. Tours in English can be arranged through the Rättvik tourist office. ◻ Free, guided tour SKr 20. ☉ Mid-June–mid-Aug., daily 11–6; tours at 1 and 2:30.

Leksand

83 18 km (11 mi) south of Rättvik (via Rte. 70), 66 km (41 mi) northwest of Falun (via Rättvik).

Thousands of tourists converge on Leksand in June each year for the Midsummer celebrations; they also come in July for Himlaspelet (The Play of the Way that Leads to Heaven), a traditional musical with an all-local cast, staged outdoors near the town's church. It is easy to get seats; ask the local tourist office for details.

Leksand is also an excellent vantage point from which to watch the "church-boat" races on Siljan. These vessels are claimed to be successors to the Viking longboats and were traditionally used to take peasants from outlying regions to church on Sunday. On Midsummer Eve, the longboats, crewed by people in folk costumes, skim the lake.

In the hills around Leksand and elsewhere near Siljan you will find the fäbodar, small settlements in the forest where cattle were taken to graze during the summer. Less idyllic memories of bygone days are conjured up by **Käringberget**, a 720-ft-high mountain north of town where alleged witches were burned to death during the 17th century.

En Route   From Leksand, drive along the small road toward Mora by the southern shores of Siljan, passing through the small communities of Siljansnäs and Björka before stopping at **Gesunda**, a pleasant little village at the foot of a mountain. A chair lift will take you from there to the top for unbeatable views over the lake.

Near Gesunda, **Tomteland** (Santaland) claims to be the home of Santa Claus, or Father Christmas. Toys are for sale at Santa's workshop and kiosks. There are rides in horse-drawn carriages in summer and sleighs in winter. ✉ Gesundaberget, S792 90, Sollerön, ☎ 0250/29000. ◻ SKr 95. ☉ Mid-June–late Aug., daily 10–5; July, daily 10–6; late Nov.–early Jan, call ahead for daily schedule.

The large island of **Sollerön** is connected to the mainland at Gesunda by a bridge, from which there are fine views of the mountains surrounding Siljan. Several excellent bathing places and an interesting Viking gravesite are also here. The church dates from 1775.

Mora

84 *50 km (31 mi) northwest of Leksand, 83 km (52 mi) northwest of Falun (via Rte. 70).*

To get to this pleasant and relaxed lakeside town of 20,000, you can take Route 70 directly from Rättvik along the northern shore of Lake Silja, or follow the lake's southern shore through Leksand and Gesunda to get a good sense of Dalarna.

Mora is best known as the finishing point for the world's longest cross-country ski race, the *Vasalopp,* which begins 90 km (56 mi) away at Sälen, a ski resort close to the Norwegian border. The race commemorates a fundamental piece of Swedish history: the successful attempt by Gustav Vasa in 1521 to rally local peasants to the cause of ridding Sweden of Danish occupation. Vasa, only 21 years old, had fled the capital and described to the Mora locals in graphic detail a massacre of Swedish noblemen ordered by Danish King Christian in Stockholm's Stortorget. Unfortunately, no one believed him and the dispirited Vasa was forced to abandon his attempts at insurrection and take off on either skis or snowshoes for Norway, where he hoped to evade Christian and go into exile. Just after he left, confirmation reached Mora of the Stockholm bloodbath, and the peasants, already discontented with Danish rule, relented, sending two skiers after Vasa to tell him they would join his cause. The two men caught up with the young nobleman at Sälen. They returned with him to Mora, where an army was recruited. Vasa marched south, defeated the Danes, and became king and the founder of modern Sweden. The commemorative race, held on the first Sunday in March, attracts thousands of competitors from all over the world, including the Swedish king. There is a spectacular mass start at Sälen before the field thins out. The finish is eagerly awaited in Mora, though in recent years the number of spectators has fallen thanks to the fact that the race is now usually televised live. You can get a comfortable glimpse of the race's history in the **Vasaloppsmuseet,** with its collection of past ski gear and photos, news clippings, and a short film. ⊠ *Vasag.,* ☎ *0250/39225.* ⌑ *SKr 30.* ☉ *Mid-May–Aug., daily 10–6; Sept.–mid-May, daily 11–5.*

Mora is also known as the home of Anders Zorn (1860–1920), Sweden's leading Impressionist painter, who lived in Stockholm and Paris before returning to his roots here, painting the local scenes for which he is now famous. His former private residence—**Zorngården**—a large, sumptuous house designed with great originality and taste by the painter himself, has retained the same exquisite furnishings, paintings, and decor it had when he lived there with his wife. The garden, also

★ a Zorn creation, is open to the public. Next door, the **Zornmuseet** (Zorn Museum), built 19 years after the painter's death, contains many of his best works. ⊠ *Vasag. 36,* ☎ *0250/16560.* ⌑ *Museum SKr 30, home SKr 30.* ☉ *Museum mid-May–mid-Sept., Mon.–Sat. 9–5, Sun. 11–5; mid-Sept.–mid-May, Mon.–Sat. 10–5, Sun. 1–5; home (guided tours only) mid-May–mid-Sept., Mon.–Sat. 10–4, Sun. 11–4; mid-Sept.– mid-May, Mon.–Sat. 12:30–4, Sun. 1–4.*

On the south side of town you'll find **Zorns Gammalgård,** a fine collection of old wooden houses from local farms, brought here and donated to Mora by Anders Zorn. One of them was converted in 1995 into the **Textil Kammare** (Textile Chamber), the first exhibit of Zorn's collection of textiles and period clothing. ⊠ *Yvradsv.,* ☎ *0250/16560 (summer only).* 🎨 *SKr 20.* ☉ *June–Aug., daily 11–5.*

Lodging

$$ 🏨 **Kung Gästa.** This modern, reasonably sized hotel is 2 km (1 mi) from town center and only 330 ft from the Mora train station. ⊠ *Kristeneberg, S792 32,* ☎ *0250/15070,* 🅵🅰🆇 *0250/17078. 47 rooms. Restaurant, no-smoking rooms, indoor pool, sauna, exercise room, meeting rooms. AE, DC, MC, V.*

$$ 🏨 **Mora.** A pleasant little Best Western chain hotel is in town center and 5 km (3 mi) from the airport. Its comfortable rooms are brightly decorated and have minibars and radios. ⊠ *Strandg. 12, S792 01,* ☎ *0250/71750,* 🅵🅰🆇 *0250/18981. 138 rooms. Restaurant, bar, minibars, no-smoking rooms, indoor pool, sauna, meeting rooms. AE, DC, MC, V.*

$$ 🏨 **Siljan.** Part of the Sweden Hotel group, this small, modern hotel affords views over the lake. Rooms are standard, with radio, television, and wall-to-wall carpeting; most are single rooms with sofa beds. ⊠ *Morag. 6, S792 22,* ☎ *0250/13000,* 🅵🅰🆇 *0250/13098. 45 rooms. Restaurant, bar, no-smoking floor, sauna, exercise room, dance club, meeting room. AE, DC, MC, V.*

$ 🏨 **Moraparken.** This modern hotel sits in a park by the banks of the Dala River, not far from town center. ⊠ *Parkgarten 1, S792 25,* ☎ *0250/17800,* 🅵🅰🆇 *0250/18583. 75 rooms. Restaurant, no-smoking rooms, sauna, convention center. AE, DC, MC, V.*

Outdoor Activities and Sports
SKIING

Dalarna's principal ski resort is **Sälen,** starting point for the Vasalopp, about 80 km (50 mi) west of Mora.

Nusnäs

❽❺ *6 km (4 mi) southeast of Mora (via Rte. 70), 28 km (17 mi) northwest of Falun.*

The lakeside village of Nusnäs is where the small, brightly red-painted wooden Dala horses are made. These were originally carved by the peasants of Dalarna as toys for their children, but their popularity rapidly spread with the advent of tourism in the 20th century. Mass production of the little horses started at Nusnäs in 1928. In 1939 they achieved international popularity after being shown at the New York World's Fair, and since then they have become a Swedish symbol—today some of the smaller versions available in Stockholm's tourist shops are, however, made in East Asia. At Nusnäs you can watch the genuine article being made, now with the aid of modern machinery but still painted by hand.

Shopping

Naturally you'll be able to buy some painted horses to take home; the place to visit is **Nils Olsson** (⊠ Edåkerv. 17, ☎ 0250/37200). Shops are open every day except Sunday.

Gävle

❽❻ *176 km (109 mi) east of Mora (via Rtes. 70 and 80), 92 km (57 mi) east of Falun (via Rte. 80).*

The port town of Gävle achieved dubious renown at the time of the Chernobyl nuclear accident in 1986 by briefly becoming the most radioactive place in Europe. A freak storm dumped large amounts of fallout from the Soviet Union on the town. For a while farmers had to burn newly harvested hay and keep their cattle inside. Yet the scare soon passed and today you can visit the town in perfect safety. Gävle is worth a stopover for a glimpse of its two relatively new museums.

The **Joe Hill Museet** (Joe Hill Museum), dedicated to the Swedish emigrant who went on to become America's first well-known protest singer and union organizer, is in Hill's former home in the oldest section of Gävle. Once a poor, working-class district, this is now the most picturesque and highly sought-after residential part of town, with art studios and crafts workshops nearby. The museum—furnished in the same style as when Hill lived there—contains very few of his possessions but does display his prison letters. The house itself bears witness to the poor conditions that forced so many Swedes to emigrate to the United States (an estimated 850,000 to 1 million between 1840 and 1900). Hill, whose original Swedish name was Joel Hägglund, became a founder of the International Workers of the World and was executed for the murder of a Salt Lake City grocer in 1914, but he maintained his innocence right up to the end. ⊠ *Nedre Bergsg. 28,* ☎ *026/613425.* ☐ *Free.* ☉ *June–Aug., daily 11–3.*

The **Skogsmuseet Silvanum** (Silvanum Forestry Museum) is on the west end of town, by the river. Silvanum, Latin for "The Forest," was inaugurated in 1961; it was the first such museum in the world and is one of the largest. The museum provides an in-depth picture of the forestry industry in Sweden, still the backbone of the country's industrial wealth: trees cover more than 50% of Sweden's surface area, and forest products account for 20% of national exports. Silvanum includes a forest botanical park and an arboretum that contains an example of every tree and bush growing in Sweden. ⊠ *Kungsbäcksv. 32,* ☎ *026/614100.* ☐ *Free.* ☉ *Tues. 10–2, Thurs.–Fri. 10–4, Wed. 10–7, weekends 1–5.*

Dalarna A to Z

Arriving and Departing

BY BUS
Swebus/Vasatrafik (☎ 020/640640) runs tour buses to the area from Stockholm on weekends.

BY CAR
From Stockholm, take E18 to Enköping and follow Route 70 northwest. From Göteborg, take E20 to Örebro and Route 60 north from there.

BY PLANE
There are 11 flights daily from Stockholm to **Dala Airport** (⊠ 8 km/5 mi from Borlänge, ☎ 0243/64510). **Mora Airport** (⊠ 6 km/4 mi from Mora) is served by **Holmström Air** (☎ 0250/30175), with five flights daily from Stockholm Monday through Friday, fewer on weekends.

Between the Airport and Town: There are half hourly **bus** connections on weekdays between Dala Airport and Falun, 26 km (16 mi) away. Bus 601 runs every half hour from Dala Airport to Borlänge; the trip costs SKr 15. There are no buses from Mora Airport.

A **taxi** from Dala Airport to Borlänge costs around SKr 100, to Falun approximately SKr 215. A taxi into Mora from Mora Airport costs SKr 90. Order taxis in advance through your travel agent or when you make an airline reservation. Book the **DalaFalun** taxi service by calling ☎ 0243/229290.

There is regular daily train service from Stockholm to both Mora and
Falun.

Contacts and Resources

CAR RENTALS

Avis has offices in Borlänge (☏ 0243/87080) and Mora (☏ 0250/16711).
Europcar/InterRent has its office in Borlänge (☏ 0243/19050). **Hertz**
has offices in Falun (☏ 023/58872) and Mora (☏ 0250/28800).

DOCTORS AND DENTISTS

Falun Hospital (☏ 023/82000). **Mora Hospital** (☏ 0250/25000). **24-
hour medical advisory service** (☏ 023/82900).

EMERGENCIES

For emergencies dial ☏ 112.

GUIDED TOURS

Sightseeing Tours: Call the Falun tourist office for English-speaking guides
to Falun and the region around Lake Siljan; guides cost about SKr 900.

LATE-NIGHT PHARMACIES

There are no late-night pharmacies in the area, but doctors called to
emergencies can supply medication. **Vasen** pharmacy in Falun (✉
Åsg., ☏ 023/20000) is open until 7 PM weekdays.

VISITOR INFORMATION

Falun (✉ Stora Torget, ☏ 023/83050). **Leksand** (✉ Norsg., ☏ 0247/
80300). **Ludvika** (✉ Sporthallen, ☏ 0240/86050). **Mora** (✉ Ångbåt-
skajen, ☏ 0250/567600). **Rättvik** (✉ Railway Station House, ☏ 0248/
70200). **Sälen** (✉ Sälen Centrum, ☏ 0280/20250).

8 NORRLAND AND NORRBOTTEN

THE NORTH OF SWEDEN, Norrland, is a place of wide-open spaces where the silence is almost audible. Golden eagles soar above snowcapped crags; huge salmon fight their way up wild, tumbling rivers; rare orchids bloom in Arctic heathland; and wild rhododendrons splash the land with color.

In the summer the sun shines at midnight above the Arctic Circle. In the winter it hardly shines at all. The weather can change with bewildering speed: A June day can dawn sunny and bright; then the skies may darken and the temperature drop to around zero as a snow squall blows in. Just as suddenly, the sun comes out again and the temperature starts to rise.

Here live the once-nomadic Lapps, or Sami, as they prefer to be known. They carefully guard what remains of their identity, while doing their best to inform the public of their culture. Many of the 17,000 Sami who live in Sweden still earn their living herding reindeer, but as open space shrinks, the younger generation is turning in greater numbers toward the allure of the cities. As the modern world makes its incursions, the Sami often exhibit a sad resignation to the gradual disappearance of their way of life. A Sami folk poem says it best: "Our memory, the memory of us vanishes/We forget and we are forgotten."

Yet there is a growing struggle, especially among younger Sami, to maintain their identity, and, thanks to their traditional closeness to nature, they are now finding allies in Sweden's Green movement. They refer to the north of Scandinavia as *Sapmi,* their spiritual and physical home, making no allowance for the different countries that now rule it.

Nearly all Swedish Sami now live in ordinary houses, having abandoned the *kåta* (Lapp wigwam), and some even herd their reindeer with helicopters. Efforts are now being made to protect and preserve their language, which is totally unlike Swedish and bears far greater resemblance to Finnish. The language reflects their closeness to nature. The word *goadnil,* for example, means "a quiet part of the river, free of current, near the bank or beside a rock."

Nowadays many Sami depend on the tourist industry for their living, selling their artifacts, such as expertly carved bone-handle knives, wooden cups and bowls, bark bags, silver jewelry, and leather straps embroidered with pewter thread.

The land that the Sami inhabit is vast. Norrland stretches 1,000 km (625 mi) from south to north, making up more than half of Sweden; its size is comparable to that of Great Britain. On the west there are mountain ranges, to the east a wild and rocky coastline, and in between boundless forests and moorland. Its towns are often little more than a group of houses along a street, built around a local industry such as mining, forestry, or hydropower utilities. Thanks to Sweden's excellent transportation infrastructure, however, Norrland and the northernmost region of Norrbotten are no longer inaccessible and even travelers with limited time can get at least a taste of the area. Its wild spaces are ideal for open-air vacations. Hiking, climbing, canoeing, river rafting, and fishing are all popular in summer; skiing, skating, and dog-sledding are winter activities.

A word of warning: In summer mosquitoes are a constant nuisance, even worse than in other parts of Sweden, so be sure to bring plenty of repellent (you won't find anything effective in Sweden). Fall is perhaps the best season to visit Norrland. Roads are well maintained, but be careful of *gupp* (holes) following thaws. Highways are generally traffic free, but keep an eye out for the occasional reindeer.

Dining and lodging are on the primitive side in this region. Standards of cuisine and service are not nearly as high as prices—but hotels are usually exceptionally clean and staff scrupulously honest. Accommodations are limited, but the various local tourist offices can supply details of bed-and-breakfasts and holiday villages equipped with housekeeping cabins. The area is also rich in campsites—but with the highly unpredictable climate, this may appeal only to the very hardy.

Norrbotten is best discovered from a base in Kiruna, in the center of the alpine region that has been described as Europe's last wilderness. You can tour south and west to the mountains and national parks, east and south to Sami villages, and farther south still to Baltic coastal settlements.

Kiruna

87 *1,239 km (710 mi) north of Stockholm.*

About 145 km (90 mi) north of the Arctic Circle, and 1,670 ft above sea level, Kiruna is the most northerly city in Sweden. Although its inhabitants number only around 26,000, Kiruna is one of Sweden's largest cities—it spreads over the equivalent of half the area of Switzerland. Until an Australian community took the claim, Kiruna was often called "the world's biggest city." With 20,000 square km (7,722 square mi) within the municipal limits, Kiruna boasts that it could accommodate the entire world population with 150 square ft of space per person.

Kiruna lies at the eastern end of Lake Luossajärvi, spread over a wide area between two mountains, Luossavaara and Kirunavaara, that are largely composed of iron ore—Kiruna's raison d'être. Here is the world's largest underground iron mine, with reserves estimated at 500 million tons. Automated mining technology has largely replaced the traditional miner in the Kirunavaara underground mines, which are some 500 km (280 mi) long. Of the city's inhabitants, an estimated fifth are Finnish immigrants who came to work in the mine.

The city was established in 1890 as a mining town, but true prosperity came only with the building of the railway to the Baltic port of Luleå and the northern Norwegian port of Narvik in 1902.

Like most of Norrland, Kiruna is full of remarkable contrasts, from the seemingly pitch-black, months-long winter to the summer, when the sun never sets and it is actually possible to play golf round-the-clock for 50 days at a stretch. Here, too, the ancient Sami culture exists side by side with the high-tech culture of cutting-edge satellite research. In recent years the city has diversified its economy and now supports the Esrange Space Range, about 40 km (24 mi) east, which sends rockets and balloons to probe the upper reaches of the earth's atmosphere, and the Swedish Institute of Space Physics, which has pioneered the investigation of the phenomenon of the northern lights. The city received a boost in 1984 with the opening of Nordkalottvägen, a 170-km-long (106-mi-long) road to Narvik.

One of Kiruna's few buildings of interest is **Kiruna Kyrka** (Kiruna Church), on Gruvvägen, near the center of the city. It was built in 1921, its inspiration a blending of a Sami *kåta* with a Swedish stave church. The altarpiece is by Prince Eugen (1863–1947), Sweden's painter prince.

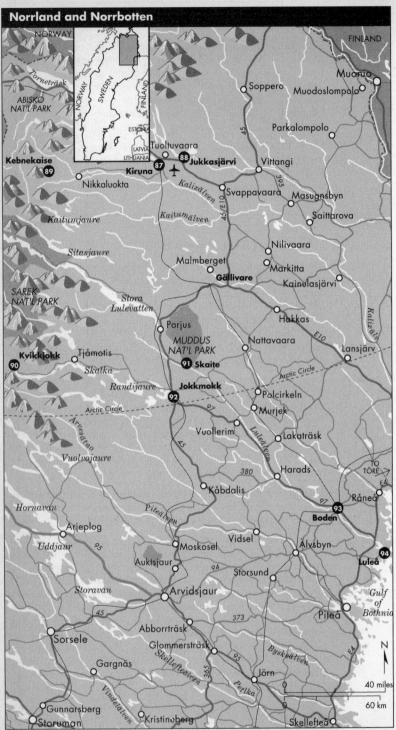

NORWAY

FINLAND

Tornetrask

ABISKO
NAT'L PARK

Kebnekaise
89

NORWAY
SWEDEN
FINLAND
ESTONIA
LATVIA
LITHUANIA

Soppero

Muonio

Muodoslompolo

Parkalompolo

Tuoltuvaara

88 Jukkasjärvi

Vittangi

Kiruna 87

Nikkaluokta

Kalixälven

Svappavaara

Masugnsbyn

Saittarova

Kaitumjaure

Kaitumälven

Nilivaara

Malmberget

Markitta

Gällivare

Kainulasjärvi

Sitasjaure

SAREK
NAT'L PARK

Stora
Lulevatten

Porjus

Hakkas

Kalixälv

MUDDUS
NAT'L PARK

Nattavaara

E10

Lansjärv

Kvikkjokk
90

Tjåmotis

91 Skaite

Arctic Circle

Skalka

Randijaure

Jokkmokk

92

97

Polcirkeln

Murjek

Arctic Circle

Arvesådno

Vuollerim

Lakaträsk

Luleälven

Vuolvojaure

45

380

Harads

TO
TÖRE

E4

Kåbdalis

Hornavan

Piteälven

Råneå

Arjeplog

Uddjaur

25

Moskosel

Vidsel

97

Boden 93

Älvsbyn

Luleå 94

Auktsjaur

94

Storsund

Storavan

Arvidsjaur

Gulf
of
Bothnia

45

373

Piteå

Sorsele

Abborrträsk

N

Gargnäs

Glommersträsk

85

365

Jörn

Byskeälven

Petka

E4

0

40 miles

Gunnarsberg

Storuman

Vindelälven

Kristineberg

0

60 km

Skellefteälven

Skellefteå

Lodging

$$$ 🏨 **Ferrum.** Part of the RESO Hotels chain, this late-1960s-vintage hotel is near the railway station. Rooms have wall-to-wall carpeting and modern, standard furniture. ✉ *Lars Janssonsg. 15, Box 22, S981 21,* ☎ *0980/398600,* FAX *0980/14505. 169 rooms. 2 restaurants, bar, no-smoking rooms, sauna, exercise room, dance club, meeting rooms. AE, DC, MC, V.*

$$ 🏨 **Kebne och Kaisa.** These twin modern hotels—named after the local mountain, Kebnekaise (☞ *below*)—are close to the railway station and the airport bus stop. Rooms are bland but modern and comfortable. The restaurant is one of the best in Kiruna; it's open for breakfast and dinner. ✉ *Konduktörsg. 3 and 7, S981 34,* ☎ *0980/12380,* FAX *0980/ 82111. 54 rooms. Restaurant, no-smoking rooms, sauna. AE, DC, MC, V.*

$ 🏨 **Fyra Vindar.** Dating from 1903, this small hotel has the advantage of being close to the railway station. ✉ *Bangårdsv. 9, S981 34,* ☎ *0980/ 12050. 18 rooms. Restaurant, no-smoking rooms. DC, MC, V.*

$ 🏨 **STF Vandrarhem.** Formerly a hospital for the aged, this modernized, 1926 building now serves as a youth hostel. It faces a large park near the railway station. ✉ *Skytteg. 16A, S981 34,* ☎ *0980/17195 or 0980/ 12784. 35 2- to 5-bed rooms. No credit cards. Closed mid-Aug.–mid-June.*

En Route Driving south from Kiruna toward Muddus National Park, you'll pass several small former mining villages before coming into the **Kalixälv** (Kalix River) valley, where the countryside becomes more settled, with small farms and fertile meadows replacing the wilder northern landscape.

Jukkasjärvi

88 *16 km (10 mi) east of Kiruna.*

The history of Jukkasjärvi, a Sami village by the shores of the fast-flowing Torneälven (Torne River), dates from 1543, when a market was recorded here. There is a wooden church from the 17th century and a small open-air museum that evokes a sense of Sami life in times gone by.

If you are gastronomically adventuresome you may want to sample one of the most unusual of all Sami delicacies: *kaffeost,* a cup of thick black coffee with small lumps of goat cheese. After the cheese sits in the coffee for a bit, you fish it out with a spoon and consume it, then drink the coffee.

Dining and Lodging

$ ✕🏨 **Jukkasjärvi Wärdshus och Hembygdsgård.** The restaurant spe-
★ cializes in Norrland cuisine—characterized by reindeer, wild berries, mushrooms, dried and smoked meats, salted fish, fermented herring, rich sauces using thick creams—and is the lifework of its manager, Yngve Bergqvist. The manor has one large honeymoon suite with wood floors and antique furniture; there are 45 cabins around it, 30 with bathroom, kitchen, and two bedrooms with bunk beds. Fifteen "camping cabins" are simple shelters that share the use of a common house with toilets, showers, sauna, kitchen, and washing machine. Breakfast is not included. River-rafting and canoeing trips can be arranged. ✉ *Jukkasjärvi, Marknadsv. 63, S981 91,* ☎ *0980/66800,* FAX *0980/668090. 1 suite, 45 cabins. Restaurant, sauna, meeting rooms. AE, DC, MC, V.*

$$$ 🏨 **Ice Hotel.** At the peak of winter, tourists are drawn by the annual
★ construction of the world's largest igloo, which opens for business as a hotel from December through April, after which it melts away. Made of snow, ice, and sheet metal, the Ice Hotel offers rooms for 40 guests,

who spend the night in specially insulated sleeping bags on top of layers of reindeer skins and spruce boughs. The bar is called In the Rocks, and colored electric lights liven up the solid ice walls. Breakfast is served in the sauna, with a view of the (nonelectric) northern lights. The entire hotel is designated nonsmoking, as it takes only a few puffs to tarnish the snow-white interiors. ⊠ *Marknadsv. 63, S981 91 Jukkasjärvi,* ☎ *0980/66800,* 𝔽𝔸𝕏 *0980/668090. 40 beds, 1 suite. Restaurant, bar, sauna, cross-country skiing, snowmobiling, chapel, meeting rooms. AE, DC, MC, V. Closed May–Nov.*

Outdoor Activities and Sports
A challenging local activity is riding the rapids of the Torne River in an inflatable boat. In winter Jukkasjärvi also offers dogsled rides and snowmobile safaris. Call the Gällivare tourist office (☞ Norrland and Norrbotten A to Z, *below*).

Kebnekaise

89 *85 km (53 mi) west of Kiruna.*

At 7,000 ft above sea level, Kebnekaise is Sweden's highest mountain, but you'll need to be in good physical shape just to get to it. From Kiruna you travel about 66 km (41 mi) west to the Sami village of Nikkaluokta. (There are two buses a day from Kiruna in the summer.) From Nikkaluokta it is a hike of 19 km (12 mi) to the Fjällstationen (mountain station) at the foot of Kebnekaise, though you can take a boat 5 km (3 mi) across Lake Ladtjojaure. Kebnekaise itself is easy to climb provided there's good weather and you're in shape; mountaineering equipment is not necessary. If you feel up to more walking, the track continues past the Kebnekaise Fjällstationen to become part of what is known as Kungsleden (the King's Path), a 500-km (280-mi) trail through the mountains and Abisko National Park to Riksgränsen on the Norwegian border.

Lodging
$ 🏠 **Kebnekaise Fjällstation.** This rustic, wooden mountain station consists of seven separate buildings. Choose between the main building, with its heavy wood beams, wood floors, and wood bunk beds—five per room—and the newer annex, where more modern rooms each contain two or four beds. All guests share the use of a service house, with toilets, men's and women's showers, and sauna. The facility is 19 km (12 mi) from Nikkaluokta and can be reached by footpath, a combination of boat and hiking, or helicopter. Guided mountain tours are available. ⊠ *S981 29 Kiruna,* ☎ *0980/55042,* 𝔽𝔸𝕏 *0980/55048; off-season, contact Abisko tourist office (☞ Norrland and Norrbotten A to Z, below). 200 beds. Restaurant, bar, sauna. AE, V. Closed mid-Aug.– mid-Mar.*

Outdoor Activities and Sports
All the regional tourist offices can supply details of skiing holidays, but never forget the extreme temperatures and weather conditions. For the really adventuresome, the Kebnekaise mountain station offers combined skiing and climbing weeks at SKr 3,795. It also offers weeklong combined dogsledding, skiing, and climbing holidays on the mountains, which vary in price from SKr 4,225 to SKr 5,395. Because of the extreme cold and the danger involved, be sure to have proper equipment. Consult the **mountain station** (☎ 0980/55000) well in advance for advice.

Kvikkjokk and Sarek National Park

⑨ *310 km (193 mi) southwest of Kiruna (via Rte. 45).*

Sarek is Sweden's largest high mountain area and was molded by the last Ice Age. The mountains have been sculpted by glaciers, of which there are about 100 in the park. The mountain area totals 487,000 acres, a small portion of which is forest, bogs, and waterways. The remainder is bare mountain. The park has 90 peaks some 6,000 ft above sea level.

The Rapaätno River, which drains the park, runs through the lovely, desolate Rapadalen (Rapa Valley). The area is marked by a surprising variety of landscapes—luxuriant green meadows contrasting with the snowy peaks of the mountains. Elk, bears, wolverines, lynx, ermines, hare, Arctic foxes, red foxes, and mountain lemmings inhabit the terrain. Birdlife includes ptarmigan, willow grouse, teal, wigeon, tufted ducks, bluethroat, and warblers. Golden eagles, rough-legged buzzards, and merlins have also been spotted here.

Visiting Sarek demands a good knowledge of mountains and a familiarity with the outdoors. The park can be dangerous in winter because of avalanches and snowstorms. In summer, however, despite its unpredictable, often inhospitable climate, it attracts large numbers of experienced hikers. At Kvikkjokk, hikers can choose between a trail through the Tarradalen (Tarra Valley), which divides the Sarek from the Padjelanta National Park to the west, or part of the Kungsleden trail, which crosses about 15 km (9 mi) of Sarek's southeastern corner.

Skaite and Muddus National Park

⑨ *192 km (119 mi) south of Kiruna (via E10 and Rte. 45).*

Established in 1942, Muddus National Park is less mountainous and spectacular than Sarek, its 121,770 acres comprising mainly virgin coniferous forest, some of whose trees may be up to 600 years old. The park's 3,680 acres of water are composed primarily of two huge lakes at the center of the park and the Muddusjåkkå River, which tumbles spectacularly through a gorge with 330-ft-high sheer rock walls and includes a waterfall crashing 140 ft down. The highest point of Muddus is Sör-Stubba mountain, 2,158 ft above sea level. From Skaite, where you enter the park, a series of well-marked trails begins. There are four well-equipped overnight communal rest huts and two tourist cabins. The park shelters bears, elk, lynx, wolverines, moose, ermines, weasels, otters, and many bird species. A popular pastime is picking cloudberries in autumn.

Jokkmokk

⑨ *205 km (127 mi) south of Kiruna (via E10 and Rte. 45).*

Jokkmokk is an important center of Sami culture. Each February it is the scene of the region's largest market, nowadays an odd event featuring everything from stalls selling frozen reindeer meat to Sami handcrafted wooden utensils. If you're an outdoor enthusiast, Jokkmokk makes perhaps the best base in Norrland for you. The village has three campsites and is surrounded by wilderness. The local tourist office (☞ Norrland and Norrbotten A to Z, *below*) sells fishing permits, which cost SKr 50 for 24 hours, SKr 100 for 3 days, SKr 150 for 1 week, and SKr 300 for the entire year. The office can also supply lists of camping and housekeeping cabins.

Lodging

$$$ 🏨 **Hotel Jokkmokk.** A modern hotel of this level of luxury seems in-
 ★ congruous in this remote region but is welcome nevertheless. Rooms
are carpeted, and six of them are designated as "Ladies' Rooms," ba-
sically all with pastels and florals. The hotel is in town center, but the
staff can arrange dogsled rides and helicopter trips to the Sarek and
Muddus national parks; there is excellent fishing nearby. ✉ *Solg. 45,
S962 23,* ☎ *0971/55320,* 📠 *0971/55625. 75 rooms. Restaurant, no-
smoking rooms, indoor pool, sauna, meeting rooms. AE, DC, MC, V.*

 $ 🏨 **Gästis.** This small hotel in central Jokkmokk opened in 1915.
Rooms are standard, with television, shower, and either carpeted or
vinyl floors. ✉ *Herrev. 1, S962 31,* ☎ *0971/10012,* 📠 *0971/10044.
30 rooms. Restaurant, no-smoking rooms, sauna, meeting rooms. AE,
DC, MC, V.*

 $ 🏨 **Jokkmokks Turistcenter.** This complex is in a pleasant forest area,
near Luleälven, 3 km (2 mi) from the railway station. Rooms have bunk
beds, a small table, and chairs; showers, toilets, and a common cook-
ing area are in the hall. ✉ *Box 75, S962 22,* ☎ *0971/12370,* 📠 *0971/
12476. 26 rooms, 84 cabins. 4 pools, sauna, meeting rooms. MC, V.*

Boden

 93 *290 km (180 mi) southeast of Kiruna, 130 km (81 mi) southeast of
Jokkmokk (on Route 97).*

Boden, the nation's largest garrison town, dates from 1809, when
Sweden lost Finland to Russia and feared an invasion of its own ter-
ritory. The **Garnisonsmuseet** (Garrison Museum), contains exhibits from
Swedish military history, with an extensive collection of weapons and
uniforms. ✉ *Garnisonsmuseet, Sveav. 10, Boden,* ☎ *0921/68399.* 📠
Free. 🕐 *Mid-June–late Aug., Tues.–Sat. 11–4, Sun. 1–4.*

Luleå

 94 *340 km (211 mi) southeast of Kiruna (via E10 and E4).*

The most northerly major town in Sweden, Luleå is an important port
at the top of the Gulf of Bothnia, at the mouth of the Luleälv (Lule
River). The town was some 10 km (6 mi) farther inland when it was
first granted its charter in 1621, but by 1649 trade had grown so much
that it was moved closer to the sea. The development of Kiruna and
the iron trade is linked, by means of a railway, with the fortunes of
Luleå, where a steelworks was set up in the 1940s. Like its fellow port
towns—Piteå, Skellefteå, Umeå, and Sundsvall—farther south, Luleå
is a very modern and nondescript city, but it has some reasonable ho-
tels. A beautiful archipelago of hundreds of islands hugs the coastline.

The **Norrbottens Museet** (Norrbotten Museum) has one of the best col-
lections of Sami ethnography in the world. ✉ *Hermelinsparken 2,* ☎
0920/220355. 📠 *Free.* 🕐 *Mid-June–mid-Aug., Thurs.–Tues. 10–6, Wed.
10–8.*

Dining and Lodging

$$$ ✕🏨 **Arctic.** Right in town center, the Arctic is known locally for its restau-
 ★ rant, which serves local specialties. The hotel is warm and cozy, with
tastefully decorated, rustic rooms. ✉ *Sandviksg. 80, S972 34,* ☎ *0920/
10980,* 📠 *0920/60980. 94 rooms. Restaurant, no-smoking rooms, hot
tub, sauna, meeting rooms. AE, DC, MC, V.*

$$$$ 🏨 **Luleå Stads Hotell.** This large, central Best Western hotel has nightly—
sometimes boisterous—dancing. Rooms in the building dating back to
1901 are spacious and carpeted, with turn-of-the-century furnishings.
✉ *Storg. 15, S972 32,* ☎ *0920/67000,* 📠 *0920/67092. 135 rooms, 3*

suites. Restaurant, café, no-smoking rooms, sauna, dance club, meeting rooms. AE, DC, MC, V.

$$$$ ⊞ **SAS Luleå Hotel.** As you might expect of a Radisson SAS hotel, this one is large, modern, and central. Each floor is different: the third floor is done in blue tones; the English Colonial–style second floor has ceiling fans and dried flowers; and the ground floor is art deco. ⊠ *Storg. 17, S971 28,* ☎ *0920/94000,* 🖷 *0920/88222. 216 rooms. Restaurant, no-smoking rooms, indoor pool, sauna, exercise room, nightclub, meeting rooms. AE, DC, MC, V.*

$$$ ⊞ **Scandic.** This hotel on Lake Sjö has an extremely pleasant setting and is 2 km (1 mi) from the railway station. ⊠ *Banv. 3, S973 46,* ☎ *0920/228360,* 🖷 *0920/69472. 157 rooms. Restaurant, no-smoking rooms, indoor pool, sauna, exercise room, meeting rooms. AE, DC, MC, V.*

$$ ⊞ **Amber.** A particularly fine old building, listed on the historic register, houses this hotel close to the railway station. Rooms are modern, with plush carpeting, minibars, and satellite television. ⊠ *Stationsg. 67, S972 34,* ☎ *0920/10200,* 🖷 *0920/87906. 16 rooms. No-smoking rooms. AE, DC, MC, V.*

$$ ⊞ **Aveny.** Rooms are of varying sizes and colors, but all are spotless and fresh. It's close to the railway station. ⊠ *Hermelinsg. 10, S973 46,* ☎ *0920/221820,* 🖷 *0920/220122. 24 rooms. No-smoking rooms. AE, DC, MC, V.*

Norrland and Norrbotten A to Z

Arriving and Departing

BY PLANE

There are two nonstop SAS flights a day from Stockholm to **Kiruna Airport** (⊠ 5 km/3 mi from Kiruna, ☎ 0980/68001) and three additional flights via Luleå. Check **SAS** (☎ 020/727000) for specific times.

Between the Airport and Town: In summer, **buses** connect the airport and Kiruna; the fare is about SKr 50. A **taxi** from the airport to the center of Kiruna costs about SKr 75; book through the airline or call ☎ 0980/12020.

BY TRAIN

The best and cheapest way to get to Kiruna is to take the evening sleeper from Stockholm on Tuesday, Wednesday, or Saturday, when the fare is reduced to SKr 595 for a single. The regular one-way price is SKr 695 plus SKr 90 for the couchette, double for return. You'll arrive at around lunchtime the next day.

Getting Around

Since public transportation is nonexistent in this part of the country, having a car is essential. The few roads are well built and maintained, although spring thaws can present potholes. Keep in mind that habitations are few and far between in this wilderness region.

CAR RENTALS

Kiruna: Avis (⊠ Kiruna Airport, ☎ 0980/16030). **Europcar/InterRent** (⊠ Växlareg. 20, ☎ 0980/14365). **Hertz** (⊠ Industriv. 5, ☎ 0980/19000).

Contacts and Resources

DOCTORS AND DENTISTS

Jokkmokk Health Center (⊠ Lappstav. 9, ☎ 0971/44444). **Kiruna Health Center** (⊠ Thuleg. 29, ☎ 0980/73000). Medical advisory service, **Luleå** (☎ 0920/71400).

EMERGENCIES

For emergencies dial ☎ 112.

GUIDED TOURS

Local tourist offices have information on guided tours.

Lapland Tours: **Same Lañs Resor** (✉ c/o Rental Line I Jokkmokk, Hermelinsg. 20, 962 33, Jokkmokk, ☎ 0971/10606) arranges tours to points of interest in Lappland.

Sami Tours: Call **Swedish Sami Association** (✉ Brog. 5, S90325, Umeå, ☎ 090/141180).

LATE-NIGHT PHARMACIES

There are no late-night pharmacies in Norrbotten, but doctors called to emergencies can dispense medicine. The pharmacy at the Gallerian shopping center in Kiruna (✉ Föreningsg. 6, ☎ 0980/18775) is open weekdays 9:30–6 and Saturdays 9:30–1.

VISITOR INFORMATION

Regional Tourist Office: Norrbottens Turistråd (✉ Stationsg. 69, Luleå, ☎ 0920/94070) covers the entire area.

Local Tourist Offices: Abisko (✉ S980 24 Abisko, ☎ 0980/40200). **Jokkmokk** (✉ Stortorget 4, ☎ 0971/12140 or 0971/17257). **Kiruna** (✉ Folkets Hus, ☎ 0980/18880). **Luleå** (✉ Kulturcentrum Ebeneser, ☎ 0920/293500). **Gällivare** (✉ Storg. 16, ☎ 0970/16660).

9 PORTRAITS OF SWEDEN

Sweden at a Glance: A Chronology

Reflections of Stockholm

Astrid Lindgren

Books and Videos

SWEDEN AT A GLANCE: A CHRONOLOGY

c 12,000 BC   The first migrations into Sweden.

2,000 BC   Southern European tribes migrate toward Denmark. The majority of early settlers in Scandinavia were Germanic.

c AD 770   The Viking Age begins. For the next 250 years, Scandinavians set sail on expeditions stretching from the Baltic to the Irish seas and to the Mediterranean as far as Sicily, employing superior ships and weapons and efficient military organization.

c 800–c 1000   Swedes control river trade routes between the Baltic and Black seas; establish Novgorod, Kiev, and other cities.

830   Frankish monk Ansgar makes one of the first attempts to Christianize Sweden and builds the first church in Slesvig, Denmark. Sweden is not successfully Christianized until the end of the 11th century, when the temple at Uppsala, a center for pagan resistance, is destroyed.

1248   Erik Eriksson appoints Birger as Jarl, in charge of military affairs and expeditions abroad. Birger improves women's rights, makes laws establishing peace in the home and church, and begins building Stockholm.

1250   Stockholm, Sweden, is officially founded.

1319   Sweden and Norway form a union that lasts until 1335.

1370   The Treaty of Stralsund gives the north German trading centers of the Hanseatic League free passage through Danish waters. German power increases throughout Scandinavia.

1397   The Kalmar Union is formed as a result of the dynastic times between Sweden, Denmark, and Norway, the geographical position of the Scandinavian states, and the growing influence of Germans in the Baltic. Erik of Pomerania is crowned king of the Kalmar Union.

1477   University of Uppsala, Sweden's oldest university, is founded.

1520   Christian II, ruler of the Kalmar Union, executes 82 people who oppose the Scandinavian union, an event known as the "Stockholm blood bath." Sweden secedes from the Union three years later.

1523   Gustav Ericsson founds Swedish Vasa dynasty as King Gustav I Vasa. He makes Lutheranism the state religion during his reign.

1611–1613   The Kalmar War: Denmark wages war against Sweden in hope of restoring the Kalmar Union.

1611–1660   Gustav II Adolphus reigns in Sweden. Sweden defeats Denmark in the Thirty Years' War and becomes the greatest power in Scandinavia as well as in Northern and Central Europe.

1660   Peace of Copenhagen establishes modern boundaries of Denmark, Sweden, and Norway.

1668   Bank of Sweden, the world's oldest central bank, is founded.

1700–1721   Sweden, led by Karl XII, first broadens then loses its position to Russia as Northern Europe's greatest power in the Great Northern War.

1807 During the Napoleonic wars, Gustav III joins the coalition against France and accepts war with France and Russia.

1809 Sweden surrenders the Åland Islands and Finland to Russia, Finland becomes a Grand Duchy of the Russian Empire, and the Instrument of Government, Sweden's constitution, is adopted.

1813 Sweden takes a Frenchman as King: Karl XIV Johann establishes the Bernadotte dynasty.

1814 Sweden, after Napoleon's defeat at the Battle of Leipzig, attacks Denmark and forces the Danish surrender of Norway. The Treaty of Kiel, in 1814, calls for a union between Norway and Sweden despite Norway's desire for independence.

c 1850 The building of railroads begins in Scandinavia.

1889 The Swedish Social Democratic party is founded.

1901 Alfred Nobel, the Swedish millionaire chemist and industrialist, initiates the Nobel prizes.

1905 Norway's union with Sweden is dissolved.

1914 At the outbreak of World War I, Sweden declares neutrality but is effectively blockaded.

1918 Women gain the right to vote.

1920 Scandinavian countries join the League of Nations.

1929–1937 The first social democratic government takes office in Sweden.

1939 Sweden declares neutrality in World War II.

1949 Sweden declines membership in NATO.

1952 The Nordic Council, which promotes cooperation among the Nordic parliaments, is founded.

1975 Sweden's Instrument of Government of 1809 is revised. This constitution reduces the voting age to eighteen and removes many of the king's powers and responsibilities.

1980 Fifty-eight percent of Sweden's voters advocate minimizing the use of nuclear reactors at Sweden's four power plants.

1986 Sweden's prime minister, Olof Palme, is assassinated for unknown reasons. Ingvar Carlsson succeeds him.

1991 The Social Democrats are voted out of office and a conservative coalition government takes over.

1992 Sweden's Riksbank (National Bank) raises overnight interest rates to a world record of 500% in an effort to defend the Swedish krona against speculation.

1995 Sweden and Finland join the EU in January.

1998 Stockholm is the 1998 Cultural Capital of Europe, hosting arts, culture, and nature events throughout the year.

REFLECTIONS OF STOCKHOLM

AT A RECEPTION for visiting dignitaries, the mayor of Stockholm surprised his guests by serving them glasses of a clear liquid that turned out to be water. It came, he explained, from the water surrounding this island city, and the purpose of the tongue-in-cheek gesture was to demonstrate that modern cities can afford clean environments. In fact, Stockholm has won the European Sustainable City Award in competition with 90-odd other cities, and a large swathe of Stockholm, including the vast royal domains, has been declared a national park for the benefit and enjoyment of the populace.

There were sound practical reasons to build Stockholm on the fourteen islands that command access from the Baltic Sea to Lake Mälaren. Back in the 13th century, after the Vikings had retired from plunder and discovery, Estonian pirates had taken to pillaging the shores of the lake, which extends deep into the Swedish heartland. Birger Jarl, the ruler who founded Sweden's first dynasty, put a stop to all that by stockading the islands the pirates had to pass. His effigy lies in gilded splendor at the foot of the city hall tower.

Stockholm without water would be unthinkable. It's the water that gives it beauty, character, life. The north shore and the south are, to be truthful, rather Germanic in character, not too different from, say, Zürich or Berlin. But watch them from across a busy waterway, mirrored in the blue lake, and they become invested with a lively charm.

The pearl in the oyster, however, is the small island known as Gamla Stan, or Old Town, dominated by the tawny colored, massive Royal Palace, designed by Nicodemus Tessin in the 17th century and completed in the 18th. In the Middle Ages, so many German merchants settled here that a law was proclaimed to limit their number on the city council to less than half of the members. The winding streets are lined with old houses in yellow, ochre, and occasional oxblood red. Some of the city's most attractive small hotels, gourmet restaurants, and lively jazz clubs are here. To many people, the greatest treasure is found inside Storkyrkan, the Stockholm cathedral, next door to the palace: a larger-than-life, polychrome wooden statue of St. George slaying the dragon from 1489.

Skeppsholmen, a smaller island east of Gamla Stan and once the nation's principal navy base, is an idyllic place for a stroll, and great for art lovers. The Museum of Modern Art by the Spanish architect Rafael Moneo opened in 1998 and is one of the great contemporary museums. It blends in well with other structures, such as the "old" modern museum, a former armory and a trendsetter since its opening in 1958; it is now becoming the Museum of Architecture. Also on Skeppsholmen is the exquisite East Asiatic Museum, another Tessin creation, which houses one of the world's finest collections of Chinese art.

After you cross the bridge from Skeppsholmen on your way back to the city center you'll walk past the National Museum and you'll do well to stop there—not just for its Rembrandts and Swedish masters of centuries past but also for its new atrium restaurant, one of the city's best, in the piazzalike inner courtyard.

The piers of Stockholm's islands are lined with so many vessels of every category, from cruise ships and seagoing roll-on/roll-off vessels to island-hopping steamboats and pocket-size ferries, that it would seem impossible to squeeze in another motorboat, sailboat, or sloop. There were more than 100,000 of them at last count, and still the number keeps growing. The waterborne traffic jam when they return on a Sunday night in summer after a weekend at sea is something to behold.

Most of the Stockholm sailors travel no farther than to one of the 25,000 islands and skerries that make up the Stockholm archipelago, extending 73 km (45 mi) east into the Baltic Sea. A red timbered cottage on one of these islands in the Baltic is most Swedes' idea of ultimate bliss, and there they seek to re-create the simple life as they imagine their forefathers to have lived it.

A fair approximation of archipelago life is just a 25-minute ferry ride away from the city center. This is Fjäderholmarna, or Feather Island, an islet that not long ago was a navy munitions dump. The rock is worn smooth by retreating Ice Age glaciers, there's a clump of yellow reeds at the water's edge, and on the rock the inevitable red cottage, windows and corners trimmed with white, against a backdrop of dark green foliage. There's a restaurant serving excellent Swedish specialties and a small colony of craftsmen making high-quality souvenirs.

Take a boat trip west from the city, and you're in a different world, verdant and tranquil. An hour away and you're at Drottningholm Palace, also designed by Nicodemus Tessin and now the residence of the royal family. The palace and its formal French garden are impressive and the little Chinese Pavilion enchanting, but the real gem is the 200-year-old and perfectly intact Drottningholm Court Theater, where period performances of operas by Mozart, Gluck, and other 18th-century composers are presented every summer. The orchestra wears wigs, the singers appear in original costumes, and the ingenious old stage machinery produces thunder and storms.

As you wander through the reception areas and dressing rooms you'll be struck by the sparse, cool elegance of the decor and furnishings, a style borrowed from Louis XV but stripped down to the bare essentials. It may strike you, too, that this is not very different from modern Swedish interiors and design. Then you will have discovered a well-hidden truth: the Swedes, who take such pride in being modern, rational, and efficient, are secretly in love with the 18th century.

–Eric Sjogren

Eric Sjogren, a Swedish travel writer based in Brussels, is a frequent contributor to the New York Times and other publications.

ASTRID LINDGREN

APPROPRIATELY, the career of Astrid Lindgren, Sweden's best-known children's writer, author of the *Pippi Longstocking* books and many others, has a fairy-tale beginning. Once upon a time, Karin, her seven-year-old daughter, ill in bed with pneumonia, begged her: "Tell me a story . . . tell me the story of Pippi Longstocking."

"Neither she nor I know where on earth she got that name from," says Lindgren. "That was the first time I ever heard it. I made up the character right there and then, told her a story, and only wrote it down much later."

Thus was born one of the most memorable characters in children's fiction, her adventures translated from Lindgren's native Swedish into more than 50 languages.

"A few years later, I was awarded a prize for the stories and offered to share it with Karin," recalls Lindgren, "but by then she decided that she was too old. She said she was bored with Pippi."

With younger children all over the world, however, Pippi continues to strike a responsive chord: a little girl of indeterminate age with a gap-toothed smile, freckle face, and a wild mop of ginger hair from which a braid juts lopsidedly out over each ear.

Phenomenally strong, irrepressibly cheeky, she lives independent of adults, with a horse and monkey in a tumbledown house, supporting herself from a hoard of gold coins. She has no table manners and doesn't go to school. She does just what she likes, when she feels like doing it.

"Bertrand Russell once said that children dream of power the way that adults dream of sex," says Lindgren. "I was impressed with that at the time, and I think I must have had it in mind when I created Pippi."

Despite vociferous protests from educationalists and child psychologists, Pippi won immediate favor with kids. Lindgren has since created several other memorable characters, but Pippi remains the basis of her enormous popularity in her home country.

It would be well-nigh impossible to find a Swede who has not heard of Lindgren. She is *Tant Astrid*, Aunty Astrid, a gray-haired, near-sighted little old lady who is a symbol of hearth and home, of faith in traditional values and love of rural Sweden, with its deep, dark pine forests, wide blue lakes and meadows dotted with red-painted wood houses.

The independent spirit that created such an unconventional character as Pippi Longstocking still exists within this grandmother, however, and using her awesome popularity, Lindgren has been partly responsible for the fall of one Swedish government and for forcing a second one in 1989 to draft radical new legislation protecting the rights of pets and farm animals, about which she has a bee in her bonnet.

She remains refreshingly unspoiled by all the adulation and attention she receives.

"When I go out, people come up to me in the street and tell me how much they've enjoyed my books, and children will hug and kiss me," she says. "Of course, that's very nice, but you know somehow I always feel it's not happening to *me*.

"It's as though someone else had all that celebrity and I am standing alongside her."

The mere suggestion that she wields power bring a steely glint to her blue eyes. "Power? I have only the power of the word," she says. "I wouldn't want power in the real sense. That's the worst thing I know. People always abuse it."

Yet there is more than suspicion that, Pippilike, she revels in the influence she, an ordinary (or perhaps one should say, extraordinary) citizen can use to inject rebellious ideas into the heads of her youthful public and bend Sweden's rulers to her will.

One of her characters is *The World's Best Karlson*. Lovable figment of a little boy's imagination, Karlson is a jovial type who laughs at reality and flies around the house aided by a propeller set in the middle of his back. The Karlson books have become particularly popular in Russia, where *Literaturnaja Gaseta,* a literary review, has described the character as "the symbol of innocent, uncorrupted childhood, the childhood we as adults find so difficult to remember and accept."

The Satirical Theater in Moscow staged a play based on the character in the 1960s, and Lindgren says that when she visits Russia, taxi drivers always talk to her about Karlson.

When former Swedish Prime Minister Ingvar Carlsson visited Moscow, she was delighted to hear that many Russians were disappointed because he wasn't the *real* Karlson.

HOWEVER, SAYS LINDGREN, it is the stories of the Bullerby children that most closely approximate her own childhood. These feature the adventures of children from three families in a little village somewhere in Sweden and eulogize rural life set against a fondly painted picture of seasonal contrast. The Bullerby children are Lindgren's *nicest* characters: playful but, unlike Pippi, unwilling to overstep the line.

Bullerby is based on the little village of Sevedstorp, set amid the dense pine-and-spruce forests that cover the southern Swedish province of Småland, birthplace of her father, Samuel August Ericsson, who by the time Astrid was born, in 1907, had moved to the nearby town of Vimmerby.

Home was a simple clapboard house, painted red and with a glassed-in porch, surrounded by well-tended flower beds, daisy-strewn lawns, and apple trees. Her father had started life as a hired hand but wound up running his own farm. The family was reasonably well off, though there was rarely money left over for luxuries. Samuel Ericsson was an excellent storyteller, and many of the anecdotes he told his children surfaced later in Lindgren's books. Her mother, Hanna wrote poetry in her youth and at one time dreamed of becoming a schoolteacher.

Lindgren was one of four children. She had an elder brother, Gunnar (born 1906), and two younger sisters, Stina (born 1911) and Ingegerd (born 1916). All displayed literary talents of some kind or another: Gunnar became a member of parliament

renowned for his political satires; Stina a translator, and Ingegerd a journalist.

The innocent childhood fun and games described in the Bullerby books are, by and large, those of Astrid herself and her brother and sisters. "We played the whole time from morning to night, just like the children in the Bullerby stories," she says.

She enjoyed a warm relationship with Samuel August, a fact that is reflected time and again in her books, people in the main with warm, understanding, though often gruff fathers. She describes their mother, on the other hand, as a rather distant person, recalling that as a child Hanna hugged her only once. It was from her that she inherited her willpower, energy, and stubbornness, she says.

The creator of Pippi Longstocking rebelled against Hanna's authority just once as a child: "I was quite young—perhaps three or four—and one day I thought she was stupid so I decided to run away and hide in the outside toilet. I wasn't there for too long, and when I came back in my brother and sisters had been given sweets. I thought this was so unfair that I kicked out in mother's direction. I was taken into the front room and beaten."

When she started at the local school at the age of seven, in 1914, she was overcome with shyness (a traditional Swedish handicap) when the teacher called out her name and, instead of answering "yes," burst into tears.

The priest in charge of registering the new arrivals told her she could go and sit down instead of standing with the other children. "I wanted to be with the others," she says. "I absolutely didn't want to go and sit down." The tears subsided, and she now sees the incident as the day she broke through her "wall of shyness."

She was a conscientious pupil, remembered by classmate Ann-Marie Fries, the model for Madicken, another of her characters, as "unbelievably nimble. I remember her in the gym; she could climb from floor to ceiling like a monkey."

Astrid also began to show evidence of literary talents. Her essays were frequently read to the rest of the class, and, when she was 13, one of them was even published in *Wimmerby Tidning,* Vimmerby's local newspaper. This was titled "Life in Our

Backyard" and described two small girls and the games they played. "They joked and called me Vimmerby's answer to Selma Lagerlöf, and I decided that if there was one thing I would never be it was an author."

She recalls her teens as a melancholy episode. "Like most teenagers, I thought I was ugly," she says, "and I just *never* fell in love. Everyone else was in love."

She left school at 16 and was given a job on *Wimmerby Tidning,* reading proofs and even covering some local events such as weddings and funerals as a reporter.

In 1926 Astrid's blissful childhood came to a very definite end, when, at the age of 18, she had an affair with a man and became pregnant. In recent years Sweden has developed a reputation for liberality in such matters, but in those days, pregnant and unmarried, she created a huge scandal in Vimmerby, a small town steeped in traditional Lutheran values.

Astrid left home and traveled to the capital, Stockholm. "Of course, my parents weren't pleased, but I wasn't thrown out or anything like that," she explains; "wild horses wouldn't have kept me there."

She knew nobody in Stockholm. "I was terribly alone at first," she says. "I had left behind all my friends. I was very unhappy. Childhood is one thing," she says philosophically; "youth is something else."

She took solace in reading the works of Norwegian author Knut Hamsun. Hamsun's book *Hunger* made a deep impression on her. She still names it as her principal literary influence. Lonely and poor herself, she identified strongly with Hamsun's graphic descriptions of the life of a starving young writer in Norway.

In an essay for the mass-circulation Stockholm evening newspaper *Expressen* in 1974, she recalled sitting under a bird-cherry tree outside a church, reading *Hunger.* "That was the greatest literary experience I've ever had," she said.

She gave birth to a son, Lars, whom she handed over to foster parents in Copenhagen, returning to Stockholm to study shorthand and typing and to land a job at a local firm working for the father of Viveca Lindfors, the Swedish actress.

"I soon started to make friends in Stockholm, and I went to Copenhagen as often as I could to see Lars. There was never any question of his being adopted. He was my son and I loved him deeply," she says.

On one occasion she left her job during working hours to take the train to Copenhagen, only to be spotted by her boss. She was sacked.

However, her luck seemed to have turned. Astrid found an editorial job with KAK, the Swedish automobile association. There she met Sture Lindgren, whom she married in the spring of 1931. Her son came to live with them, and in 1934 she gave birth to her daughter, Karin.

THE FAMILY LIVED IN the part of Stockholm known as Vasastan, at first in a small apartment close to the main railway line to the north of Sweden, later in a spacious, light apartment overlooking a park. Lindgren still lives there today, surrounded by her books and memorabilia of her lifetime as an author.

It was in the winter of 1941 that Karin asked her to tell the story of Pippi Longstocking. "Much later I was out walking in the park when I slipped and sprained my ankle," she recalls. "I was forced to lie in bed, so I began to write down the stories I had told to Karin."

She typed a manuscript and sent it to Bonniers, one of Sweden's leading publishing houses. It was refused. Undaunted, she wrote a girl's story, *The Confidences of Britt-Mari,* which she entered for a contest organized by another, much smaller, publishing house, Rabén and Sjögren. She won second prize, and in 1944 the story was published. Lindgren also began working for the company as an editor.

The following year Rabén and Sjögren published her follow-up, titled *Kerstin and I.* Then in 1945 the company announced a new contest for books aimed at children age 6–10.

Lindgren revised her Pippi Longstocking manuscript and entered it for the contest, along with a new effort, *All About the Bullerby Children,* in which she lovingly recreated her childhood in Vimmerby. *Pippi Longstocking* won first prize. *All about the Bullerby Children* failed to take an award but was bought for publication.

The first Pippi Longstocking book was well received by both critics and public and soon sold out. However, a year later, the follow-up, *Pippi Goes Aboard,* caused a furor, with Lindgren accused of undermining the authority of parents and teachers.

Professor John Landquist, writing in the evening newspaper *Aftonbladet,* accused Lindgren of "crazed fantasy" and said Pippi's adventures were "something disagreeable that scratches at the soul."

Today there is a different perspective. Viví Edström, professor of literature at the University of Stockholm, has described Pippi as "a child's projection of everything that is desirable" and claims her as a major influence on Swedish literature.

"In the still prim and moralizing children's literature of the 1940s, Astrid Lindgren's breakthrough meant that children had a literature on their own terms," says Edström.

The third and last Pippi Longstocking book, *Pippi in the South Seas,* was published in 1948. In this, Pippi sails away to a Pacific island for a reunion with her father, returning to Sweden for Christmas, which she spends alone. It could be an allegory on the fate of nonconformists in Sweden, a country where the good of the collective has always been prized above that of the individual.

Physically, the model for Pippi was a red-haired, freckle-faced friend of daughter Karin, Sonja Melin, who today sells vegetables in Hötorgshallen, one of Stockholm's few surviving indoor markets. "I meet her now and again when I go out shopping," says Lindgren. "She was just so lively as a child. As soon as I saw her, I thought, 'that's my Pippi!'"

Lindgren has created many other well-loved and sometimes controversial characters in the 30 books she has written since.

Mio My Son, written in 1954 (perhaps significantly, two years after the death of husband Sture) is one of Lindgren's most ambitious books: a highly advanced fairy story that explores difficult themes such as fear and death.

In 1985 a journalist asked Lindgren on Swedish Radio: "Isn't *Mio My Son* actually a pretty nasty book?"

She replied, "Of course; that's why children love it."

HILE SHE HAS never attempted a "serious" adult novel ("I never really wanted to. I'm not sure I'd be any good at it."), she has not fought shy of exploring themes considered improper for children. In 1973 controversy raged once more over *The Brothers Lionheart,* in which a dying child dreams of meeting, in another world, the brother he idealizes who has died heroically in a fire. The two boys ride off to fight the forces of evil.

Shortly after this, in 1976, Lindgren, a lifelong voter for the Social Democrats, caused a still greater fuss when she became embroiled in a row with Sweden's Socialist government.

It all started with a demand from the tax authorities, which, she calculated, would, along with her social-insurance contributions, exceed her actual income. She wrote a fairy story for *Expressen,* the Stockholm newspaper. Its main character, Pomperipossa, has always loved her country and respected its rulers. Now she turns against them: "'O you, the pure and fiery social democracy of my youth, what have they done to you?' thought Pomperipossa, 'How long shall your name be abused to protect a dictatorial, bureaucratic, unjust, authoritarian society?'"

The barb went home, and in the Swedish parliament (*Riksdag*) the then finance minister, Gunnar Sträng (his surname translates into English as "Strict") reprimanded Lindgren. "The article is a combination of inspired fantasy and total ignorance of tax policy," he said. "Astrid Lindgren should stick to what she knows, namely making up stories."

Lindgren hit back: "He may not be good at arithmetic, but he's certainly good at telling fairy-tales. I think we should trade jobs, he and I."

In that year's general election the Social Democrats lost power, after more than 40 years in office. An analysis of the result by the influential Sifo public-opinion research institute named the controversy over Lindgren's story as a major contributory factor.

Ronia, the Robber's Daughter, published in 1981, returned to a "straight" fairy-tale format, the story of a boy and girl from two different, warring bands of robbers, who run away together. This was turned into an award-winning Swedish film by co-median/director Tage Danielsson. Eleven of her books have been filmed, and Lindgren herself still takes an active interest in each project.

She has been positively deluged with prizes, including in 1989 the Albert Schweitzer Award, for her work on behalf of animal rights. At a time in life when most people would be content to wind down, she joined forces with veterinary surgeon Kristina Forslund in a campaign to persuade Sweden to introduce more stringent rules on animal husbandry.

A string of articles and open letters soon brought the government to its knees. Prime Minister Carlsson announced new legislation that he dubbed "Lex Astrid" and called on Lindgren personally to tell her about it.

Despite the fact that the laws are considered the most advanced in the world, Lindgren is not satisfied. She describes them as "toothless." "They are full of loopholes," she says. "Now we have to fight to get them tightened up."

Although hampered by failing eyesight, she began the 1990s with a new children's play written for Stockholm's Royal Dramatic Theater, plans to film *The Brothers Lionheart,* and has thoughts of writing a new book.

"It depends whether I feel inspired. I write quite quickly, in shorthand at first, then I type it. I do a chapter, then re-write until it flows properly. After that I continue with the next one. A word processor? I couldn't use one of those; I'm not a bit technically minded, I'm afraid.

"I really don't know what I would have been if I had not become an author." She smiles, perhaps thinking of her battles with authority, the Pippi Longstocking side of her personality coming to the fore. "Maybe I could have been a lawyer. I might have been rather good at that."

–By Chris Mosey

BOOKS AND VIDEOS

Books

One of the easiest and certainly most entertaining ways of learning about modern Swedish society is to read the Martin Beck detective series of thrillers by Maj Sjöwall and Per Wahlöö, all of which have been translated into English. One of these, *The Terrorists,* was even prophetic, containing a scene in which a Swedish prime minister was shot, a precursor to the assassination of Olof Palme in 1986.

Similarly, an entertaining insight into how life was in the bad old days when Sweden was one of the most backward agrarian countries in Europe can be obtained from Vilhelm Moberg's series of novels about poor Swedes who emigrated to America: *The Emigrants, Unto a Good Land,* and *The Last Letter Home.*

The plays of Swedish writer August Strindberg greatly influenced modern European and American drama. Perhaps the most enduringly fascinating of these, *Miss Julie,* mixes the explosive elements of sex and class to stunning effect.

One of the most exhaustive and comprehensive studies in English of the country published in recent years is *Sweden: The Nation's History,* by Franklin D. Scott (University of Minnesota Press). Chris Mosey's *Cruel Awakening: Sweden and the Killing of Olof Palme* (C. Hurst, London, 1991) seeks to provide an overview of the country and its recent history seen through the life and assassination of its best-known politician of recent times and the farcical hunt for his killer.

A History of the Vikings (Oxford University Press, 1984) recounts the story of the aggressive warriors and explorers who during the Middle Ages influenced a large portion of the world, extending from Constantinople to America. Gwyn Jones's lively account makes learning the history enjoyable.

Videos

Of course, Sweden was home to Ingmar Bergman, who produced such classics as *The Virgin Spring* (1959), *Wild Strawberries* (1957), and *Fanny and Alexander* (1982).

SWEDISH VOCABULARY

English	Swedish	Pronunciation

Basics

English	Swedish	Pronunciation
Yes/no	Ja/nej	yah/nay
Please	Var snäll; Var vänlig	vahr snehll vahr vehn-leeg
Thank you very much	Tack så mycket	tahk soh **mee**-keh
You're welcome	Var så god	vahr shoh **goo**
Excuse me (to get by someone)	Ursäkta	oor-**shehk**-tah
(to apologize)	Förlåt	fur-**loht**
Hello	God dag	goo **dahg**
Goodbye	Adjö	ah-**yoo**
Today	I dag	ee **dahg**
Tomorrow	I morgon	ee **mor**-ron
Yesterday	I går	ee **gohr**
Morning	Morgon	**mohr**-on
Afternoon	Eftermiddag	**ehf**-ter-meed-dahg
Night	Natt	naht

Numbers

1	ett	eht
2	två	tvoh
3	tre	tree
4	fyra	fee-rah
5	fem	fem
6	sex	sex
7	sju	shoo
8	åtta	oht-tah
9	nio	nee
10	tio	tee

Days of the Week

Monday	måndag	mohn-dahg
Tuesday	tisdag	tees-dahg
Wednesday	onsdag	ohns-dahg
Thursday	torsdag	tohrs-dahg
Friday	fredag	freh-dahg
Saturday	lördag	luhr-dahg
Sunday	söndag	sohn-dahg

Useful Phrases

Do you speak English?	Talar ni engelska?	tah-lahr nee ehng-ehl-skah
I don't speak Swedish.	Jag talar inte svenska.	yah tah-lahr **een**-teh **sven**-skah
I don't understand.	Jag förstår inte.	yah fuhr-**stohr** **een**-teh
I don't know.	Jag vet inte.	yah **veht** **een**-teh

I am American/ British.	Jag är amerikan/ engelsman.	yah ay ah-mehr-ee-**kahn** **ehng**-ehls-mahn
I am sick.	Jag är sjuk.	yah ay **shyook**
Please call a doctor.	Jag vill skicka efter en läkare.	yah veel **shee**-kah **ehf**-tehr ehn **lay**-kah-reh
Do you have a vacant room?	Har Ni något rum ledigt?	hahr nee noh-goht **room leh**-deekt
How much does it cost?	Vad kostar det?/ Hur mycket kostar det?	vah **kohs**-tahr deh/hor **mee**-keh **kohs**-tahr deh
It's too expensive.	Den är för dyr.	dehn ay foor **deer**
Beautiful	Vacker	**vah**-kehr
Help!	Hjälp	yehlp
Stop!	Stopp!/Stanna!	stop, **stahn**-nah
How do I get to . . .	Kan Ni visa mig vägen till . . .	kahn nee **vee**-sah may **vay**-gehn teel
the train station?	stationen	stah-**shoh**-nehn
the post office?	posten	**pohs**-tehn
the tourist office?	en resebyrå	ehn-**reh**-seh-**bee**-roh
the hospital?	sjukhuset	**shyook**-hoo-seht
Does this go to . . . ?	Går den här bussen till..?	gohr dehnbus hehr **boo**-sehn teel
Where is the W.C.?	Var är toalett/ toaletten	vahr ay twah-**leht** twah-**leht**-en
On the left	Till vänster	teel **vehn**-stur
On the right	Till höger	teel **huh**-gur
Straight ahead	Rakt fram	rahkt **frahm**

Dining Out

Please bring me . . .	Var snäll och hämta åt mig	vahr snehl oh hehm-tah oht may
menu	matsedeln	maht-seh-dehln
fork	en gaffel	ehn gahf-fehl
knife	en kniv	ehn kneev
spoon	en sked	ehn shehd
napkin	en servett	ehn sehr-veht
bread	bröd	bruh(d)
butter	smör	smuhr
milk	mjölk	myoolk
pepper	peppar	pehp-pahr
salt	salt	sahlt
sugar	socker	soh-kehr
water	vatten	vaht-n
The check, please.	Får jag be om notan.	fohr yah beh ohm **noh**-tahn

INDEX

NOTES

NOTES

NOTES

NOTES

NOTES

NOTES

NOTES

NOTES